WITHDRAWN

D1158317

WORDSWORTH AND THE POETRY OF SINCERITY

WORDSWORTH AND THE POETRY OF SINCERITY

David Perkins

The Belknap Press

of

Harvard University Press

Cambridge, Massachusetts

1964

The author makes grateful acknowledgment to Mrs. W. B. Yeats,
The Macmillan Company, New York, Messrs. Macmillan & Co.
Ltd., London, and the Macmillan Company Ltd. of Canada for
permission to reprint "Three Movements," from The Collected
Poems of W. B. Yeats (*copyright 1933 by The Macmillan*
Company; renewed 1961 by Bertha Georgie Yeats), and to
quote from "The Circus Animals' Desertion," "Sailing to By-
zantium," "The Tower," and "The Coming of Wisdom with
Time," from The Collected Poems of W. B. Yeats (*copyright*
1928, 1933, by The Macmillan Company; copyright 1940, 1956
by Georgie Yeats; copyright 1961 by Bertha Georgie Yeats);
to Holt, Rinehart and Winston, Inc. and Jonathan Cape Limited
for lines quoted from "Birches" from Complete Poems of Robert Frost (*copyright 1916, 1921, by Holt, Rinehart and Win-*
ston, Inc.; renewed 1944 by Robert Frost); and to Oxford Uni-
versity Press for permission to quote from Poems of Gerard
Manley Hopkins (*New York: 1930*).

TO DOUGLAS BUSH

PREFACE

DURING THE latter part of the eighteenth century in England, poets and readers began to be influenced by a relatively novel assumption: that poetry should be written with a personal sincerity. Even a classicist like Johnson could find "Lycidas" unsatisfying because it is not "the effusion of real passion . . . Where there is leisure for fiction there is little grief."

The new premise of sincerity is, of course, only a part of the large transition into the modern world that took place in the romantic age, but it is an enduring and important part. It has presented a serious challenge to poetry ever since. This book studies the concrete effects in the work of one major poet, and diverse apologies are in order. On the one hand, there is no attempt to offer a complete description of Wordsworth; for he is viewed from a particular standpoint. On the other hand, I have obviously not tried to write a history of this premise and its ramifications in the poetry of the modern world. It seemed that the general meaning for poetry of this new challenge should emerge concretely and in detail, and that the best way is to watch a man struggling with it in the circumstances of his own age and his own life. The standpoint does allow, however, for a placing of Wordsworth in a continuous poetic succession from the eighteenth century to the present.

No general discussion of Wordsworth can conscientiously omit his later poems. It has seemed to me that they are especially relevant to the present subject — that the perennially debated problem of Wordsworth's decline and his lifetime preoccupation with sincerity shed light on each other. On the other hand, there is the fact that these poems are substantially different from the earlier ones. This is one reason why they are discussed as a unit. Another reason is that the approach or mode of the discussion has had to be slightly different: because they are so much less known, it seemed desirable to take up a few typical examples in some detail.

Any student of Wordsworth owes an enormous debt to other scholars and critics. I am especially indebted to the work of Ernest de Selincourt, Helen Darbishire, Mary Moorman, M. H. Abrams, W. J. B. Owen, F. W. Bateson and John Jones. I am also grateful to friends and powerful arguers — William Alfred, Jerome Buckley, Alfred Harbage — who will see that their views sometimes rescued me from my own. My final thanks are to Douglas Bush, W. J. Bate, and Mark Van Doren, who took time to read, question, correct, and help.

D. P.

CONTENTS

WORDSWORTH AND THE POETRY OF SINCERITY

I

THE CHALLENGE
OF SINCERITY

WORDSWORTH IS the central figure of English romanticism, and, with the exception of Goethe, he is probably the greatest writer of the romantic age. He is also a moving example of a man dominated by a moral ideal. In the transformation of poetry throughout the eighteenth century, nothing is more remarkable than the emergence of sincerity as a major poetic value, and, indeed, as something required of all artists. One can hardly overstress the novelty of this demand. Neither Pope nor his predecessors would have dreamed of asking themselves the dreadful question: is my poetry sincere? It is true that Pope often puts on a character of downright honesty — "he cannot flatter, he,/ An honest mind and plain, he must speak truth," to borrow what Cornwall says of Kent in *Lear*. But Pope invites no one to value his poetry by the actual truth of this pose. Cornwall's further remarks also apply. The plainness is obviously craft, one main reason for Pope's diminished prestige in the nineteenth century. Nowadays we may attach more numerous and complex meanings to sincerity than did readers a century ago, but we still make the same demand. That all effective poetry must be sincere is a premise so widely accepted that we seldom discuss it, though in fact it is questionable. Today it is almost impossible to feel our way back into a state of mind, which once existed, wherein the sincerity of an artist was not an issue — not because it was taken for granted, but because no one was thinking about it. The vocabulary of criticism in the Renaissance included neither "sincerity" nor synonyms that come near our modern concept. The subsequent elevation of sincerity accompanied the profound changes that led us to think of poetry as something close to self-expression. It has resulted in far-reaching revisions of poetic content and style, of the process of composition and the basis of enjoyment.

For example, the ideal of sincerity has made poetry much more difficult to write by introducing an extra dimension of self-consciousness. Even if sincerity suggests to a poet only truthfulness or earnestness, he is still tempted to question his poem as he creates it, and to question it from a point of view not strictly relevant to its success as poetry: is the emotion genuinely his own? does he really mean what he says? As soon as such questions are raised, we are no longer sure. If, in addition, a poet attempts to describe some event or moment of feeling in his past life, he becomes still more entangled in scruples. To imagine experience is one thing. To reproduce it is a very different matter, and the more one strives to do so, the more difficult it seems. Nothing is more likely to perplex us than exhortations to be sincere. For readers of poetry, on the other hand, the ideal of sincerity tends to shift the ground on which poetry appeals, or add another source of appeal. For one finds what might be called the drama of sincerity, a poetry that displays or implies the struggle, and the cost, when a man tries to be honest with himself and completely faithful to his experience. As one reads this poetry, classical values of form may seem less important, and the same thing is true of the more romantic values of richness and suggestion. In fact, by the early twentieth century things had so turned around that simply because he strove for such qualities a writer might be thought insincere. He might even suspect himself.

There is, it seems to me, only one sense in which it is even possibly appropriate to say that a poem must be sincere. It may be that in order to write well a poet must deeply feel the emotion he expresses as he creates the poem, though he need not feel it ever before or after. This is what Wordsworth meant by sincerity, but not all that he meant; and if sincerity suggested nothing more, it would have little influence on poetry or criticism. For in this sense sincerity would be merely a sufficient power of sympathetic imagination. It would have nothing to do with personal honesty, and the whole sting and effect of the poetic ideal of sincerity proceed from the fact that it refers to moral qualities — veracity, earnestness, integrity. To expect that a poet will write with a personal truthfulness is obviously naïve, as virtually all poets have recognized. But their more sophisticated views have not prevented them from making the effort. In describing the particular response of Wordsworth to the challenge of sincerity, one also suggests how the ideal of sincerity has influenced poetry throughout the last century and a half; for at the opening phase of this new development, Wordsworth already confronted most of the large dilemmas it engenders, and he felt his way to stylistic expedients that later poets would continue and refine. Moreover, if we stand at a distance, a personal drama of the widest relevance unfolds itself in Wordsworth. He reveals at least one way in which the ideal of sincerity may work itself out in the life of a man — the achievement it may inspire, and the limitations to which it may finally contribute. The achievement is obvious in Wordsworth. Apart from his constant effort to be honest, there would have been neither the power of phrase nor the liberating originality of thought. An ideal that might crush other poets made Wordsworth a great one.

— 2 —

We might remind ourselves at the start of some of the chief obstacles that puzzle any effort to write a poetry of sincerity, obstacles not theoretical or academic, but felt by poets as urgent, practical problems to be overcome, so far as possible, by devising an appropriate style or technique. Three of them seem especially important; for they result from some of the elementary facts about poetry: that it is an affair of language; that it compels selectivity, limiting the scope of experience that can be subsumed; that it must be learned as an art with traditions and conventions of its own. One can hardly explain the history of poetic style or, indeed, of literature since Wordsworth unless one keeps in mind that there has been a continuing mistrust of language. By words, it is feared, we chop reality into categories. The categories are arbitrary, or, even if they are not, their generality strips our experience of its unique aspects. In an extreme development of this line of thought, words may be viewed not as a human enterprise in approaching reality, but as a defence against it. As Sartre brilliantly suggests in *La Nausée*, words obscure the reality, the utter absence of meaning or determinate character in things:

The root of the chestnut tree thrust itself into the earth, just under my bench. I no longer remembered that it was a root. The words had vanished, and, with them, the significance of the things, their methods of use, the feeble guide-marks that men have traced on their surface. I was sitting, a little bent over, head lowered, alone confronting that black, knotty, and utterly raw mass, and I was frightened.[1]

For Sartre, words actually contribute to insincerity, or *mauvaise foi*. In most writers, the ideal of sincerity leads to a suspicion that language is inadequate. We always feel that we mean more and mean it more precisely than we have been able to say, and are troubled with a perpetual restlessness and dissatisfaction, as though we were itching in some internal organ that could not be scratched. All speech will seem to some extent a violation; we can keep ourselves from distorting our experience and feeling only by not speaking of it. These scruples are not simply part of the pathology of sincerity; at least, they are very common. They have not much prevented poets from writing, but they have infected poetry with an endemic sense of guilt. Spinning his lines of elaborate workmanship, Tennyson achieved an ample output, but when the matter lay near his heart, even he would confess that

> I sometimes hold it half a sin
> To put in words the grief I feel;

for words "half reveal/ And half conceal the Soul within."

Anyone who contemplates his own thoughts and feelings finds that they are always in process, changing as they recombine with different elements. Even our past is not settled, but constantly assumes new shapes and meanings in the shifting lights of the present. Yet a poem can only exist by solidifying a moment in the flux of consciousness. In order to write at all, a poet must commit himself, at least temporarily, to some dominant concepts or feelings. In "Sailing to Byzantium," for example, Yeats rebels against the "mackerel-crowded" sea of nature and seeks the unchanging life modeled in works of art, but in other poems of the same period his mood and choice are very different. Either mood is true to Yeats, and the point is that any poem, however complex, will be purer, simpler, and more consistent than the personal consciousness of the writer. Knowing this, and prizing sincerity, a poet may feel that he cannot achieve it simply because he must limit and select in order to write at all. This dilemma so troubled Yeats that he developed complex theories of personal identity, theories that would, in effect, allow him to write without the question of sincerity interfering. He argued that the self always involves the anti-self, and thus contradictory expressions may be equally sincere. Or he speculated that one achieves an identity by maintaining a pose, as though the features of the face would mold themselves to a mask, and thus it is not necessary to know what one is, but only what one wishes to become. But this was an unusually intricate defense thrown up because of an exceptional alertness to the threat. Yeats desperately wanted to be sincere yet knew that the ideal could stifle his poetry. In general, poetry — including Yeats's — has tried to meet the dilemma by more practical expedients of style and form.

We find, then, that sincerity requires both an utmost precision and a wide inclusiveness, an ability to catch both the exact shade and the whole scope of meaning. If both these aims have affected poetic style separately, they affect it still more when they are taken together. They are not necessarily inconsistent. There is no reason why speech cannot be both ample and exact. But these aims come into practical conflict when they are joined, as generally they have been during the last century and a half, with the romantic ideal of intensity, and especially when intensity is sought in the current guise of compression. For how can one be not only exact in discriminating, but also inclusive, and simultaneously condensed? One answer lies in the thought, so pervasive in contemporary poetry and criticism, that in a poem every word must be individually watched and weighted. There is also the desire to exploit or recognize in the language of poetry devices that allow words to sustain multiple meanings. At the same time, we require that everything said or implied in a poem somehow hang together, making up a unified expression; yet an over-all integration may become more difficult to achieve to the extent that each part or element has been packed with many implications. That all these demands are not irreconcilable is proved by a few contemporary lyrics that can stand comparison with almost any in English. But it is no wonder that so many of our most ambitious attempts crumple under the strain, lapsing into a new vagueness that can be far more extreme than the mistiness we may deplore in romantic verse.

Furthermore, as we try to straddle divergent ideals the very uses of language to which we are forced may come to seem insincere. The doubts of the modern poet are especially felt in the use of symbols. For if, as Yeats said, "it is only by ancient symbols" that a lyric poet can summon the "abundance and depth of nature," it is also true that symbols are, at best, only a "winding stair" in the poet's struggle to come to grips with his experience. In his old age Yeats could feel that his gaudy images and symbolisms must be given up, however desirable or even necessary they might be to his art. As he puts it in "The Circus Animals' Desertion,"

> Winter and summer till old age began
> My circus animals were all on show,
> Those stilted boys, that burnished chariot,
> Lion and woman and the Lord knows what;

but he now wonders whether such symbols, though they contain "Heart-mysteries," do not themselves "engross" and

enchant the heart into a "dream," leading it away from
that reality of which they were only intended to be "em-
blems." Hence the circus animals have deserted, the poet's
"ladder" of symbols is "gone," and he must, as Yeats says,
"lie down where all the ladders start,/ In the foul rag-and-
bone shop of the heart." In "East Coker," Eliot composes
a lyric in a densely intricate, symbolic manner, and at once
rejects it. "That," he writes, "was a way of putting it — not
very satisfactory:/ A periphrastic study." For such indirect
or "periphrastic" symbols do not resolve the "intolerable
wrestle/ With words and meaning" as the poet strives to
express and meditate his own experience. And, significantly,
Eliot at once resorts to a more direct, Wordsworthian vein
of meditative statement.

The challenge of sincerity also affects poetic form in the
larger sense of over-all structure. Granted the wish to express the whole of one's experience and feeling, it is obviously more difficult to think oneself sincere while writing
a short poem. Lyrics have certainly been dominant for the
last hundred and fifty years, but most poets have become
impatient with them. Pasternak is an example. He finally
devoted himself to fiction and poetic drama because, as he
explained, he could fully deal with his own experience and
that of his time only in the larger genres; the lyrics of his
youth — indeed the lyric as a form — seemed doomed to
insignificance by their brevity. Even Keats, who in his odes
achieved the greatest lyrics of the nineteenth century, always
aspired to write a long poem, one that would permit more
experience to be included. A really capacious work cannot,
of course, be intense in every moment. But a further and
subtler liability is that, even in writing a long poem, one
must still impose an order; one must relate things to each
other in some particular way, to the exclusion of other pos-

sible relations that may seem equally true. Mere length does not elude the difficulty: how even in a long poem can we be honest not only to the scope, but also to the fluid, changing character of our emotions, and the uncertainty of our beliefs?

Poetic drama might seem to offer a way out. Diverse points of view are represented, and we need not commit ourselves to any one of them. But at least for English writers, poetic drama has not been a profitable option in the modern world. Poets themselves have usually had little experience and less understanding of the theater. The uses of language that have now become habitual from writing poetry cannot be successfully transposed to the stage. And there is always the looming figure of Shakespeare. Poets cannot hope to rival his example, and yet his influence can be evaded only by a struggle and an immense cost in self-consciousness. What is needed, then, is a poetic form that provides space without petrifying or stratifying the poet's experience, or his interpretation of it. The history of poetry since Wordsworth shows a constant groping for such a form. The *Prelude* was an early attempt; its eddying flow shows Wordsworth's central preoccupations in changing lights. Another early manifestation occurred when Wordsworth had the thought that all of his poems might be considered as making up one whole, the shorter pieces being outworks and vestibules to the vast cathedral (which was never finished). For there have been repeated experiments with more extensive poetic structures in the modern world, and they mostly come down to the same general hope: a series of lyrics that can be linked to form a larger whole. In these works — such as Eliot's *Four Quartets* or Tennyson's *In Memoriam* — each poem can approach the same central concern or subject matter, but from shifting moods and points of view. Thus, with no loss of intensity in any part, the whole can achieve the depth and significance of a major work, while remaining honest to the flux and diversity the poet knows in himself.

Finally, the wish to be sincere is challenged and baffled by the fact that poetry is a learned performance, that all poetic expression depends on traditions and conventions peculiar to the art and inherited from the past. Every poet knows that you cannot simply look into your heart and write. As Yeats put it, the "soul" can learn to sing only by studying "Monuments of its own magnificence." Yet if you imitate the great achievements of the past, how can your poem be thought a sincere personal utterance? The question of imitation is only the most obvious result of this anxiety. For a fanatic sincerity may suppose that merely to be influenced by other writers — in fact, to be influenced by anything at all — somehow clouds the purity of self-expression. There is plainly no answer to this dilemma, except to say that it rests on a fallacy: the self is realized not by exclusion but by assimilation; sincerity is not achieved by casting off influences — an attempt both impossible, and, were it possible, dishonest to one's experience — but rather by integrating them with each other and with all that one has encountered in the past. But though we have to do with a fallacy, it has nevertheless had pervasive effects. Poetry since Wordsworth reveals a continuing temptation to confuse sincerity with originality, and then originality with idiosyncrasy, as though one were most oneself by being most unlike other people.

Again, it is obvious that poetry must exploit conventions. But how can you use a poetic language or method that lies in the common stock if you are concerned for the integrity of some personal emotion, and proceed on the assumption that every moment of feeling is unique? From this point of view, the technique of *symboliste* verse, which influenced English poetry for about fifty years beginning in the 1890's, can be seen as a natural response to the continuing challenge of sincerity. Abstract and discursive speech, it was supposed, can only lower the temperature of poetry; but a graver objection was that such language plasters over the truth, reducing an individual perception to a common thought. Traditional grammar with its embodied logic was equally suspect; for any logic or order imposed by the medium of expression may seem to involve a distortion. Hence discursive statement was abolished and syntax liberated, and poetry dealt in concrete images placed to interact suggestively with each other. With this technique in hand, poets could hope to explore realms of experience hitherto inaccessible, and, ideally speaking, every poem might disclose a new perspective. In the surrealist offshoot, the attempt was to reproduce states of mind, either associative and dream-like or simply unconscious, that seemed closer to the final reality, to reality as it is in itself, unmediated by the forms of language, art, and logic. *Symboliste* poetry was an extension of the romantic revolt against discursive logic and rhetoric. Like romantic poetry, it was a protest in the name of truth, and it too located "truth" in the inward consciousness rather than the external norm. But, of course, the *symboliste* writers developed conventions of their own.

Even though the ideal of sincere personal utterance can never be wholly fulfilled in practice, poets since Wordsworth must still come to terms with it. They may, of course, reject it, perhaps swinging to the opposite extreme. We have witnessed desperate flights of fancy in which poets try to assert that poetry has nothing to do with self-expression. One thinks of Arnold's Preface to the *Poems* of 1853, or of

Eliot's meditation on "Tradition and the Individual Talent," in which it appears that tradition does virtually all the work of writing. If Shakespeare "unlocked his heart" in his sonnets, "the less Shakespeare he," says Browning, who devoted himself to dramatic monologues. But Browning's characterizations often remain only ideas with costumes and historical settings, and the same may be said of much poetic drama or dramatic poetry in the modern world (with the exception of those monologues where the speaker is simply the writer, plainly visible behind an assumed name). That this writing seems too conscious indicates perhaps that if a modern poet refuses personal utterance, he must strain to avoid it. Though in greater or less degree, most poets have accepted the challenge of sincerity. But the poetry has usually been shaped by a doubleness of motive that would have interested Browning; for it can also involve a deliberate artfulness in trying to seem sincere. If readers have naïve but eager expectations, poets are influenced to give what is required. In poetry such as his seemingly autobiographical *Life Studies*, Robert Lowell says, "You want the reader to say, this is true." For him the wish created a problem of technique: "There was always that standard of truth . . . the reader was to believe he was getting the *real* Robert Lowell." [2] Poetic style, then, can result from the struggle to be sincere united with the desire to seem it.

— 3 —

Granted the wish to be and seem sincere, we can attempt a general sketch of the poetry that emerges. Classical art, with its clear and obvious form, its loftiness and simplification to essences, preserves a strong sense of the difference between art and the world we know in actual experience. The same thing is true of neo-classical art except that, being reverential and intimidated, it tends to reduce the procedures of the classics to a rigid code of proprieties, to form by conforming, so to speak. In this self-conscious use of models, the literature of Queen Anne's England, as of France in the seventeenth century, achieved an uncanny finesse, while at the same time the greater English writers never dwindled into mere formalism. They were invigorated by their bold predecessors in the Renaissance, and, on another side, by their brawling, Philistine age. But the achievement, however impressive, was confining. Various reactions were well under way by the time of Wordsworth. Among them, the ideal of sincerity especially tends to narrow the distance between art and ordinary speech. When in the Preface to the *Lyrical Ballads* Wordsworth addresses himself to the fundamental question, "What is a Poet?" and answers that a poet "is a man speaking to men," he devises a formula for the change. The older view, after all, had been that a poet is a "maker," with the implication that he may exploit established materials and customary arrangements, and that to some extent a work of art may be detached from the human being who shapes it. Wordsworth would have a poet speak not from the traditions of a craft, but from his full experience and concern as a man. Compared with classical and neoclassical verse — which offer a clearer contrast than any other — the poetry of sincerity will seem personal rather than typical, intimate rather than public, spontaneous or natural rather than heightened and planned.

For its subject matter, this poetry turns to the actual world in which we live, and presents something said to have been done or experienced by the writer. In this sense, it tends to be realistic and autobiographical. It usually centers upon some event or feeling in a close, concrete, and amply circumstantial way. One thinks of Wordsworth's encounter with the leech-gatherer, or of moments in the *Prelude* such as the encounter with the veteran soldier, or of such famous later episodes in English poetry as Arnold visiting (after Wordsworth) the Grande Chartreuse, Hardy listening to the darkling thrush, or Eliot making pilgrimages, from ancestral and religious piety, to East Coker and Little Gidding.

It is an odd law that, other things being equal, a poem is more likely to seem sincere if it describes actions or objects not usually treated in poetry, or treats them from a new point of view. For the simple-minded assumption is that when a poem does not obviously come from the common stock of poetry, it must issue from the writer's own experience. Here is one benefit to Wordsworth from talking about aging pedlars, leech-gatherers, and feeble-minded children. It is partly because of such novel subject-matters that a poetry of sincerity tends to be detailed and circumstantial. Arnold's "Philomela" and Hardy's "Darkling Thrush" are both influenced by literary sources (Hardy obviously builds on Keats's "Ode to a Nightingale"), and their themes are perhaps equally conventional. But Arnold merely refers to an image traditional in poetry, "the nightingale — / The tawny-throated," while Hardy takes a long look at something unexpected — "An aged thrush, frail, gaunt, and small,/ In blast-beruffled plume." As a result of this and similar differences, the poems appeal in very different ways. While Arnold's poem is academic, though in a good sense of the word, Hardy plucks whatever special attraction we feel to sincerity. Because of his particularity and strangeness, he seems to focus on something that actually happened. Hardy and Housman can be compared in a similar way. Both writers are pessimists, yet Hardy's feeling seems more sincere. The reasons lie partly in Hardy's diction and versification. He has a gnarled awkwardness that makes his naïvetés more convincing than those of Housman, though they are equally deliberate. Another reason, however, is that, while both poets invent brief tales of tragic irony, Hardy often invents with richer detail in a less conventional setting, situation or plot. Because the occasion of his feeling seems convincingly real, the feeling itself may seem authentic and inevitable. In Hardy's poetry, emotion seems to rise from events; in Housman, emotion may seem wilfully to imagine events by which it can be nourished.

− 4 −

Though it is concerned more for *mimesis* than *harmonia*, a poetry of sincerity can still be acutely aware and scrupulous in questions of form and technique. Its formal purposes differ, however, from those of earlier poetry. In speaking of *harmonia*, Aristotle referred to our instinct for imposing order or rhythm on our experience, for giving it a clear shape or design. In a general way, this seems to express the motive and effect of poetic form down to the romantic age. In the Aristotelian tradition, our desire for both *harmonia* and *mimesis* (the representation of reality) could not result in a conflict. "Reality" was conceived to lie in the internal logic of things, the course or development that things would take if they were free from accident. It follows that one cannot contemplate "reality" in the world of common experience so well as in works of art, and the *harmonia*, the clear and shapely form, is itself mimetic; it inheres in the essence or truth of things. But if one applied Aristotle's diagnosis — art rests on our instincts for both *mimesis* and *harmonia* — to the modern scene, one would expect to find exactly the sort of split that now troubles all of the arts. When "reality" is no longer located in ideal norms, but instead in the unique accidents of individual experience, one cannot satisfy the yearning for *harmonia* without seeming to violate the angularities of truth. When a work of art still stresses form, it does so as a specialized interest, and the form tends to become its own content. Hence art seems compelled either to shrink into mere abstraction and formalism, or else to load itself with everything in sight, paralyzing its digestive organs. Of course, no work of art falls into either extreme. We are concerned only with tendencies, and it is obvious that the poetry of sincerity must take the path of exact representation. Its stylistic problem, then, is to develop techniques that will permit the highest degree of *mimesis*.

The object of this *mimesis* is twofold. On one hand, it reproduces events in the outer world — the realism of Wordsworth's "Michael." On the other, it discloses the writer's inward consciousness, his feelings, beliefs, and state of mind. The ode on "Intimations of Immortality" is an example. But beginning with Wordsworth, it is more generally accurate to say that art tends less to distinguish between the outer world of events and the inner world of consciousness. Instead, it renders their meeting point or interfusion. For we can know outward things only as they are reflected and modified in some particular consciousness or "point of view"; and we can know our inner world only as we are responding to something outside. To disclose the experiencing self in its full individuality, poetic style must above all be free. It must be free from the control of an audience, of traditions, of forms determined at the start. The freedom is claimed at every level, in the large structure of a poem and the least details of diction and versification.

Since Wordsworth there has been a periodic and cumulative effort to expand the vocabulary of poetry. The general hope is, of course, to provide a language by which any or all experience can be handled directly. But many poets have also been eager to develop a highly personal diction, a speech smacking of their individual selves. The results are sometimes spectacular. They include the extreme elipsis of Hopkins, the country dialect, archaisms, neologisms, and gawky compounds of Hardy, the obvious and extreme melodiousness of Swinburne (there was an unusual ferment of innovation in poetry near the turn of the century), and, in our own day, the peculiarities of Cummings and Pound. Even Yeats and Frost, who use a relatively traditional language, pretend to a regional English. In a footnote to one of his poems Yeats tells us that the line, "My fanatic heart," contains only two beats, because "I pronounce 'fanatic' in what is, I suppose, the older and more Irish way." And Frost exploits a conscious homeliness. "Where's this barn's house?" he begins one poem. For these developments Wordsworth and Coleridge set the stage in their opposition to the "poetic diction" of the Augustans. They argued that its obliquities prevented a natural or truthful presentation, and also that it was exploited as a group language of poets only. Wordsworth and Coleridge did not go so far as to desire a speech flavored with personal idiosyncrasies. They simply sought to use the words men might speak over the dinnertable. Keats felt a similar impulse when he gave up the Miltonic diction of *Hyperion* ("Miltonic verse cannot be written but in the vein of art") and tried instead to catch what he called the "true voice of feeling."

Much of this stylistic experiment that breaks away from tradition and loosens form involves a desperate eagerness to be almost anything rather than "poetic." It may be that the eagerness is reflected in the business attire of contemporary poets, and the varied occupations by which they support themselves. Yeats was perhaps the last significant figure who looked, dressed, talked, and acted in a way that satisfies our stock idea of the poet, though the stock idea is largely a continental product. English and American poets have seldom been so tempted as their European counterparts to act out in their lives a special role, whether as *poète maudit*, or as a disciple to occult knowledge dwelling in a tower, or simply as a sensibility too refined for the world, like Shelley at Eton. (Appropriately enough, Rilke died of the prick of a rose.) But at least we often think of the major English writers of the last century as variations on the Longfellow type, students browsing the newest shoots of knowledge in all fields, their libraries crammed with volumes in many languages, and with busts of "Daunty, Gouty, and Shopkeeper," as Auden brashly puts it, staring from the top shelves. These writers lived as professional men of letters, but poets now live as doctors, business executives, agriculturists, teachers, or bar-flies. Poetry has become a part-time job, and though output has dwindled (the *Collected Works* may be a thin book these days), there are compensations. If poetry deals with one's own experience and feeling, it may be an advantage to have some stance in life other than as a professional writer.

The vogue of free verse has been inspired by much the same feelings that excited Wordsworth when he attacked poetic diction — exasperation with an arbitrary notion of what is or is not poetic, fear that prescribed forms seal off aspects of reality. Thus our contemporary free verse may be seen as only a later manifestation of the drive toward freedom inherent in the poetry of sincerity. Coleridge pointed out that Wordsworth could not be entirely himself except in blank verse, the most flexible form available, for practical purposes, in his day. For of the major romantic poets only Coleridge, in *Christabel*, discovered a looser meter, which, however, was used only for narrative. Indeed, what Coleridge said of this meter could be used, with only a little rephrasing, as a better than average statement of the principle at work in our free verse: it is "rather dramatic than lyric, i. e. not such an arrangement of syllables, not such a metre, as acts a priori and with complete self-subsistence . . . but depending for it's beauty always, and often even for it's metrical existence, on the *sense* and *passion*." [3] Arnold, Newman, and many others later explored the possibilities of a cadenced, mainly iambic line of varying lengths. Of course, most poets still wrote in stanzas, as they do today, but they proliferated an astonishing variety of stanzaic forms. In fact, this variety is the first thing one notices about the poetry of the nineteenth century; and the accumulation of diverse patterns equally reveals the constant working of the urge to freedom. To the extent that these diverse patterns originated as *ad hoc* adjustments of form to content, they are prototypes of free verse; for it is a cliché of criticism that free verse enables a poet precisely to render the unique contour of his emotion. But free verse allows sincerity not simply by offering a particular form, or lack of form. Stanzas and meters tend to eloign a poet from himself: because they are traditional, they fill his imagination with reminiscences of past poetry; because they are set forms with clear-cut exigencies, they divert his attention. Free verse, on the other hand, leaves a poet to confront his experience with little help, suggestion, or intrusion from the form. "All that is personal soon rots," says Yeats, and hence tells why he avoided free verse:

If I wrote of personal love or sorrow in free verse, or in any rhythm that left it unchanged, amid all its accidence, I would be full of self-contempt because of my egotism and indiscretion, and foresee the boredom of my reader.[4]

Yeats does not deny that poetry is made out of the personal life of the writer. He simply feels that personal emotion must be packed in the "ice and salt" of traditional form. And then one finds Robert Lowell explaining why he used free verse in *Life Studies*:

When I was writing *Life Studies*, a good number of the poems were started in very strict meter, and I found that . . . regularity just seemed to ruin the honesty of sentiment, and became rhetorical; it said, "I'm a poem" . . . I felt that the meter plastered difficulties and mannerisms on what I was trying to say to such an extent that it terribly hampered me.[5]

In one respect, these conflicting opinions are a model for many of the literary wrangles of the last sixty years: both writers make the same assumptions about the effect of free verse in coming closer to the personal life of the writer. Whether we praise convention or deplore it, say that poetry should be impersonal or personal, admire the rich minutiae of a formal integration or a large access to experience, is only the internecine quarrel of people in the same boat. We can take one side or the other, but the issue in debate is still the romantic ideal of sincerity.

– 5 –

Our struggle to be sincere must influence art simply because art cannot be isolated from our moral and intellectual life. Hence we can try for a moment to consider the hunger for sincerity as it affects not only art in a narrow sense, but the way we aspire to use our minds generally. A man trying to be sincere is likely to move in two directions at once. On the one hand, he may strive to meet his experience without preconceptions, or to keep them from distorting his sense of things, so that he may draw and accept whatever inferences would naturally arise. On the other hand, no man ever struggled to be sincere unless he hoped finally to come to a more settled view of things, however tentative and provisional it may still be. (A Nihilist may be sincere; but he has no reason to strive for sincerity.) Our open-mindedness, then, is a means toward beliefs in which we can have a greater confidence, that is, toward a state of mind somewhat less open.

Nevertheless, the first gesture of sincerity is likely to be what one might call a divestment. A sincere man would not think other men's thoughts. He might agree with others, but only after independent consideration. Neither, as we see in Emerson, would he wish, lacking a creed, to think his own thoughts over again unless they well up freshly from experience. He will suppose that truth — the only truth of which he can be certain — must be sought in his own immediate experience, which he must grasp just as it is. And so in the yearning for sincerity a man may try to rid himself of all interpretations that seem given from without, just as a poet may resist the conventions of his art. He may be tempted to turn his back on culture, tradition, consensus; for he dreams of seeing more directly, with the clarity of innocence. It is naturally hard to describe this position with much sympathy, but then we are being unsympathetic only to an idea presented in an extreme way; obviously no one ever carried out these views without compromise. Yet they have had a large influence on modern poetry. There has been a wish to go back to a pure source. It is the drive to interrogate what Lear calls "unaccommodated man," to find again and start once more from some unchallengeable reality.

In one aspect, the search for a pure source is an effort to find those interpretations of experience that would naturally occur to a fresh mind, a mind not imbued with prior opinions and violated by them. Plainly no one since Adam can have a completely fresh mind, least of all by the time he is old enough to write poetry. But a writer can pretend to be more open and undetermined than he is, thus lending a spurious obviousness to his interpretation of things. Hardy is an example. At least, his deliberate naïveté can suggest a fresh gaze. Or, recognizing that he himself is regrettably provided with ideas, a writer may seek to go back in time or down the scale of education, to beings who, he imagines, see and feel with an immediacy he canot match: children, or memories of childhood; savages, or, at least, members of primitive societies; the Middle Ages or other times equally remote and romanticized; peasants, beggars, even half-wits, and, in Hardy, animals and vegetable life. The impulse is still vividly alive. One thinks of Yeats's Crazy Jane. The looking back need not be merely nostalgic or escapist, or a ruse for presenting one's own opinion. It can also involve an earnest effort to recover a knowledge, truth, or way of seeing that is fundamental, yet likely to be forgotten amid present-day distractions.

In another aspect, the return to a pure source can mean that we try to seize experience before it has been interpreted at all. Here one can think of the encouragement given by German idealistic philosophy: man can know only the content of his own mind, which may or may not correspond to what (if anything) exists outside. Furthermore, the mind, it was supposed, proceeds by a sequence of regular steps from perception to synthesis and inference, and so one can try to reach back as far as possible to the initial stages of the process. This philosophy (or the British empiricist tradition from which it was developed) reinforced the romantic attempt to write spontaneously, and the frequent equation of sincerity with spontaneity. If a writer can catch experience as it is before he reflects upon it, and his feelings in the same instant of time, he is touching on the purest source of whatever knowledge and understanding he can hope to have. The results for poetry depend, of course, on the way perceptions come to us, and various opinions may be held on this matter. We may believe, as Eliot seems to do, that an event is experienced in parts, in distinct and separate images that imply the total event, before it is conceived as a whole — "brown hair over the mouth blown,/ Lilac and brown hair." Or with Wordsworth one may feel that an event is experienced as a whole before it is analyzed into parts. When Wordsworth describes scenes and actions, he often takes extreme measures — incremental repetition, for example, or proliferation of conjunctions and prepositions — to keep us from breaking them into disconnected elements as we read. In any case, one assumption that dominates much modern poetry is that a perception is truer, at least more fundamental and certain, than the inferences we build on it, and we must go back to primary perceptions, seizing them in their full immediacy, if we have any hope of obtaining a reliable interpretation of things.

Yet, to repeat, the hope in being sincere is to come to a better understanding of one's experience. More than that, one seeks generalizations, principles of wide applicability. Hence the poetry of sincerity is likely to be meditative. It embodies the twofold striving of a sincere mind to be open to experience and to obtain beliefs by which we can guide ourselves. Accordingly, this poetry begins in a concrete object, event, or perception, realized in vivid detail and immediacy, and goes on to ponder it in discursive terms. Out of particular experience and reflection upon it, the poetry builds toward a moment of insight, when a general truth seems to break upon the mind with compelling force. Since, moreover, the conclusions of a sincere mind are independent, they are likely to be original, not duplicating the views and beliefs accepted by most people. For this reason, the poetry of sincerity must often be meditative if it is going to be understood — that is, it must embody whatever experience and process of thought lead the writer to his distinctive insight. One can note a remark Keats made when he was thinking of Wordsworth's poetry: "We read fine things but never feel them to the full until we have gone the same steps as the Author." [6]

– 6 –

When we read Wordsworth today, it is not likely to be for the beliefs or dogma to which he subscribed at any stage of his life, and least of all for the religion of Nature that pervades his greatest poetry. This poetry took the lead in a major theme of sensibility in the nineteenth century. It encouraged readers to imagine that they felt a sympathy and communion with the natural world, and, in such communion, a quasi-religious experience. For if the natural world was not itself divine, it was haunted by a divine presence. But this particular religious movement has run its course and the sect is disbanded. We now have to read Wordsworth in the same way, and for the same reasons, that we read other poets whose theology we may not share. Partly, of course, we read him for his phrasing — the unforgettable lines and stanzas. We still turn to the Wordsworth finely presented by Arnold and Mill, the poetry that awakens us to sources of happiness in the common things of life. There is the brooding weight and sanity of his wide moral concern, and the manly pathos of poems that are, in Hazlitt's phrase, "mournful *requiems* over the grave of human hopes." We can also go to Wordsworth for a poetry of visionary symbolism, a few passages mostly in the *Prelude*. Then, too, no poet gives a more vivid picture of the mind encountering and building up its world, and reading Wordsworth we see more clearly the modes and processes of our own consciousness. There is also the Wordsworth who senses the aura of strangeness around any act or object, the sheer inexplicability of it, the mystery and unfathomable depth.

Behind all of these partial descriptions there is the writer who, whenever he is taken seriously, troubles the conscience of poetry. He seems to suggest that even in writing poetry some commitments must be put before art.

−7−

He did not look like a poet. He had nothing of Shelley's ethereal delicacy of feature; unlike Byron, he could not be portrayed as a corsair; he had not even the large, expressive eyes and lofty brow of Coleridge. He was, Dorothy admitted, "certainly rather plain than otherwise," [7] and in his middle years many persons described him simply as a hale English gentleman — sturdy, sociable, unaffected. Yet Wordsworth's countenance could be romanticized. There was something formidable about it. The "nose announces a wonder," [8] said Haydon. It was high, curved, massive, like a projecting crag of rock. The mouth, a feature much softened in portraits, was a long slash, with a noticeable "swell and protrusion of the parts above and around." [9] The eyes were small and set far apart. Occasionally they kindled into an expression that seems to have been memorable yet hard to describe: "a light which seems to come from unfathomed depths"; "a fire in his eye (as if he saw something in objects more than the outward appearance)"; eyes "like fires, half burning, half smouldering, with a sort of acrid fixture of regard." [10] Joanna Hutchinson referred to his Schedoni glance,[11] in allusion to the malign monk of Mrs. Radcliffe's *The Italian*,

whose "eyes were so piercing that they seemed to penetrate
. . . into the hearts of men . . . few persons could support their scrutiny." The cheeks were lanky and carved
with a deep, vertical furrow, like a seam running up a cliff.
The general expression of the face could be lively, even with
a childlike jollity, and in his later years it often suggested a
luminous kindliness. For the most part, however, the expression was grave and reflective. Hazlitt speaks of a "severe,
worn pressure of thought about his temples." [12] The impression on many people seems to have been of something
granite and forbidding. His look, said Carlyle of the seventy-
year-old poet, was "not bland or benevolent so much as
close impregnable and hard." [13] Haydon was more exuber-
ant. "His head is like as if it was carved out of a mossy rock,
created before the flood." [14] Sir Henry Taylor saw "a rough,
gray face, full of rifts and clefts and fissures, out of which,
some one said, you might expect lichens to grow." Wordsworth, he said, did not resemble a poet because "there was
so much of a man that you lost sight of superadded distinctions." [15]

He was, at least after his youth, incapable of romantic il-
lusions. His pamphlet on the *Convention of Cintra*, it was
agreed in his circle, combined the philosophical and psychological depth of Burke with the moral passion of Milton.
Thundering from a summit of idealism, Wordsworth was
to recall the English people to strenuous principle in the
conduct of foreign affairs. But while the pamphlet was at
the printer's, he began to fear that portions of it might ex-
pose him to prosecution for sedition or libel. The heroic
mood evaporates like a morning mist. The publisher is begged
to read it over. "If any such passages occur, let the leaf
be cancelled — as to the expense, that I disregard in a case
like this." [16] (The last clause is a tremendous proof of

Wordsworth's alarm.) Wordsworth reflects that the pamphlet has been long delayed. It will probably have little effect. There is no reason why he should endanger himself. Except that there was little risk, the reaction is quite sensible. It is not the reaction of a Shelley, however. The contrast with Shelley holds in another sphere as well. No man was more "tenderly attached" to family and friends than Wordsworth, but, according to Coleridge, he could not fall in love in a romantic way. He does not "understand what Love is," and "ridicules the existence of any other passion, than a compound of Lust with Esteem & Friendship, confined to one Object." [17] For he had become, as Sara Hutchinson puts it, "such a *wary* man." His advice to one thinking of marriage is "let a wife *drift* toward you"; for "if you go positively in search you are sure to create the necessary qualities where they may not exist." [18] What does a "tenderly attached" man do when in a shipwreck it seems that he, his wife, and his sister are in danger of drowning: "My Brother, thinking it would be impossible to save his wife and me, had stripped off his coat to be ready to swim." [19] Doubtless any man would save himself. But there is something strange in this — and altogether characteristic of Wordsworth. It lies, perhaps, in the fact that he stated his intention to Dorothy, and that she noted it without comment. The same grim common sense or realism played a part in interrupting his friendship with Coleridge. Without going into the history of their quarrel, it can simply be said that what with drink and laudanum Coleridge was a psychological wreck and Wordsworth despaired of him. "I give it to you as my deliberate opinion . . . that he neither will nor can execute any thing of important benefit either to himself his family or mankind." [20] The prophecy was incorrect. Coleridge's major prose works were still to come. At the time (1809), however, any man of sense would have shared Wordsworth's opinion. But Wordsworth of all men had the least right to despair of Coleridge, a friend to whom he owed so much, to whom he was bound by the strongest pledges, especially when Coleridge was struggling against his own habits and when, as Wordsworth understood, to lose hope for him would make Coleridge despair of himself. As Shakespeare shows in Enobarbus or Kent, common sense is not an appropriate governor of human loyalties.

But Coleridge knew that "In all human beings good and bad Qualities are not only found together . . . but they actually tend to produce each other."[21] The same obstinate veracity, the habit of admitting to himself and saying to others what he held to be true, was one of the things that attracted Coleridge in the first place and still attracts readers to Wordsworth's poetry. He was a person one could trust. According to Coleridge, it was Wordsworth's "practice & almost his nature to convey all the truth he knows"; his "words always *mean* the whole of their possible Meaning."[22] Even the vanity and egotism with which Wordsworth was charged could be explained as a refusal to fake. There are other explanations too. For a long time Wordsworth was miserably uncertain of the value of his work. That did not prevent him from being stiff-necked about it. When James Tobin told him that if "We Are Seven" appeared in print, it would make him "everlastingly ridiculous," he answered "Nay . . . that shall take its chance, however."[23] Years later, when his fame was beginning to spread, he had the obstinacy to publish *Peter Bell*, a step which Crabb Robinson thought would set back his reputation ten years. But a man may easily be both obstinate and insecure, and if he is insecure about himself he can seldom be generous to others. Moreover, as Wordsworth urges his own claims, one should remember that they were denied and ridiculed in the popular journals. "I know but *one* instance," said Coleridge, "(that of Benedict Spinoza) of a man of great Genius and *original* Mind who on those very accounts had been abused, misunderstood, decried and (as far as the several ages permitted) persecuted, who has not been worried at last into a semblance of Egotism." [24]

Perhaps Sir Henry Taylor had the truest explanation. Wordsworth simply disdained the conventions of modesty. He had not more vanity than other men, but "what there was, like everything else in him, was wholly undisguised." [25] Nothing is more likely to seem original and eccentric than an absolute honesty. Moreover, in Wordsworth the honesty was not simply a way of speaking, of telling "all the truth he knows." He had, said Coleridge, a striking "Homogeneity of character." Many others noticed something similar. They were pointing to what might be called will-power, though better terms may be integrity or wholeness. It is a possibility in human nature that gives point to Pythagoras' noble saying, that one has only to pitch upon that course of life which is most excellent, and custom will render it the most desirable.

In any kind of work, the union of hard common sense with tenacity would have made Wordsworth effective. The addition of an immense high-mindedness plus, of course, some unexplainable gift, made him a poet. He was intensely competitive and ambitious, as much as any captain of industry, with the difference that he would commit himself only to what he held to be best. He was willing to take money from his brother, John, for he could not "earn any money without taking off . . . attention from worthier things." John encouraged him: "I will work for you, was his language, and you shall attempt to do something for the world." [26] Even in reading, De Quincey says, he was careless "of any literature that could not be considered as enshrining the very ideal, capital, and elementary grandeur of the human intellect," though occasionally, Dorothy admits, William "wasted his mind in the Magazines." [27] Just as Milton identified himself with the great poets of the past, Wordsworth identified himself with Milton. If, like Milton, he felt a certain contempt for persons less dedicated, that is only natural. For it is easy enough to feel, at moments, that one may sometime try to achieve something great; but most of us are not willing to make the sacrifices, or, perhaps, we do not clearly realize the necessity. In his youth, when he had almost no money, Wordsworth was jealous above all of his independence. He might have won a fellowship at Cambridge, but he would not drive his intellect along the academic track. When he graduated, he might have become a cleric, but he would not subscribe to the articles of the church to "vegetate on a paltry curacy." When by good luck he received a small legacy, he husbanded it and wrote, "living upon air and the essence of carrots, cabbages, turnips, and other esculent vegetables, not excluding parsley." [28]

Indeed, he was a sort of Cincinnatus of poetry, who could interrupt the writing of the great ode on "Intimations of Immortality" to spread manure on the garden. [29] The independence was a way of life as well as of thinking, and it was independence for the sake of achievement. For by the time he was twenty-one, Wordsworth knew as a matter of common sense that "small certainties are the bane of great talents," [30] and upon that principle he acted. As Coleridge put it, Wordsworth "knows the intrinsic value of the Different objects of human Pursuit, and regulates his Wishes in Subordination to that Knowledge . . . he feels, and with a *practical* Faith, the Truth . . . that we can do but one thing well, & that therefore we must make a choice — he has made that choice from his early youth, has pursued & is pursuing it." [31]

The choice, of course, was poetry, but poetry not as offering a momentary release from the actual concerns of life. To Wordsworth, our daily preoccupations — our "business, love, or strife" — are the distraction and escape, the dream, the illusion in which we protect ourselves, until we float out of existence, having cheated ourselves of life. Great art, he thinks, can call us back to reality. It is a record and instrument of man's questing mind seeking to grapple with truth.

Perhaps the best short description of Wordsworth is that he was an English, middle-class, limited version of Tolstoy. There was the same sensuous grip. Though Wordsworth was much more inhibited, there was the same violence of passion, and fundamental sympathy with the energies of life even when they might be lawless. Both men show a clutch for essentials and contempt of trivia. Moreover, it is a drastic understatement to say that they took things hard. Whatever they went through, there was a passionate concern that dwarfs most writers. Neither did they dwindle as they grew older. If their art gradually withered, the reason lies not so much in any increasing numbness as in their power to care so much about other things. To take some trivial examples: Wordsworth's interminable tirades in his later years against political reform, or his vehement opposition to his daughter's marriage, are not edifying passages in his life, but they show that the fire was not spent. Aubrey de Vere wondered that the aging poet should "speak with passionate grief of the death of a child, as if a bereavement forty years past had befallen him the day before, detailing the minutest circumstances of the illness." [32] In his youth, after the French Revolution, Wordsworth went through a spiritual and intellectual crisis that reminds one of Tolstoy. Both men could commit titanic energies in the struggle for some final certitude, with a questioning that leaves nothing unchallenged, and then, if they thought they had an answer, they would impose it upon their art.

II

SINCERITY AND
COUNTER IDEALS

ONCE THE term "sincerity" established itself in the vocabulary of poets and critics, it could hardly be weeded out.
No one except Oscar Wilde would wish to defend an insincere art. For example, even T. S. Eliot, who insists that
in creation an artist goes through an "extinction of personality," also speaks of the "duty, the consecrated task, of sincerity." Eliot's endorsement can remind us that "sincerity,"
like most critical slogans, obviously embraces different meanings. At least from the early nineteenth century, it could suggest one thing to the general audience for poetry, and something more qualified to poets themselves, who were forced
to confront the problem of combining open sincerity with
aesthetic value. At the same time, there has been an historical evolution in the literary use of the term, a shift from
more immediate, simple senses to derived, complex ones,
the process reaching a late stage when I. A. Richards prescribed meditative exercises for testing the sincerity of a
poem — sincerity still being regarded as "the quality we
most insistently require" in poetry and criticism. To discover what Wordsworth meant by sincerity is relatively
easy — partly because he put the common meanings fore-
most, partly because he discussed it at some length. But as
soon as we understand what he meant, we see why sincerity
was not by itself a sufficient ideal for poetry. It had to be

supplemented by other claims, with which it immediately conflicted.

In the nineteenth century some assumptions about poetry seemed obvious that have now vanished, together with the large, unsophisticated audience that held them: poetry is personal utterance; therefore it is or should be veracious; it is passionate and spontaneous. It would, of course, be granted that a poet may invent episodes or speak through an imaginary mouthpiece. Also, like any one else, a poet could be affected, hypocritical, or simply not himself for a moment, and John Keble reminded his contemporaries that "the feelings the writer expresses should appear to be specimens of his general tone of thought, not sudden bursts and mere flashes." [1] But on the whole the emotions expressed in a poem arise from the writer's personal life and refer back to it. As a result, appreciation involved a response to the character of the writer. "I confess," says Leslie Stephen, "that I at any rate love a book pretty much in proportion as it makes me love the author." [2] The statement could have been made by almost any critic in the nineteenth century. That it should be a confession is also typical; when they thought about it, critics and writers knew that the premise was overly simple. But they seldom kept this in mind, and poetry appealed to much the same interests in them as in the average reader.

That criticism so much concerned itself with a writer's character was of enormous advantage to Wordsworth, granted the sort of character that appealed to our ancestors and their ignorance of Annette Vallon. Hazlitt might rebuke his egoism. Liberals might condemn him as a turncoat. Wordsworth has "exchanged the company of leech-gatherers for that of tax-gatherers," remarked Jeffrey.[3] Other grumbles would inevitably be heard from time to time. For example, one of Wordsworth's *Lyrical Ballads* tells how poverty forced a virtuous rustic to sell all his sheep one by one. "If the author be a wealthy man," remarked a reviewer in 1799, "he ought not to have suffered the poor peasant to part with the last of the flock." [4] But as the nineteenth century wore on, most readers would have agreed with Grosart: "The closer one gets to the man, the greater he proves, the truer, the simpler." [5] Wordsworth himself knew that a poet may adopt a pose or pretended identity. "On the basis of his human character" Burns "reared a poetic one" that was "strikingly attractive." The example of Burns is especially interesting because Wordsworth, with his more strenuous morality, might not be expected to relish this particular poetic identity in its amorous and convivial aspects. Perhaps Wordsworth could respond to Burns's "poetic character" because he could see a morally sympathetic being underneath. "Enough of the real man appears to show that he was conscious of sufficient cause to dread his own passions, and to bewail his errors." [6] When a writer seemed likable or admirable, other aspects of poetry became less important, so that a poem might win an audience despite technical lapses that would have sunk it in a previous age. Dorothy Wordsworth tells Lady Beaumont that "We have just read a poem called *The Sabbath* written by a very good man . . . but it wants harmony, the versification indeed being very unpleasing. I say it is written by a *good man*; but I know nothing of him except from his poem; but a good man I am sure he is." [7] Wordsworth's *Excursion* should be viewed in this context. Since Dorothy was a drum majorette of the *avant garde*, she reminds us again that to think of poetry as personal utterance was the more radical premise in her day.

Few critics today are likely to forget that poetry exploits

conventions. Still less do we fear that conventions may be a sort of lie. Yet Wordsworth was much troubled by them. Throughout his life, he shows a curious anxiety to explain that they are not meant to deceive. For example, "Mr. Crowe, in his excellent loco-descriptive Poem, 'Lewesdon Hill,'" pretends that the whole poem was uttered "on a May-morning, before breakfast . . . No one believes, or is desired to believe," that the poem was "actually composed within such limits of time." On the other hand, there is no reason "why a prose statement should acquaint the Reader with the plain fact, to the disturbance of poetic credibility." [8] Such distress is clearly unnecessary; however it may relate to "truth," art can be made up of fictions. Even though Wordsworth ends with a more sophisticated remark about "poetic credibility," we may feel nowadays that the question need not have come to mind. This is especially true when we recollect that he was not reassuring Miss Fenwick, to whom the thought was dictated, but reassuring himself, for feigning that the River Duddon sonnets were spoken through the course of one day. Wordsworth understood, of course, that in art literal veracity is an empty scruple; but he could not convert that understanding into heart-knowledge — into an assent he could possess without continuing to return to it. "I do not ask pardon," he says, "for what there is of untruth in such verses, considered strictly as matters of fact," [9] a statement so absurd in a poet that it is a complete exposure. At bottom, Wordsworth deplored the principle of "poetic credibility." He much preferred a poetry that needs no such excuse.

– 2 –

Wordsworth's most extended and practical discussion of sincerity, in which he struggles to apply the concept in evaluating particular poems, occurs in the often neglected

Essay on Epitaphs (1810), originally written for Coleridge's periodical, *The Friend*. The question arises in an undeniably quaint way in this *Essay*. He imagines himself in a village churchyard. With strange simplicity, he forgets that the form and substance of epitaphs are strongly influenced by convention. We know that the dead must have possessed their share of human failings, yet in a churchyard we hear nothing of them. Wordsworth at once labors to explain this deviation. For one thing, the epitaphs may be more truthful than we suppose. From various causes — for example, vice is more noticeable than virtue — we tend to underestimate the prevalence of goodness, especially in rural communities. But however far we push the reflection, we are still left with a teasing recognition that epitaphs do not tell the whole truth.

Wordsworth employs two major arguments in justification, both of them indispensable to him throughout his life. First he distinguishes between total representation and a selectivity that preserves what matters most. For even if on a tombstone things are not mentioned "which did exist," the epitaph still remains a "faithful image." It "*is* truth, and of the highest order . . . it is truth hallowed by love." The truth presented is of the "highest order" because — to speak plainly — love fogs the mind. It is a "luminous mist" through which only the essential "parts" of the "object" will be seen. (There is also a purely poetic gain. As a result of this selective process, the epitaph will "impress and affect the more.") [10] It appears, then, that when a poet sets out to re-create some particular experience, sincerity need not bar him from eliminating details and aspects. Anticipating a bit, we can add that the selection is less likely to conflict with sincerity when it is carried on unconsciously, long before the poem is written and without reference to its needs. In the second place, Wordsworth explains the absence of "detraction" in graveyards by an appeal to psychological probability. An epitaph should be composed only by be-reaved mourners (no one else can hope to be sincere), and they would certainly not enter into minute explorations of character. "To analyse the characters . . . of those whom we love, is not a common or natural employment of men at any time," least of all "do we incline to these refinements" under the pressure of grief. [11] And, of course, death would inspire no one to recollect traits of character less admired. Sincerity requires, then, that you express your own feelings and impressions, and there is the added implication that, in some sense, what you honestly feel to be true must be true.

Here, indeed, we touch a chief point in Wordsworth's description of sincerity. It is not clearly said in the *Essay on Epitaphs*. It is implied through the whole of his work. There are senses in which "truth" and "sincerity" could be opposed, "truth" referring to things as they are, "sincerity" to our opinions and feelings. The split could easily result in per-plexities; one might ask whether a poet has earned the praise of sincerity when he misunderstands his experience, a question that especially occurs to those who cannot accept Wordsworth's doctrine of nature. But Wordsworth strenu-ously resists both this particular distinction and the way of thinking that leads to such antitheses. He shows that our individual minds diffuse shape, tone, and meaning through whatever comes to us from without as the raw data of an experience. In fact, we have no knowledge of things as they are in themselves, but only of our impressions. And yet we live by these impressions. To stop at this point would be to concede what Santayana calls "normal madness," that is, the subjective filtering and distortion of reality that no fi-nite being can avoid. But Wordsworth held that our impres-sions can correspond to reality. To explain how this can be, he put on, with Coleridge, metaphysical wings, and, like

Coleridge, he also kept an introspective interest in the creative process itself.

Wordsworth assumed that the quality of a poem as an aesthetic object — its richness, organic integration, and power — measures the truth of what it conveys, meaning by "truth" a harmony with ultimate realities. The reasons for this have to do with the synthesizing habits of the poetic mind and also with the general criteria or tests of "truth" Wordsworth accepted, two points of his doctrine that will come up in more detail later on. Most of us, if we hope to arrive at "truth" or even a good opinion, might feel that we ought to pause and rummage among our impressions. We want to be judicious because we have to be inferential. To Wordsworth — at least, if he is faithful to one of his dominant premises — such fumbling and creaking up a mental ladder simply evidence a state of mind that is far from truth and will never get there. The mind of a great poet does not hesitate in self-division or doubt — not in those moments when it can create poetry. It assimilates and integrates all its experience; it is complete and ready. But the assimilating and integrating can be fully carried out only when they are grounded in truth, only when our inward impressions correspond to outward realities. When this accord is absent, we will be plagued by feelings of uncertainty and inward strife, as most of us usually are, and in such times we will not be able to write poetry. One can say, then, that the impressions we entertain will correspond to reality when they are integrated with each other, or when they exist in a mind that organically interrelates all its functions and contents. This, indeed, is perfect sincerity in the highest sense of the term. But it is a sense extremely difficult to apply in discussing or distinguishing works of art.

In a more practical sense, Wordsworth was urging a fidelity to inward impression or feeling, as it is or was on a particular occasion. Anyone who had done this much could not be reproached. And without this, a lyric could not give satisfaction. What Wordsworth said of epitaphs he would think true for all poetry of personal utterance: "Literature is here so far identified with morals, the quality of the act so far determined by our notion of the aim and purpose of the agent, that nothing can please us, however well executed in its kind, if we are persuaded that the primary virtues of sincerity, earnestness, and a moral interest in the main object are wanting." [12] It was a commonplace of classical rhetoric, more than ever repeated in the eighteenth century, that you will not be able to move others unless you are yourself moved. But the same verbal formulas often survive from one age to the next while their content gradually changes. By Wordsworth's time this maxim of rhetoric had been turned around. Sincerity, which had been prescribed only as a means to effective utterance, had now become a literary value in its own right, a test by which works of art could be tried. "The writer who would excite sympathy is bound . . . to give proof that he himself has been moved." [13]

– 3 –

For this reason, Wordsworth rightly sees that he must establish a "criterion of sincerity," that is, rules by which one can judge whether a writer is sincere. As usual, he remains practical and concrete. He attempts to induce his rules from particular epitaphs by minute analysis (an "irksome" but sometimes necessary employment, he says). When we reduce his analyses to the general principles that work through them, Wordsworth (like most persons who tackle this baffling problem) appears disappointing. His few criteria cannot hold as proof. But Wordsworth would not deny this. He seems to confine himself to naming probable signs, what people will usually accept as indications of sincerity. So we can drop his own attempt to evaluate particular poems by this standard, shifting the discussion to a more profitable ground. Since his poetry had to seem sincere, and since he had considered what would make for the desired impression, it is easy to infer that what he held to be primary indications would also represent major stylistic aims. For Wordsworth not only benefits from our natural attraction to honest speech. To some extent, he exploits it.

Spontaneous utterance, a "simple effusion of the moment," practically guarantees that the sentiments vented are honestly felt. (Whether a *poem* can be spontaneous is another question.) Signs of spontaneity might be a colloquial diction, an informal syntax, a natural or psychologically probable movement of thought. But the most reliable sign of spontaneity is strong passion. The assumption issues from a simplified psychology. Some circumstance, such as the death of a loved person, presents itself to the mind; passions are excited; they collect themselves and pour out in speech, breaking through all psychological impediments and escaping in their headlong rush any prudential reserve that second thoughts might suggest. If the psychology is indeed overly simple, it still seems to influence our judgment. At least when we are directly addressed — someone "looks you in the eye" — and the speaker seems deeply moved, as indicated by tears, a light in the eye, gestures, or whatever, most of us still presume sincerity. We seem to grant that passion has no leisure to lie. On the other hand, perfect composure and a smooth tongue are often regarded with suspicion; we are likely to confuse poise with pose. Hence an epitaph that seems a "naked ejaculation" implies sincerity, and "will not be less acceptable for the rudeness of the expression." [14]

Taking spontaneous passion as a test, Wordsworth instances various signs of insincerity, signs naturally to be avoided in his own verse. An evident diligence to produce artful effects immediately condemns itself. It proves that the "better affections" of the author are "less occupied . . . than his vanity delighted" as he "curiously" constructs a "fabric to be wondered at." Pope especially proves that he writes from vanity, not only by his unnatural diction, but by the sequence of his ideas; "the connections are mechanical and arbitrary." Examples of mechanical connection are ideas suggested by words, as from alliteration, or by a habit of antithetical thinking, "words doing their own work and one half of the line manufacturing the rest," or ideas "formally accumulated" in search of a rhyme.[15] These operations prove themselves to be mechanical when the balance, antithesis, alliteration, rhyme, or whatever, obscures meaning, or violates psychological probability, or even makes the poem self-contradictory. More generally, whatever suggests that the head may have been more busy than the heart offers grounds for suspicion, and here Wordsworth thinks also of the metaphysical verse of the early seventeenth century. Far-fetched conceits imply conscious labor and the meddling interference of the intellect. In fact, any straining to match the fashionable style of a particular age has a "killing power"; for it demonstrates that the writer "is acting a part, has leisure for affectation," and, perhaps most important, "feels that without it he could do nothing." [16] Here, of course, Wordsworth stumbles over his incorrect assumption that passion will speak the same language in all ages, a language distinguished mainly by force, directness, and simplicity. Such reasonings influenced Wordsworth throughout his life. In his last years he cast a suspicious eye over Petrarch's "love verses." Many of his poems "must have flowed, I do not say from a wish to display his own talent" — Wordsworth is struggling to be charitable — "but from a habit of exercising his intellect in that way rather than from an impulse of his heart." [17]

If the major criterion is the presence of spontaneous emotion, we are more or less reduced to asking what in fact indicates emotion. One can set aside such obvious matters as exclamation or direct assertion by naming passions, though they are important in Wordsworth. In the *Essay on Epitaphs*, Wordsworth moves at once to something more subtle. A second empirical sign of sincerity in a poem would be a massive, organic integration and inevitability — "there is nothing arbitrary or mechanical, but it is an organized body, of which the members are bound together by a common life" — for strong feeling spontaneously working will produce these qualities. Of one egregious poem Wordsworth remarks, "there is no under current; no skeleton or stamina of thought and feeling. The Reader will at once perceive that nothing in the heart of the Writer has determined either the choice, the order or the expression, of the ideas." [18]

— 4 —

That poetry should be spontaneous is the most important single assumption to keep in mind if one seeks to account for Wordsworth's style. Perhaps it is the basic convention of nineteenth-century poetry. It dominates every aspect of technique, from the lesser cares of diction and versification to the handling of over-all shape or arrangement of parts — what might be called "plot" if we use the term to refer not only to the design of a narrative but also to the sequence or pattern of things said in meditative or lyric poetry. Indeed, the attempt to be spontaneous helps explain why, if considered as wholes, the longer works of romantic writers are seldom successful. However brilliant they can be in passages, they are likely to remind one of Coleridge's famous self-description: "My Thoughts are like Surinam Toads — as they crawl on, little Toads vegetate out from back & side, grow quickly, & draw off the attention from the mother Toad." [19] The inconvenience is the same that Johnson found in Thomson's *Seasons*. The "great defect" is "want of method": "The memory wants the help of order, and the curiosity is not excited by suspense or expectation." But the trouble cannot be blamed entirely on the premise of spontaneity. Any attempt to create art must cope with an intrinsic conflict between amplitude, or richness of content, and cleanliness of shape, and artists could be roughly classified by the choice they make. The romantics much preferred amplitude. There is a serious suggestion from the youthful Charles Lamb to his equally young friend, Coleridge, a suggestion that reflects much in romantic art — its daring and hope, its accompanying risk of sprawl and diffuseness — : "I have a dim recollection that, when in town, you were talking about the Origin of Evil as a most prolific subject for a long poem. Why not adopt it, Coleridge? there would be room for imagination." [20] Indeed, there might be nothing but room. The romantic dilemma is summed up in a bizarre observation of Haydon's: "In phrenological development" Wordsworth "is without constructiveness while imagination is as big as an egg." [21]

But if Wordsworth's poetry denies readers the sense of formal artistry in its construction, it offers the alternative pleasure of artlessness — those winding journeys of thought that look so unpremeditated. This sinuous progression, as of an act of mind taking place immediately, is always valued by romantic spirits. Yeats described it as "the crooked road of life," and contrasted it with the tireless mechanism of Bernard Shaw, who appeared to him in a dream as a sewing machine. "The Serpent," says Coleridge, "by which the ancients emblem'd the Inventive faculty appears to me, in its mode of motion most exactly to emblem a writer of Genius. He varies his course yet still glides onwards — all lines of motion are his — all beautiful, & all propulsive." [22] But unless a poem does vent itself in an undeliberated way, the ideal of spontaneity does not entirely free poets from the anxieties of construction. One must resolve a question as one writes: what sequence or arrangement of things said will have the look of a spontaneous flight. Wordsworth and his readers might agree that strong emotion suggests spontaneous utterance, but then what is the path of thought under the influence of emotion? He must at least feel satisfied that the course of his poem shows a psychological probability. But how is one to know? Many of the *Lyrical Ballads* suggest that he is trying to imitate motions of thought observed in others, and also that he was much influenced by the psychological treatises of his day, which were empirical and descriptive. These poems, he says, attempt to trace "the primary laws of our nature: chiefly, as far as regards the manner in which we associate ideas in a state of excitement," or, as he also phrases it, "to follow the fluxes and refluxes of the mind when agitated by the great and simple affections of our nature." [23] Needless to say, he does not seek to describe principles of association but to enact them. "The Thorn," for example, presents the way in which persons such as the narrator — a retired captain of a small trading vessel, Wordsworth explains — "cleave to the same ideas," and it shows "the turns of passion . . . by which their conversation is swayed." [24] Wordsworth could even hope that poetry might make up a "science of feelings," a science as objective in its own sphere as the Newtonian science of matter.

Wordsworth was always alert to defend his works on similar grounds. Each of his poems highlights some moral sentiment, he argues, but each also embodies some common process of the mind — "some general principle, or law of thought, or of our intellectual constitution." There is, for instance, his sonnet, "With Ships the sea was sprinkled far and nigh." Who has not, he asks Lady Beaumont,

> felt that the mind can have no rest among a multitude of objects, of which it either cannot make one whole, or from which it cannot single out one individual, whereupon may be concentrated the attention divided among or distracted by a multitude? After a certain time we must either select one image or object, which must put out of view the rest wholly, or must subordinate them to itself while it stands forth as a Head.

The sonnet begins,

> With Ships the sea was sprinkled far and nigh,
> Like stars in heaven, and joyously it showed;
> Some lying fast at anchor in the road,
> Some veering up and down, one knew not why.

As he analyzes the sonnet, Wordsworth seeks mainly to point out various stages within a continuing psychological process. "I am represented," he says,

> casting my eyes over the sea, sprinkled with a multitude of Ships . . . my mind may be supposed to float up and down among them in a kind of dreamy indifference with respect either to this or that one, only in a pleasurable state of feeling with respect to the whole prospect. "Joyously it showed," this continued till that feeling may be supposed to have passed away,

and a kind of comparative listlessness or apathy to have suc-
ceeded, as at this line, "Some veering up and down, one knew
not why."

The analysis continues at length, fondling all parts of the
poem. The sonnet concludes, he quaintly explains, by invit-
ing the reader "to rest his mind as mine is resting." [25]

Wordsworth was always a most eager and prolific com-
mentator on his own poetry, and he exploits all sorts of
critical approaches. He tells the literary sources of particular
lines or poems, connects them with incidents in his life, interprets them in the light of his general premises, and points
out felicities. He can also undertake systematic accounts or
explications, discussing the poem as a whole made up of
parts and disclosing the over-all meaning to which the parts
contribute. He does not, however, examine the parts with
a scrupulous attention to verbal meanings; minute analysis
took another line. This, indeed, is the point. When he "ex-
plicates," he does not apply the conventions of our own
age, but rather those we have attempted to describe, especially that a poem is a spontaneous, generative act of expression taking place through a moment of time. The comment
cited above is one example. Close analysis does not exhaust
itself on the verbal texture so much as on what, in a sense,
lies behind it. Language is scrutinized mainly as an index to
successive states of feeling evolving in a natural way; and
it is these states of feeling that are analyzed at length. For
another example, one can turn to a notebook interpretation
of "To Joanna," one presumably made for Wordsworth's
private use.

I begin to relate the story, meaning in a certain degree to divert
or partly play upon the Vicar. . . . my mind partly forgets its
purpose, being softened by the images of beauty in the descrip-

tion of the rock, and the delicious morning, and . . . [then] I am caught in the trap of my own imagination. I entirely lose sight of my first purpose. I take fire in the lines "that ancient woman." I go on in that strain of fancy [at the phrase] "Old Skiddaw" and terminate the description in tumult.[26]

Wordsworth naturally looked at earlier writers through his own conventions. It was easy enough to do so. Most lyric poetry can be interpreted as a sequence of spontaneous emotions, if that is what one has in mind. The difference is partly that romantic poets were careful to preserve the impression, and partly that they exploited it to waive the necessity for any other model or guide — for example, a movement based on formal logic, or on the pattern of a devotional exercise (both familiar in seventeenth-century verse), or on a literary genre so far as it may dictate a sequence of moods, as in the pastoral elegy. The conventions of romantic poetry were thoroughly understood and accepted throughout the nineteenth century, and it often happened that by the expectations derived from them even Wordsworth seemed deficient. There is a "taint of duty" in his verse, thought Bagehot. "Things seem right where they are, but they seem to be put where they are." [27] To Mill, his poetry had "little even of the appearance of spontaneousness," [28] and John Wilson felt that even in Wordsworth's great ode "the movements are sometimes too slow and laborious." [29] Curiously enough, many of the things often deplored today in Shelley — the random association, the jungle of metaphor, the vague outcries, the primitive architecture, shapeless and insubstantial — were accepted by nineteenth-century readers as evidence of genuine passion and spontaneity. They did not think these traits beautiful, but viewed them with a sympathetic toleration, thinking them inseparable from a true poetic temperament.

– 5 –

There is no compelling reason, needless to say, why in reading Wordsworth we should share or even think of the conventions he accepted. Indeed, any calculated attempt to use them once more could only be speculative, and a reading based on such effort would seem a mere curiosity, like most archaeological reconstruction. In one sense, a poet must be our contemporary or he means nothing to us. But to restore the past — so far as one can — has at least the value that it challenges the present, and helps emancipate one from the needless anxieties and limitations it may impose. The ultimate gain is that, delivered from stock values of the moment or the militancies of theory, one can make a more independent and more simply human response to the poetry of any time. It seems that two things, important for a full appreciation of Wordsworth, tend to be submerged in our own conventional approaches to poetry. In the first place, a romantic poem especially exploits and depends upon our sense of time passing. Less than most poetry should romantic verse be conceived as a spatial design or mosaic into which each part has been fitted, thus encouraging cross-reference back and forth. Often, in fact, it exhibits the drama of a man gradually discovering his meaning.[30] Since Wordsworth can be condensed and elliptical, we may often have to pause, puzzling out some phrase or line. But the full meaning of a phrase can be obtained only by sensing the process of feeling and thought that evolves through it. If this seems a truism, it is often forgotten in our analytic exercises. It may be that the highest enjoyment of Wordsworth is not well served by the diligence of minutely analytical reading as we practice it nowadays. In theory there should be no difficulty; we are inspecting each expression to see how it fits into the evolving process. In fact, however, the sense of organic movement disappears. Putting it another way, we might remind ourselves that every poem dictates the speed at which it ought to be read. By going too slowly we would show ourselves insensitive to the verse, and we would miss effects vital to the poem. Of course, there is no reason why a critical discussion of Wordsworth's poetry should not analyze slowly. The trouble comes in actually reading this way, and in Wordsworth's case it might be better to stick with what is always a more natural way of enjoying a poem — that is, to appreciate what one can as one reads through it, and then to read it again many times, and to read other poems by the same writer, until the meaning of every part clarifies and deepens itself, as it will do, while the poem continues to be felt as a massive experience.

In the second place, according to Wordsworth and his contemporaries, poetic style must be appropriate to the speaker in his supposed state of mind. This would be a critical commonplace in any age. It takes on significance mainly as it is mixed with other premises or pursued in isolation. For at least in principle, romantic writers could make it virtually the sole ideal of style. In practice, needless to say, they kept many other things in mind. But the ideal of naturalness could always be exploited as a defense. Whatever a poet's manner of expression might be, it was allowable so long as it seemed organic to his feelings at the moment. For example, mixed metaphors are generally decried, and Wordsworth can match any eighteenth-century or modern critic in destructive analysis from the standpoint of good sense. But the wildest mixtures could be permitted when they seemed to proceed from uncalculating enthusiasm. Hence when we read romantic verse we often confuse ourselves or call forth needless ingenuity. We try, that is, to establish a pattern — usually a pattern of metaphor — much more consistent than the writer thought necessary. Or, as one final example of the way later assumptions may collide with those of the romantics, the imagist poets admired an economy of words that may seem excessive to others, and they sometimes made the rather spinsterish virtue of thrift a necessary trait of all good poetry. If we seek economy, Wordsworth will prove a disappointment, except in a few, uncharacteristic poems — the fine "A Slumber did my Spirit Seal," for example, which for a while attracted as much comment as "Tintern Abbey." Wordsworth more rightly considered that even "repetition and apparent tautology are frequently beauties of the highest kind." His reasons are typical. Among them is that

Words, a Poet's words more particularly, ought to be weighed in the balance of feeling, and not measured by the space which they occupy upon paper. . . . every man must know that an attempt is rarely made to communicate impassioned feelings without something of an accompanying consciousness of the inadequateness of our own powers, or the deficiencies of language. During such efforts there will be a craving in the mind, and as long as it is unsatisfied the speaker will cling to the same words, or words of the same character.[31]

– 6 –

Like anyone else, a poet is never influenced solely by one ideal. Simplifying into large and general categories, one can say that Wordsworth espoused three, mutually antagonistic premises: poetry is spontaneous, personal utterance, as already described; it is a craft or art; it is an imitation of nature. The premise of craft or art should be associated especially with Wordsworth's later years, and that of nature with the *Lyrical Ballads*, but the three hopes or aims contended in him throughout his life. Since Wordsworth was not the man to sacrifice a poetic instinct to a poetic theory (though he would sacrifice to a moral belief), the rival pulls did not much trouble his practice. But the jostle of these diverse premises shows clearly in his theoretical remarks about style, producing both the confusion and occasional profundity. For an example, I will mention only Wordsworth's main points concerning diction and versification.

In speaking of "art," Wordsworth does not quite have in mind whatever the term may now suggest. Neither does he usually adopt the sense of the term common in the eighteenth century, when art might mean simply planned communication, a calculated effectiveness in evoking intended responses. For this notion of art was a product of the rhetorical traditions that Wordsworth wished to discard and from which we have been receding ever since. When Wordsworth deplores "art" ("the adversary of Nature"), he is usually referring to adornment, something added to "simplicity and self-presented truth." [32] When he goes so far as to praise it ("I yield to none in *love for my art*"),[33] he is usually thinking of the deliberate labor and revision that went into his own poems. He would touch up, so to speak, for the sake of logic, clarity, euphony, or whatever, but, from a militant and rigid point of view, it is precisely this process of touching up that conflicts with sincerity. Wordsworth could readily create

> a memorial which to me
> Was all sufficient, and, to my own mind
> Recalling the whole picture, seemed to speak
> A universal language.

At the same time, he knew that to write for others demands

"considerate and laborious work," if only for the sake of being intelligible.[34] Yet merely to ask whether he is intelligible compels a writer to put himself in the place of his audience, a process that immediately tempts toward insincerity; "laborious work" is not spontaneous. Wordsworth never openly acknowledges, however, that the necessity of art could threaten sincerity. He shows, instead, the typically English ability to muffle ideas and ignore contradictions that has always fascinated either clearer or sometimes only shallower thinkers on the continent, and that may be variously described as muddle-headed, hypocritical, or remarkably sagacious.

"Nature," in the sense that it could be opposed both to personal sincerity and to "art," was a concept inherited from the recent past. It was the "nature" of which, Pope said, a perfect copy could be found in Homer, the normative or universal aspect of things, the "general nature" of Johnson and Reynolds, which the poet should strive to imitate. Wordsworth uses the term in this sense only when he refers to human nature, to an inherent character that all men share. But Wordsworth habitually sought to connect abstractions with concrete experience, and, in this case, he fell into the sort of practicality and literalness that can often discredit an idea. Influenced by various considerations — by primitivistic assumptions in the wake of Rousseau, by the need of a pure sample for scientific study, and by the hope for bold contours that a poet might easily trace — Wordsworth argued that the elements of human nature, which were tangled and tinseled over in city dwellers, displayed themselves naked in country people. Thus both neoclassic and romantic trains of thought could lurk in the ample shade of the word "nature." But unless you were lucky enough to be a peasant poet, you were still obliged to render something caught from without, thus foregoing personal utterance.

$$-7-$$

Were a poet struggling only to be sincere, he might not be able even to begin to compose. In other words, the clash of contradictory premises in Wordsworth's thinking about poetry did not arise simply because he lived in a time of changing poetic values; it is inevitable in a poetry of sincerity. The reasons have to do both with the nature of poetry and with a writer's state of mind as he composes. A poem must plainly be something more than sincere talk. A writer needs habits and purposes that can limit freedom. From a purely ideal point of view, to preserve a chance for complete sincerity one would have to keep oneself undetermined, forming no customs, exercising no favorite themes, acquiring no skill in one idiom more than another. For who knows how the wind of the spirit will veer? One must be ready to speak in any way. But unless we imagine that some higher power will dictate to a poet, such vacant freedom is merely intimidating. That is why the mind deliberately leans upon a model, encastles itself in rules and conventions, frames theoretical programs and manifestoes, or sinks into fashions, being grateful, in any case, to escape so far as it can the numbing horror of mere liberty, a naked heart confronting a blank page. We are touching, in other words, upon the psychological appeal to a poet of whatever can restrict at the start the choices open to him.

The more a poet composes with a distinct consciousness of his aims and commitments, the more they ease anxiety. For obviously, to borrow the old saying, if we do not know what harbor we seek, no wind can seem favorable. But if the aims are held in mind simply as general hopes, a poet may still find himself at a loss, envisioning his port, but not knowing how to get there. Our poetic ideals become helpful to the extent that they are particular; for then they can directly inform the task of composition, suggesting a subject matter, an attitude toward it, a diction, a verse form, and so forth. Certainly a poet does not wholly envision his poem before it is accomplished; it comes right, as Yeats said, like "the closing of a box." The point is only that it helps a good deal if some things have been settled before he begins. Given his assumptions about poetry, Wordsworth had both to accept and deplore such commitments. Or rather, one should perhaps say that he managed to achieve whatever reassurance may be provided by thinking one has a ready guide, while at the same time maintaining, for practical purposes, his own freedom; the commitments he announced could intervene very little in the process of composition.

With respect to diction, as in other matters, Wordsworth rallied himself to the standard of "nature." He tried, however, to restrict the meaning of the term, so that instead of being obviously permissive and pliable, "nature," at least in self-deluding hope, becomes something close to an imperious rule from without. When Wordsworth, in the Preface to the *Lyrical Ballads*, urges that a poet must use the "very language of men" or the "language really used by men," the phrases are, as Coleridge said, vague and equivocal, though scarcely lacking in historical significance, especially when backed by the massive example of Wordsworth's achievement. But Wordsworth had in mind a more specific application; a natural language can be discovered in the speech of rustics, especially when they are passionately excited. Since a poet is not usually himself a rustic, it seems fair to ask how he obtains this language. Wordsworth has few precise directions, but an analogy may help us to answer. Since a poet should also express natural thoughts and emotions, he must know when his feelings are normally human, and when they are possibly eccentric. In a letter to John Wilson, Wordsworth supposes himself asked where we may find our "best measure" of human nature. Finding himself in a tight squeeze, he becomes vehement and oracular: "I answer, [from with]in; by stripping our own hearts naked" — something scarcely possible — "and by looking out of ourselves to- [wards men] who lead the simplest lives, and those most according to nature." [35] If this comes close to tautology, Wordsworth thinks it is still a practical help. He is urging us to cast our eyes in a certain direction. And Wordsworth thought his "measure" of naturalness was firm and clear. He even supposed a poet might copy it in a "slavish and mechanical" way. [36] So also with the language of poetry. Wordsworth talks of "adopting" the speech of simple or rustic persons, and certainly implies collecting it from without, presumably through the ear. To the end of his life, Wordsworth seems never to have changed his mind on this point, even after Coleridge's destructive analysis in the *Biographia Literaria*, which, however, Wordsworth had merely skimmed, at least by 1817 and according to his own statement (though he saw enough of it to be offended). In 1836 he told Justice Coleridge that "many incidents" in his poems were "drawn from the narration of Mrs. Wordsworth" or of Dorothy, he himself giving "the oral part as nearly as he could in the very words of the speakers." [37] If Mary and Dorothy were not quite persons in "humble and rustic life," Wordsworth might still trust they would be "less under the influence of social vanity" and hence would "convey their feelings and notions in simple and unelaborated expressions." [38]

But Wordsworth had abundant good sense and introspective honesty. He knew that even in adopting the speech of Dorothy or Mary he was in the habit of "dropping . . . all vulgarisms or provincialisms." These, he explained, are merely "accidents," and a poet must still "separate" his "composition from the vulgarity and meanness of ordinary life." [39] The premise that a poem imitates nature must be modified, in other words, by the reminder that it is also a work of art. Wordsworth would only use the language of rustics after having "purified" it, and if the purifying does not involve deliberate elevation, it at least requires "selection" from the speech you actually hear. But since nature must be purified of its "accidents," it can hardly be used as a guide in the process. [40] Hence it is not surprising that Wordsworth's poems — even the most extreme experiments — never duplicate rustic speech, as Coleridge pointed out. Had Wordsworth described his attempt in another way, as an effort within the province of art to *approximate* the "very language" of a class of men, no one could object; for that is what poems such as "The Thorn" accomplish. But had Wordsworth admitted this, he would have had to abandon "nature" as a strict test or guide in the process of writing, thus also relinquishing whatever psychological reassurance he may have obtained. At best, however, the guide could only be elusive, no more than a shadowy idea in the mind. For granted the need to purify, the standard of nature can only mean the speech of rustics as reconstituted by the poet, and the poet must finally surrender himself to his own taste and judgment.

With regard to the diction of poetry, then, the general stylistic aims announced in the Preface to the *Lyrical Ballads* might supply some positive directions, but nothing very detailed or helpful. In view of the evidences of insincerity we mentioned, it might seem that Wordsworth could at least help himself to rules of avoidance. Certain mannerisms might be considered untouchable, but this was not the case.

It is true that whatever seems artfully labored will intrude in a disconcerting way, but, on the other hand, there is no particular expression or type of language that cannot seem natural. For example, hyperbole is usually a "mean instrument," but if emotion is sufficiently intense, "strangeness" may become the very "order of Nature." [41] The point is simply that, as Coleridge put it, "every metaphor, every personification, should have its justifying cause in some *passion* either of the Poet's mind, or of the Characters described by the poet." [42] The only conclusion to be derived from Wordsworth's remarks about diction and figures is that he would not "trick out or elevate," but would instead apply rather strict psychological criteria. Unless we believe that Wordsworth actually composed in undeliberating spontaneity, it follows that he would have to decide for himself whether the feelings expressed in a poem would naturally vent themselves in a figurative language.

– 8 –

When Wordsworth thinks about versification, similar difficulties present themselves in a more acute way. For the plain fact is that verse cannot be either spontaneous or natural, if we mean by "nature" the way men actually express themselves. This is true even though the romantics felt that impassioned speech tends to fall into marked rhythms; a favorite example was the Song of Deborah. There is still a gap between rhythms spontaneous in passion and metrical or stanzaic forms. Wordsworth overcame the contradiction as best he could. He exploited, as I said, forms of verse that would exert the least possible control, so far as such forms were available to him. But, needless to say, he frequently used stricter forms as well. They represent the counter-spirit inevitably created by his achieved liberty. Since freedom brings anxiety, set forms are a relief. Wordsworth's dilemma reveals itself in one of his protests. In high indignation he declares that a poet who submits to a "formal mould" has "put his heart to school," yet he vents the thought in a sonnet, a rigid form which, as he elsewhere explains, eases the "weight of too much liberty." [43] It is also appropriate that Wordsworth should cast his self-dedication to "Duty" in stanzas, the same stanza, he points out, as Gray's "Hymn to Adversity." For fixed forms were adopted with a sense of grudge, as a retrenchment in the face of difficulties. They might be necessary, but they are always unfortunate; it would be much better if a poet's spontaneous impulses might be an "unerring light."

The dilemma spreads far beyond Wordsworth, reappearing in all romantic poets and vexing most poets since. To employ set forms, or, indeed, to accept any commitment to a particular idiom, tone, theme, theory or function, merely limits the scope of poetry. Moreover, if one is struggling to be sincere, one may find that aspects of one's inner life — perhaps those that come to seem most significant — can no longer be expressed. Hence the romantics much preferred not to make or, at least, to acknowledge such commitments. They yearned to be instinctive as birds, or, changing the metaphor, they wanted to counterpart the vital spirit of nature, where all is spontaneous assimilation and growth. Or, like Byron, they dramatized their wayward self-will; in *Don Juan* the drastic shifts of tone, the Hudibrastic rhymes, the endless vagaries and digressions, finally mean that the poem, like the universe of Calvin, has no law save the whim of its author. They are flounces of egotism, and, of course, they are reminders that so great a thing as a lord does not bend his mind to the drudgery of art. The crowning impertinence was that Byron appointed himself the defender of Pope.

The romantic attack on Pope was often based directly on this issue of freedom against limitation, range against confinement. The youthful Keats (himself a "tadpole of the Lakes," according to Byron) provides an example. In "Sleep and Poetry" he looks back to the poets of England before Pope and scolds the shrunk purview of neoclassic writers. Moreover, he associates their constricted theme and sensibility with their use of rigid forms. Neoclassic poets were "closely wed/ To musty laws lined out with wretched rule," and it typifies the romantic mood that this passage of ebullient scorn rhymes "wed" with "dead." [44] But from one point of view, the whole of Keats's brief career, with his constant essaying of new styles, his search for a function and justification, shows a brilliant, heroic struggle with precisely those anxieties from which neoclassic poets were spared. Much may have been closed to them, but that at least simplified choice.

There is, indeed, a vicious circle. The doubt, anxiety, and guilt rampant in the modern world result directly from the variousness of possibility still increasing before us. In comparison with any past age, our culture obviously includes and nourishes more diversities of belief, more ways of valuing, more shapings of feeling and experience. But in the intellectual world, to increase options is usually to reduce confidence in any one option; we disbelieve because so much competes for our belief. Thus one can say that the romantic or Faustian spirit is liable to doubt because it has experienced so widely; but then one can also say that it experiences so widely because it doubts in the first place. An honest agnosticism must be continually seeking or it has no right even to be agnostic. But if doubt can be a spur to activity, it is not a track for it. Referring back to Wordsworth's "Ode to Duty," we may feel that if we cannot be intuitive and spontaneous we are threatened with paralysis; for our "duty" is much easier to apostrophize than to define.

III

THE PROCESS
OF COMPOSITION

WORDSWORTH OFFERS a partial description of the way he composed in the Preface to the *Lyrical Ballads* — the well-known sentences about "emotion recollected in tranquillity" and the "spontaneous overflow of powerful feelings." Supplementary utterances are scattered in other prefaces, letters, reported conversations, and the like. Since they emerge from introspection, it seems reasonable to combine them with anecdotes about him. The data still remain scant and superficial, but to some extent it is possible to reconstruct the methods or processes that resulted in Wordsworth's poetry. It will be seen that he claimed to be more spontaneous than he was, which is not surprising. On the other hand, he fell into procedures — including unconscious ones — which at least fostered a relative spontaneity, if we compare his methods with those of other poets. And, what is more important, his working habits were likely to produce effects that would look like spontaneous composition.

That a poem might emerge spontaneously was a desperate but necessary hope. It was the only chance for resolving the otherwise impossible dilemma. In creating a poem, one must desire many things besides direct honesty of utterance and yet one may think sincerity threatened or diluted simply because other aims are kept in mind. But if a poem — a completed, metrical, and shapely expression — can be conceived without premeditation and without deliberation, sincerity can be reconciled with art. To some extent, of course, the handling of formal elements can become habitual and unconscious in a poet. Unless we remembered this, we might gape in wonder that even some of the strongest minds of the century — Newman and Mill, for example — bowed down to cant and catchword: poetry, says Mill, "is little else than a pouring-forth of the thoughts and images that pass across the mind" in a state of strong feeling.[1] If we still disagree, we can easily forgive nineteenth-century readers their slogans when we analyze our own.

The premise of spontaneous composition can also be viewed as the weakening toward literalness of a more complex insight. When Coleridge and his German contemporaries thought of a poem as an organism that grows by "evolving the germ within," they made a valuable contribution to aesthetic theory. For Coleridge, this view did not necessarily preclude conscious manipulation by the poet, but the tendency was to identify what was still called "judgment" with the spontaneous rightness of creative genius. "You feel strongly," Wordsworth tells a younger writer, "trust to those feelings, and your poem will take its shape and proportions as a tree does from the vital principle that actuates it." [2] But if a poem may be compared to a tree, or, as Coleridge once suggested, to a "Covey of poetic Partridges with whirring wings of music, or wild Ducks *shaping* their rapid flight in forms always regular," [3] the main conscious task for a poet is to initiate activity, to get all those wings into motion. Hence when Wordsworth talks about the process of composition, he is mainly concerned to describe the moment when utterance begins to flow.

– 2 –

Like many of the romantic writers, Wordsworth speculates in lifelong fascination concerning the general characteristics of a creative mind, the activities and powers that distinguish it from the minds of other men. He offers a suggestive account of genius in any kind of activity, at least to the extent that "genius" refers to a quality of mental life in the moment, rather than to the production of monumental works, which may, after all, result from the mere bricklaying of talent perpetually applied. The distinction is itself a romantic one. Coleridge, for example, appeared even more astonishingly gifted in his talk than he does in his works. To his contemporaries he was the incarnate idea, or archetype, of genius, and Hazlitt contrasts him with the merely talented William Godwin: Coleridge floated in the upper air, exposing himself to all thought and knowledge, constantly hurtling from one thing to the next ("but his wings saved him"), while Godwin had "*valves* belonging to his mind, to regulate the quantity of gas admitted into it," so that like a steamboat he always arrived at the "promised end." [4] In fact, as they list the traits of "genius" romantic writers usually include a certain prodigality which may seem spendthrift to the man of talent. It is analogous to the verbal wit of Shakespeare, which often appears to serve no strict or necessary purpose, being, as Coleridge says, "like the flourishing of a man's stick, when he is walking, in the full flow of animal spirits." [5] Yeats, for example, thinks that the Richard II of Shakespeare's play is a man of creative genius made useless to the state by his overabundance, and though the interpretation smells of the fin-de-siècle, it is not without point. At least there is a potential genius in Richard, in the self-delighting excess of his mental activity, even in his habit of responding to an immediate situation not by the practical measures it so urgently demands, but by exploring and exhausting the world of feeling it opens up to him. It has affinities with "pure research," or, to put it another way, the realm of his own mind is more vivid and exciting to him than the realm of fact.

Though the amount of play in Wordsworth's verse has been underestimated, it is certainly no match for Shakespeare's. Yet Wordsworth emphasizes that a main characteristic of any poet is his delight in his own sensations, feelings, and thoughts. He is "a man pleased with his own passions and volitions . . . who rejoices more than other men in the spirit of life that is in him." [6] Wordsworth is not saying merely that for excitement and happiness a creative mind does not require gross stimuli from without, though he assumes this to be true. The sensations and thoughts of a poet are extraordinarily vivid to him. As Wordsworth puts it, a poet possesses "more than usual organic sensibility," and he has also "a disposition to be affected more than other men by absent things as if they were present." [7] Neither is Wordsworth referring merely to a liberal use of the mind, an activity unsubdued to any particular task, aim, or morality. He is also trying to suggest something vaguer and possibly more important, that is, the pleasure of consciousness, simply of being, and of any motion of consciousness, and he adds that this is more than usually keen in a poet. In this respect, a poet resembles a child, at least as the romantics imagined or thought they remembered the feelings of childhood. The air we breathe "is to my Babe a perpetual Nitrous Oxyde," says Coleridge. "From morning to night he whirls about and about, whisks, whirls, and eddies, like a blossom in a May-breeze." [8] As it matures, genius retains a sort of

innocent wonder. It combines what the romantics supposed
to be the fresh gaze of a child with the obstinate integrity of
a man consulting his own experience, and hence thinking
outside traditional categories or interpretations.

Most of all, however, Wordsworth insists that a poet has
a connecting mind. He is not, like most of us, passive to
experience, at most a mere filing-cabinet; the sensibility of
genius reacts by linking or relating whatever it notices. The
assertion is safely commonplace, and could be endorsed
equally by an eighteenth-century associationist such as Alexander Gerard, or by T. S. Eliot, who admires in metaphysical poetry the amalgamating of "disparate experience"
and the "direct sensuous apprehension of thought." Wordsworth goes much further. A poet must have "thought long
and deeply" so that "continued influxes of feeling are modified and directed" by thoughts, "which are indeed the rep-
resentatives of all our past feelings." [9] The phrasing of these
remarks issues from psychological theories local to Wordsworth's age, but he is trying to suggest a way of relating that
involves the whole past and present life of the mind in immediate experience.

-3-

It may also be mentioned that any lasting achievement
presupposes a power of unusually sustained and intense concentration. Once when he was a very old man Wordsworth
looked back some forty-six years to compare the working
habits of Coleridge with Southey's. What he says of Coleridge helps to set right the portraits by Chambers and others,
who (following the guilt-ridden and perpetually apologiz-
ing Coleridge himself) show him as gabby and digressive,
and dwell as much on the great works he only planned or
claimed as on the ones he accomplished. Major achievement,

Wordsworth says, results from an almost obsessed state of mind, involving a poet

often times in labour that he cannot dismiss or escape from, though his duty to himself and others may require it. Observe the difference of execution in the Poems of Coleridge and Southey, how masterly is the workmanship of the former, compared with the latter; the one persevered in labour unremittingly, the other could lay down his work at pleasure and turn to anything else.[10]

When Wordsworth was himself engaged in creative activity, he could be virtually oblivious of what was happening around him. During the fatal illness of his children Catharine and Thomas, he was closely involved with the *Excursion*, and could, Aubrey de Vere was later told, hardly be brought to notice their danger.[11] As less striking testimony, there is the simple fact that his domestic circle suffered the annoyances common whenever any member of a family works creatively, or even with strong interest. Delayed dinners were a constant embarrassment to his wife and sister. "Wm. worked at *The Pedlar* all morning," Dorothy confides to her journal. "He kept the dinner waiting till four o'clock."[12] Even when visiting away from home, he made his wife uncomfortable by "similar transgressions," but Mary Wordsworth devised a remedy — her husband would not be oblivious to waste of money. According to a former servant interviewed by Rawnsley,

Mrs. Wudsworth would say, "Ring the bell," but he wouldn't stir, bless ye. "Goa and see what he's doing," she'd say, and we wad goa up to study door and hear him a mumbling and bumming through it. "Dinner's ready, sir," I'd ca' out, he'd goa mumbling on like a deaf man, ya see. And sometimes Mrs.

Wudsworth 'ud say, "Goa and brek a bottle, or let a dish fall just outside door in passage." Eh dear, that maistly wad bring him out, wad that. It was nobbut that as wad, howivver. For ye kna he was a verra careful man, and he couldn't do with brekking t' china.[13]

Like many other persons, Wordsworth found intense creative effort injurious to his general health. "William wished to break off composition, and was unable, and so did himself harm."[14] The nervous strain is suggested by the fact that, when he could not be moving about out-of-doors, creative activity was accompanied by compulsive bodily gestures. He began the *White Doe of Rylstone* walking up and down in "the shelter of a row of stacks in a field." But his shoe was too tight and rubbed the skin from his heel. He gave up walking, but "the irritation of the wounded part was kept up by the act of composition."[15] The symptoms are vague, naturally enough — "uneasiness at my stomach and side, with a dull pain about my heart."[16] As we encounter his complaints, they may sound quaint. They are, after all, phrased either by himself or by persons who loved him and wholly sympathized. One morning on a continental tour Mrs. Wordsworth "Rose at five o'clock . . . but with disturbed mind." For she had left her husband "in bed hurting himself with a sonnet." Later she joined Wordsworth in their carriage, and "have here written down the sonnet, Jones' Parsonage, so I hope he will be at rest."[17] It is suggestive that Mary Wordsworth thinks he may rest once the sonnet is written down. For Wordsworth composed in his head, and a poem existing only in the head is inevitably in a more fluid state than one in manuscript. In other words, to write out what one has mentally prepared involves a more positive commitment to it, or to a settled way of putting it, and hence can be experienced as a crisis and focal point for anxiety. This may be why Wordsworth felt a peculiar aversion to penmanship. To hold a pen gave him, he said, all kinds of bodily uneasiness, and he would usually dictate poems or even letters to various feminine transcribers.

If Wordsworth possessed an unusual gift for prolonged concentration, it is possible, I think, to speculate concerning some of its sources. William James argues that intense effort arises from novel challenge, and that a gifted mind can dwell for a long time on the same subject matter because it continues to find new aspects in it. We can also remind ourselves that though Wordsworth revised slowly, laboriously, and in agony, he usually composed a first draft with pleasurable rapidity. The sense of progress would, of course, make it easier for him to keep going. Finally, he often seems to have produced in one session either a poem or a self-subsisting block of verse, a partially independent unit. As a result, he would be invigorated as he wrote by a hope to complete something before quitting. He often speaks of being teased or haunted by a poem as he works on it. It must have seemed, at times, as though a poem were just about to come right, as though just one more push would bring it into final balance. Thus when "We Are Seven" was "all but finished, I came in and recited it to Mr. Coleridge and my Sister, and said, 'A prefatory stanza must be added, and I should sit down to our little tea-meal with greater pleasure if my task were finished.' I mentioned in substance what I wished to be expressed, and Coleridge immediately threw off the stanza." [18] In this case, Coleridge's contribution was only a temporary relief. Wordsworth later changed the stanza. But the psychological situation must have occurred frequently, and helps explain Wordsworth's obstinate hanging on, while his housemates grew hungry.

– 4 –

Granted a potentially creative mind, Wordsworth then tries to explain how it actually produces a poem. We can begin with the sources of poetry in experience, the poet powerfully impressed and moved on some occasion. The conscious mind may then forget this random moment, but it is not frozen, to revive unchanged at some later date. Instead, perhaps over many years, it fuses with other memories, blends with ideas of value, acquires representative significance. At the same time, aspects of the original perception are dropped as they become irrelevant to the growing nexus of meaningful relations. In a conversation with Aubrey de Vere, Wordsworth mentioned a poet who took rural walks armed with "his pencil and notebook." With "flashing eye and impassioned voice," Wordsworth declared that pencil and notebook should have been left at home. "Then, after several days had passed by, he should have interrogated his memory as to the scene. He would have discovered that while much of what he had admired was preserved to him, much was also most wisely obliterated. That which remained — the picture surviving in his mind — would have presented the ideal and essential truth of the scene."[19] Thus when a poet recollects past experience, he finds that it has been quietly transformed. At the end of this process a poem has prepared itself, and needs only to be put into words.

The moment of crisis and verbal precipitation, when the poem as a content of consciousness becomes a poem in words, is the most obscure in the whole process of composition. Wordsworth makes a valiant effort to describe it in the Preface to the *Lyrical Ballads*:

I have said that poetry is the spontaneous overflow of powerful feelings: it takes its origin from emotion recollected in tranquillity: the emotion is contemplated till, by a species of re-action, the tranquillity gradually disappears, and an emotion, kindred to that which was before the subject of contemplation, is gradually produced, and does itself actually exist in the mind.[20]

Wordsworth's phrasing here may be rather involved, but it is subtle and exact, though his use of the word "emotion" may be confusing. He had good reason for employing it. Emotion was the catalyst of his creative activity. More than that, in the actual moment of verbal release, it must often have seemed as though emotion were taking the lead and summoning the images required to sustain it. At the same time, however, one can hardly recollect or contemplate an emotion as such, but rather its accompanying circumstances. As both the Preface and his own poems make clear, Wordsworth means that some former occasion comes to mind, but only as modified over a lapse of time. It originally excited feeling and now does so again. "In this mood successful composition generally begins" and is spontaneously "carried on."

To make sense of Wordsworth's account — that is, to see it as a promising way of composing — one assumption is indispensable. We would have to agree with Wordsworth and the other romantic writers that strong feeling intensifies power of mind and hence readiness of words and language. A man who finds that passion clogs the channels and vents of speech, or who does his best work in a thousand slow, studied touches, cannot be a romantic poet. Though we now think of Keats as a careful and deliberate craftsman, his own view was different. "If Poetry comes not as naturally as the Leaves to a tree it had better not come at all," and, as for revision, "shall I afterwards . . . sit down coldly to criticise when in Possession of only one faculty, what I have written, when almost inspired?"[21] Wordsworth is vehement that he cannot write to order as a mere craftsman: "My verses have all risen up of their own accord"; "at no period of my life have I been able to write verses that do not spring up from an inward impulse"; "I know not how it is, I have ever striven in vain to write verses upon subjects either proposed, or imposed . . . I was once a whole twelve-month occasionally employed in vain endeavour to write an inscription upon a suggested subject." [22] In these remarks Wordsworth is, of course, turning down requests for verses, but whoever seeks additional testimony need only look at the translations Wordsworth attempted. Even Coleridge foundered in Wordsworth's translations from the *Aeneid*: "Since Milton, I know of no poet with so many *felicities* and unforgettable lines and stanzas as you. And to read, therefore, page after page without a single *brilliant* note . . ." [23] and a similar sigh may be raised over Wordsworth's modernizations of Chaucer.

It is curious how completely Wordsworth reversed the neoclassic description of the way poetry is composed. The critics of Pope's day granted, of course, that much else was necessary, but emphasized the value of deliberation and conscious labor. Wordsworth stressed unconscious creative processes, and conceded that thoughtful workmanship is also indispensable. Certainly there is no one or best way to set about writing, and the disparate effects of Pope and Words-worth correspond to vastly different working habits. On the other hand, possible and hence fostering ideals may, as a general rule, be preferred to impossible ones. Labor is com-monly in any man's power, and though it will hardly make a poet by itself, it will usually make a good poet better. The premise of unconscious creativity may be one reason why each of the romantic poets wrote and published a large amount of second-rate verse, relatively much more than one expects to find in the canon of an important poet. Moreover, the ardor for spontaneity, and the expectation of it, intensified the puzzlement, despair, and even guilt that were often present in the process of composition. The romantic poets, needless to say, did not repudiate their poetic ideals, but in practice they could not wholly carry them out, and so they confronted an unusually perplexing task. If they followed their considering mind, rather than unanalyzed promptings, their judgment had still to put on a mask and appear as its opposite, that is, in an illusion of spontaneity. It is no wonder that Keats and Shelley lament that they cannot pour forth as naturally as a nightingale or a skylark.

Moreover, it also follows from romantic premises that to write poetry can hardly be learned and certainly cannot be taught. A neoclassic artist could easily tell a novice how he should proceed. Sir Joshua Reynolds did it in his great series of Presidential Discourses to the Royal Academy, and he is only the first example that leaps to mind. And if art is taught, artists are more likely to resemble each other. But the romantic generation cannot tell you how to set about writing, for the reason that you do not set about it. It just happens. A strict adherent of Wordsworth's system could not even talk about the choice of a subject matter; the subject matter must choose him. Thus of his glum "Warning" against the Reform Bill, Wordsworth characteristically says, "It was written for one of the best reasons which in a poetical case can be given, viz. that the author could not help writing it." [24]

Once the subject matter or poem has flashed upon the mind and composition has begun, it should flow almost automatically. Wordsworth makes, in this connection, an extremely significant and revealing remark. He says that when he starts to compose, he does not always have a "distinct purpose formally conceived." He may, that is, begin simply with description, presenting as faithfully as possible "such objects as strongly excite" his feelings. He does not know in advance what course his poem may take. Nevertheless, he can proceed because

habits of meditation have so prompted and regulated my feelings, that my descriptions of such objects as strongly excite those feelings, will be found to carry along with them a *purpose*.[25]

In other words, the remembered objects will have acquired meaning or representative value. This has taken place in an unconscious digestion of experience long before the moment of composition. As Wordsworth also puts it, his feelings have been "connected with important subjects," and, trusting in this, he can compose "blindly and mechanically." [26]

−5−

But most of Wordsworth's poems were not produced this way. Even though it is based on introspection, this description of the creative process remains wishful, an ideal to which he was bound in uneasy wedlock, never quite faithful. At other times an equally introspective remark will stress something utterly different. "The logical faculty has infinitely more to do with poetry" than inexperienced writers suppose; poetry "requires an adroitness which can proceed from nothing but practice; a discernment, which emotion is so far from bestowing that at first it is ever in the way of it." When R. P. Gillies suggested that "the moment a clear idea of any kind is conceived, it ought to be brought out directly and [as] rapidly as possible," Wordsworth disagreed. "I am not sure," he replied, "that I comprehend your meaning," but he went on to scrutinize two possible meanings, quarreling with each, and finally concluded, "My first expressions I often find detestable; and it is frequently true of second words as of second thoughts, that they are the best." [27] Since these remarks come out of Wordsworth's middle and later years, and some of them have an air of recantation, we might be tempted to dismiss them as relevant only to the aging poet no longer himself. Probably his working procedures changed as he grew older — certainly his style did — but comments such as these acknowledge a lifelong necessity. Though hardly so radical or striking, they are at least as true to Wordsworth's habits of composition as the opposite account in the Preface to the *Lyrical Ballads*. A still more significant reminder occurs in a passage written between 1798 and 1800. By "patience" and "slow creation," poetry can be

> given
> A function kindred to organic power,
> The vital spirit of a perfect form.[28]

But according to romantic writers, it is precisely the organic integration and inevitable movement of a poem that usually imply spontaneity in the poet. In fact, there was no effect of spontaneous composition that could not also be achieved by deliberate thought and toil.

In the Preface of 1815, Wordsworth lists the powers or faculties needed to write poetry: observation, sensibility, reflection, imagination, fancy, invention, and judgment. The list oddly mixes neoclassic with romantic catchwords, the reason being that it is not theoretical but comes out of Wordsworth's actual experience as a writer. Among these faculties, invention and judgment especially — though not necessarily — involve conscious activities of mind. Invention displays itself when "characters are composed out of ma-

terials supplied by observation," and "such incidents" produced as are "most fitted to do justice to the characters, sentiments, and passions, which the Poet undertakes to illustrate." [29] By 1815 Wordsworth was turning out a poetry
quite different from the work of 1800. Nevertheless, throughout his life invention was busy in the creation of poems.
There is, for example, his note on "The Thorn" (1798). The
poem, Wordsworth said,

arose out of my observing, on the ridge of Quantock Hill, on a
stormy day, a thorn which I had often passed in calm and bright
weather without noticing it. I said to myself, "Cannot I by some
invention do as much to make this Thorn permanently an impressive object as the storm has made it to my eyes at this moment?" [30]

A few lines of verse, or a tag of speech, might also suggest
a poem. Thus the "Ode to Lycoris" (1817) "originated in
the four last lines of the first stanza," and in "The Idiot
Boy" (1798) a particular saying, "The Cocks did crow to-
whoo, to-whoo, And the sun did shine so cold" was "the
foundation of the whole." [31] The evidence is not clear-cut,
but such statements may imply a process of composition
analogous to the experience Housman describes in *The
Name and Nature of Poetry*. A few lines may rise up spontaneously in the poet, who then labors to weave a poem
around them.

Wordsworth possessed considerable readiness of invention,
"a highly *generative* mind," as Crabb Robinson put it. In
conversation he was frequently silent and preoccupied, especially in his earlier years, but when his emotions were roused
he could sustain long monologues, breaking forth in "passionate eloquence," as Coleridge said, "stunning you with
oratory," to cite the experience of another contemporary.

The same gift applied in composition. Invention did not necessarily precede a "spontaneous overflow." Thus after seeing the thorn, Wordsworth "began the poem accordingly, and composed it with great rapidity." In such cases there is not the unconscious assimilation, over a period of time, of particular experience to general meaning. Instead, some occasion collects and vents mental stuff, and to the extent that the process takes place rapidly, it is likely to tap preoccupations always ready to mind. In Wordsworth, then, one can sometimes discover the spontaneity by automatism that Leavis remarks in Shelley, an almost blind stamping of habitual themes (deserted mothers, for example) on whatever material comes to hand. But even if invention became virtually automatic, it was first released by an act of will, a decision or determination that was not spontaneous. And, of course, it could be carried on in a much slower, more calculating way.

Judgment is a regulatory power. It decides "how and where, and in what degree" each of the other capacities "ought to be exerted." In other words, it adapts means to ends. "By judgment, also, is determined what are the laws and appropriate graces of every species of composition." [32] A hymn expressing the "sentiments of a multitude" must employ a stanza, Wordsworth tells Southey, while a personal effusion can be allowed more irregularity. Wordsworth's purposes in "The Thorn" might, he felt, be assisted by a more "rapid Metre." He also wished to add an introductory poem to "The Thorn" presenting the character of the speaker. [33] This too was a resolve of judgment. On the whole, judgment, however necessary, was a disquieting power to Wordsworth, since it especially suggested second thoughts. It forced him to revise his phrasing, a job that nagged and frustrated, and made him an irritable member of his household, "only agreeable by fits," as Sara Hutchinson put it. Or the "judicious recommendation of Mrs. Wordsworth" or some other intimate might cause him to divide one poem into two, thus requiring that he find other matter as a setting for each half. All of these considerations were inspired by the wish that a poem might have its "due effect" on the reader. Thus judgment involves a scrutiny of the poem, either during or after its composition. The inspection can only be willed and conscious, because the poet must study his work from the standpoint of some person other than himself.

– 6 –

In theory, then, the composition of a poem might be spontaneous. In practice, it involved a mingling of impulse with conscious will. But Wordsworth also adopted a practical method that might help sustain the state of mind he required, namely a headlong readiness accompanied by strong feeling. He composed aloud and usually outdoors without pen and paper. "I sauntered," he says, along the public way "like a river murmuring/ And talking to itself." [34] He would produce his verses on walking tours, or in the shelter of a big stone by the public road, or mostly as he paced back and forth on some level path — irregularities in the ground broke his trains of thought. Unless we remember that, for example, the day-long rambles described in Dorothy's *Journals* were not usually holidays, we would have no adequate sense how much of his time was spent working. Since walking was also Wordsworth's main sport, one might speculate that there would not be the sort of cleavage between labor and play suggested by settling into an office at 8:30 A.M., and hence not the same mute groan. As a matter of fact, Wordsworth kept no regular working hours. He sometimes granted himself vacations, but otherwise he was likely to be on the job at any time of day.

That Wordsworth composed aloud ("booing," his rustic neighbors called it), could give rise to odd situations. According to one of the local observers interviewed by Rawnsley, night passers-by could be terrified:

> I've knoan folks, village lads and lasses, coming ower by t'auld road aboon what runs fra Gersmer to Rydal, flayt a'most to death there by t'Wishing Gate to hear t'girt voice a groanin' and mutterin' and thunderin' of a still evening . . . fwoaks could hear sounds like a wild beast coming fra t'rocks, and childer were scared fit to be dead a'most.[35]

Wordsworth sometimes perceived the humor. For a while his family kept a turtledove, and the bird would "begin cooing and murmuring whenever it heard me making my verses." At Coleorton a laborer used to follow the noisy author about, trying to catch his words.[36] It is a droll picture, and at the time Wordsworth was unaware of his caboose, one more instance of his oblivious concentration. But the habit had other results as well. We know that when Wordsworth recited his poems he had a habit of chanting, and it is a fair presumption that he did the same thing as he composed. Moreover, he would be saying the same words many times over, so that in creating he probably fell into a chant-like repetition. Such repetition, kept up over a period of time, can naturally induce a half-trance. At such times, sensory impressions are likely to be dim, while objects of the mind acquire peculiar vividness. The flow of sound in which he submerged himself would tend to muffle inhibitions and release him from scruples of perfectionism. The march of rhythm dinned into his ears would hasten his mental step; for if we hear what we are saying, it is painful to

leave a clause hanging or a rhythm unfulfilled, and the tendency is to insert something at once. Thus to compose aloud
may often lead one to compose rapidly; and mere speed itself
tends to sustain feeling. As Coleridge puts it, the wheels of
the mind catch fire by whirling. That is one reason why revision so tormented Wordsworth. "He is always very ill
when he tries to alter an old poem," says Dorothy, "but new
composition does not hurt him so much." [37] It is hard to
feel any passion save irritation while you are bargaining with
yourself over a phrase.

In a typical session, then, one would find Wordsworth
out for a walk, "his jaws workin' the whoal time," as a
rural neighbor told Rawnsley, rather rapidly producing a
substantial unit of verse. Whether this should be called spontaneous composition is perhaps a matter of definition. But
such habits in creating are likely to result in a verse that
reads as though it might be spontaneous. For when from the
start phrases or tags of verse are jotted down, and the whole
process of composition goes on through successive drafts,
the poetry cannot help differing from that mainly created in
the head. For one thing, a pencil poet, so to speak, can more
easily start with scraps and try to patch them together. Secondly, because the poem is before him on the page, he tends
to revise as he writes, jacking up every phrase to meet his
own standards or ideals. From his constant watchfulness,
his expression may become more condensed, as accumulating meanings are not unrolled by progressive amplification,
but packed into increasingly tight phrasal pellets or nuggets.
The virtues of such poetry are likely to be compression, taut-
ness, intellectual intensity. Its danger is disconnection. On
the other hand, poetry composed in the head ordinarily
moves by amplification. In adding a new phrase, the poet
usually repeats what he has done from the opening line,

obtaining push from what has gone before, and hence his poetry may achieve a more plastic and natural sweep. Grammar is likely to be complicated and loose. Because the verse must satisfy the ear more than the eye, rhythms tend to become more emphatic. This, however, is not the place for a summary of Wordsworth's style. The point is only that many of his stylistic individualities should be related to the fact that he was composing aloud without pen and paper.

In addition to such general characteristics, Wordsworth's methods in composition could result in particular tricks of phrasing that support or agree with the notion of spontaneous utterance. He often appears to be revising as he writes, and a word or phrase that he professes to find inexact is not struck out but corrected in the course of the poem: "These hedge-rows, hardly hedge-rows, little lines/ Of sportive wood run wild"; "Entrenched, say rather peacefully embowered"; "Those walks well worthy to be prized and loved — / Regretted! — that word, too, was on my tongue." He talks to himself ("Aye, think on that, my Heart, and cease to stir"), comments on his own sentiments (I "would resound/ Your praise . . . presumptuous thought!"), rallies his wandering impulses to the task at hand ("My drift, I fear,/ Is scarcely obvious"; "But these, I fear,/ Are falsely catalogued"; "But let me now, less moved, in order take/ Our argument"), and changes his mind as he writes.[38] These and similar gestures can often be surprisingly effective. Certainly they show an attempt in verse to render or yield to impulsive processes of mind, and may be contrasted with Wordsworth's description of a speech that is not impulsive. When in "Resolution and Independence" he meets the leech-gatherer with his steady self-possession, the old man speaks a different sort of poetry, his words following each other in "solemn order," with

> something of a lofty utterance drest —
> Choice word and measured phrase, above the reach
> Of ordinary men; a stately speech.

-7-

Wordsworth certainly desired to be thought more spontaneous that he actually was. He took frequent occasion in his poems to tell his readers that they were enjoying unpremeditated effusions:

> Along the mazes of this song I go
> As inward motions of the wandering thought
> Lead me;

>   thus flowed my thoughts
> In a pure stream of words fresh from the heart;

> All nature seems to hear me while I speak,
> By feelings urged that do not vainly seek
> Apt language, ready as the tuneful notes

of birds.[39] If in these passages Wordsworth seems a trifle flat, it may be that he was tongue-tied by embarrassment. Of them one might say what Wordsworth once remarked of the poet he most admired. "Milton talks of 'pouring easy his unpremeditated verse.' It would be harsh, untrue, and odious, to say there is anything like cant in this; but it is not true to the letter." [40] Moreover, such extreme assertions often contradict what we know of the actual creation of the poems in which they appear. The poem called "Desultory Stanzas" concludes the *Memorials of a Tour on the Continent* and was written while the volume was in proof. Crabb Robinson had suggested its subject — a commemoration of "those patriotic and pious bridges at Lucerne" — and Dorothy tells Robinson that the suggestion set Wordsworth's "mind to

work; & if a happy mood comes on he is determined . . .
to add a poem on that subject." [41] Yet in the poem itself
Wordsworth says he writes on a sudden impulse occasioned
by viewing the completed book:

> Is then the final page before me spread,
> No further outlet left to mind and heart?
> Presumptuous Book! too forward to be read,
> How can I give thee licence to depart?
> One tribute more; unbidden feelings start
> Forth from their coverts; slighted objects rise;
> My spirit is the scene of such wild art
> As on Parnassus rules. [42]

Wordsworth's obsession with creating an aura of spontaneity could hardly be put more nakedly than in these awkward lines, protesting so explicitly, and yet so remote from
the "wild art" of Parnassus in result and also in the occasion
that really prompted them.

It would seem, then, that in claiming bird-like spontaneity
Wordsworth knew he was exploiting a convention. This
would, of course, be taken for granted, except that one remembers Wordsworth's guilty attitude toward such poses.
He must have felt that this particular one was desperately
necessary. In the first place, spontaneity can function as an
excuse. We do not expect or demand a high finish in the
free notes of nature. We may accept or even relish Wordsworth's occasionally awkward, homely, or grotesque phrasing, his mixed metaphors, his prolixity as he gropes for his
meaning. In the second place, a convention of spontaneity
allows freedom. It disburdens the poet of any stylistic rigidi-
ties. He can speak in any way he chooses. Like every established poet, Wordsworth was frequently obliged to comment
on the verses of acquaintances or aspiring youngsters. Many

instances occur in his letters, and the detailed suggestions or cautions show, as clearly as anything else, that Wordsworth really favored no party or school of poetic stylists. He does not feel, as Keats once did, that a poet should "load every rift with ore." He is not militant for any slogan — concreteness, intensity, suggestion, magic, poetry richly figurative, or plain. He tries merely for a pure, intelligible English, and so smooths over an awkward rhythm, or crosses out redundancy, or puts a confused expression in a clearer way. Most of all, he seems to be on guard against mannerisms that call attention to themselves. The ideal is a style defecated, to use Coleridge's words, to a pure transparency. For the aim of his art is truth — not truth made more attractive or persuasive as with neoclassic poetry, but truth starkly rendered and powerfully felt. Or, as he puts it in a great phrase, poetry is "truth . . . carried alive into the heart by passion," truth becoming formative in character and activity.

IV

THE ADEQUACY
OF LANGUAGE

VEXED IN so many ways, our hope for sincerity is perhaps most puzzled by the dilemma of form. The dilemma is
obvious with respect to aesthetic form in particular. Even
if a poet avoids ready molds — stanzas, meters, a poetic diction — he still coaxes his expression toward economy, climax,
or whatever, and thus compromises the ideal of sincerity.
But poets have increasingly felt themselves challenged by
something more fundamental. Clearly no act of expression
— perhaps no event in consciousness — can take place except as it flows into form, and yet we have no guarantee that
forms indispensable to us will also correspond to realities
(except by a special definition of reality). Sometimes we
may feel confident they do not. The forms of grammar are
an example. Moreover, any particular form pre-empts and
excludes. It forces us to take just one path, so to speak,
when perhaps it would be truer to take a great many at
the same time. And there are also things to which no path
can take us.

Words themselves may be viewed as a system of forms
which produce, channel, and partially censor the consciousness of each individual. Even a wail or grunt becomes a form
to the extent that it isolates some aspect of consciousness,
rendering more distinct whatever it isolates and suppressing
what it does not. Accordingly a few aspects of the gen-

eral problem of form may be brought to a more specific focus in questioning the adequacy of language. Any poet — indeed, anybody with a mind not merely brutish — commonly has a feeling that he struggles with words. The effort can be explained in alternative ways, depending upon what relation one supposes between words and consciousness. If we assume that nothing becomes an object of consciousness until it is mediated in a form, we can argue that mankind posits or builds up the sole cosmos available to it (which might as well be called reality) in various systems of forms — words or language being only one such system. Among others, one might mention pictorial art and science.[1] From this point of view, the range and variety of experience open to any individual would be limited by what might be called his vocabulary, if we use the word to describe not only verbal resources but also analogous resources in other systems of forms. When we grapple with words, we may be straining to reproduce in one form or system what first became actual for us in another. Discussion of music or painting is an obvious example. But within the system of words we can also distinguish between a possessed consciousness or reality that is nuanced and extensive, and one that is less so. And we can strive to create a reality richer and more variegated. This, indeed, is a function of poetry. It especially makes new conquests for all mankind. On the other hand, we may assume that words do not constitute or produce consciousness, but simply designate what is already present to us in our own minds. In this case, how can a word, a puny tag or label, convey the vividness of an image? And how can any number of words, culled and stitched with the utmost skill, begin to suggest the idea-swarming depth of any single moment of consciousness? Yet so far we have supposed that words refer only to the contents of our minds. If they refer also to things in themselves, the rivalry would be hopeless.

— 2 —

These and similar questions may be said to have haunted Wordsworth. He is not always pessimistic. Sometimes he shows a rather booming confidence in language, at least as used by himself. These are usually his shallower moments, but only in his shallower moments can we use Wordsworth as a sample of the common opinion of his time. He then assumes three heaps or piles, so to speak: there are "things," "thoughts," and words. In a poem, as in any expression, the mind should function as a careful porter, transferring "things" to words with nothing lost and nothing added. As Wordsworth puts it, words must be brought "rigorously to the test of thoughts; and these again to a comparison with things, their archetypes." [2] He will occasionally adopt metaphors that imply a more idealist position, and it would be possible (though mistaken, I believe) to align him with Shelley or especially Coleridge. At least at moments, Shelley seems to have regarded language as something loosely analogous to a Kantian form:

> Language is a perpetual Orphic song,
> That rules with Daedal harmony a throng
Of thoughts and forms, which else shapeless and senseless were.[3]

Coleridge does not go so far. He does, however, stress far more than Wordsworth how much we depend on language. On the one hand, the language available to us (or the way we use it) actively qualifies what we apprehend as reality. Words, he says, "are living powers, by which the things of most importance to mankind are actuated, combined, and humanized." Conversely, the scope and quality of our mental life naturally shape our language. "Every man's language varies, according to the extent of his knowledge, the activity of his faculties, and the depth or quickness of his feelings." [4] The more we are capable of discriminating reflection, the more words we need; the more words we have, the more we are capable of discriminating reflection. Coleridge — here is the point — would never suggest that words were necessary only for communication, or that the relation between thoughts and words could be a mere matter of counterparting, as though two independent spheres were somehow to be superimposed. Words are not mere indicators. They are the organs of thought, without which our minds could not stir. Coleridge makes this assertion in his grandly picturesque way when he comments on Horne Tooke's *Epea Pteroenta*, "winged words: or language, not only the vehicle of thought but the wheels." "The wheels of the intellect I admit them to be," says Coleridge, "but such as Ezekiel beheld in *the visions of God* as he sate among the captives by the river of Chebar. *Whithersoever the Spirit was to go, the wheels went, and thither was their Spirit to go; for the Spirit of the living creature was in the wheels also.*" [5]

When Wordsworth falls into similar utterances, they do not have quite the same meaning. He is altogether capable of saying that words must be "not what the garb is to the body but what the body is to the soul, themselves a constituent part and power or function in the thought," and the last phrase might well have been written by Coleridge. Like Coleridge, he takes it for granted that "language and the human mind act and re-act on each other," and that "words are not a mere *vehicle*," but "*powers* either to kill or to animate." And he certainly agrees with Coleridge that language ill-used is "unremittingly and noiselessly at work, to subvert, to lay waste, to vitiate, and to dissolve." [6] Pope's style actually prevents clear thinking or deep feeling. The point of view has affinities with Auden's remark that language is a theological question, or with Eliot's, when he discusses "The Social Function of Poetry," that the "direct duty" of a poet "is to his language."

But all of this still leaves Wordsworth a long way from Coleridge and moving in a different direction. Wordsworth insists again and again that thought — especially what could be called insight or vision — can be non-verbal and hence far more subtle, profound, and comprehensive than the words found to represent it. Expression is a process of fitting — unconsciously and spontaneously, he hopes — language to what we already apprehend. When he says that words must be not a "clothing" for the thought, but an "incarnation" of it, the context is one in which he is hooting at Pope, who uses words to bedizen his thoughts. At other times, Wordsworth will talk about his own writing as an effort to "clothe" his meanings. On the whole, in such remarks Wordsworth's main points are that we can communicate our thoughts only by their minutely appropriate words, and that the words should not call attention to themselves. Language should "uphold, and feed, and leave in quiet, like the power of gravitation or the air we breathe." [7] A poet's highest verbal skill manifests itself when we are unconscious of his words, being involved in a living, immediate experience or act of mind.

Putting it somewhat differently, one can say that when Wordsworth feels optimistic about the powers of language, it is often because he momentarily reposes on the air-mattress of a theory, or of theoretical thinking. He forgets his own desperate, defeated battles with words, and, like virtually everyone who thought about language in the century before him, falls under the influence chiefly of Locke. We

know only our own percepts or ideas, but ideas can be collected with varying degrees of care and adequacy. Here,
indeed, is one implication of Wordsworth's repeated boast,
"I have at all times endeavoured to look steadily at my subject." Moreover, this effort or intention may, he says at times,
account for his style. Our words, Locke taught, can denote
our ideas and should do nothing more, and if they do anything more, they obstruct knowledge. Language exists for
communication, not for thinking, and it allows us to mud-
dle our heads more than we could without it. We can, for
example, use words to which we attach no ideas, as the
youthful Coleridge did. "Unrelentingly possessed by thirst/
Of greatness, love, and beauty," he could turn to no objects that would satisfy these emotions because he lived in
London. (Wordsworth here assumes, like most persons in
the century before him, the existence of innate particular
emotions.) As a result, Coleridge was driven to substitute
"words for things" in

> endless dreams
> Of sickliness, disjoining, joining, things
> Without the light of knowledge.[8]

Or we can, like Pope, be seduced by the pleasures of verbal
artifice. The patterns of sound and rhetoric, the periphrasis,
personification, and antithesis of Pope's style ("words doing
their own work") give proof to Wordsworth of a mind at-
tentive more to words than things. Even if we avoid these
and other dangers, there are still obstacles to communication. Our words, Locke had pointed out, are always the
signs of *our* ideas and not those of someone else. As Wordsworth puts it, "my associations must have sometimes been
particular instead of general," and the same thing would be
true for each of his readers. Moreover, words may evoke dif-

ferent ideas from one age to the next, so that language is "subject to endless fluctuations and arbitrary associations." [9] But such reminders are only pin-pricks; they do not dislodge Wordsworth's basic assurance that adequate speech can take place. But the confident mood — on this basis — refers mainly to descriptive poetry. Wordsworth's attitude to language changes radically when he moves into his great theme, the introspective quest on "shadowy ground" as he explores the "Mind of Man — / My haunt, and the main region of my song."

– 3 –

Wordsworth is certain that at moments cognition may become utterly direct and unmediated. He knows this from his own experience. His poetry, with its incomparable, concrete grasp of mental events, tries to describe such states of consciousness. They are characterized by the absence not only of words and unnoticed verbalizing, but of any other mediating form or language, and of thought as well. No sensation, image, concept, or whatever is in the mind at such moments, only a blank and featureless diffusion. The first time he entered London, Wordsworth says in the *Prelude*:

> A weight of ages did at once descend
> Upon my heart; no thought embodied, no
> Distinct remembrances, but weight and power.
> (VIII, 552–554)

To convey such inward experiences Wordsworth usually fell back on metaphor. One can especially cite the recurrent metaphor that compares the imagination exerting its power to a mist spreading within and without. There is, for example, the famous passage in Book VI of the *Prelude* where the imagination rises like an "unfathered vapour," and the mind, that "lonely traveller," is at once "halted" and "lost." It is, Wordsworth says, a "usurpation" in which the "light of sense/ Goes out." But these fleeting moods and flashes are knowledge, immediate, unimpeachable, possessing and scarcely sayable. Or if one rejects the term "knowledge," it can only be to make a higher claim, and one must talk about the direct intuition of truth. And, of course, these moments implicate not random insights we could just as well do without, but the truths man most seeks to know, the destiny of the soul and the being of God.

Wordsworth also takes for granted that we use languages other than words — such as mathematics. But what far more concerns and distinguishes him is his assumption that nature — mountains, lakes, clouds, winds — can become a language for the human mind. On the one hand, the "Wisdom and Spirit of the Universe" speaks to us through the forms of nature. Stated thus briefly, this conviction, fundamental to Wordsworth's doctrine, could imply only the first premise of natural theology. Certainly natural theology flows into the religion of Nature, and hence into Wordsworth, but it utterly transforms itself in doing so. He does not claim that religious knowledge or truth can be inferred from the natural world. He feels, instead, that in nature such knowledge is mediated to us as in a language. Hence it can be far more vivid, ample, and satisfying than any series of inferences. The conviction was so deeply rooted that it emerged not only as a conscious theme but in countless phrases that, in any poet but Wordsworth, might seem only vague metaphors: "the speaking face of earth"; "notes that are/ The ghostly language of the ancient earth"; the "forms/ Perennial of the ancient hills" and "changeful language of their countenances";

                          the earth
          And common face of Nature spake to me
          Rememberable things;

and the great lines, as he speaks of moments when in childhood he "hung alone" on some perilous ridge "Shouldering
the naked crag" —

          With what strange utterance did the loud dry wind
          Blow through my ear! [10]

On the other hand, the human mind can use the forms
of nature as a language for self-expression. There are,
Wordsworth says, men who are "framed" for contemplation
but have little power to express themselves in words — "un-
practised in the strife of phrase." But they have a language,
not, of course, for communication, but for the self-manifesta-
tion of consciousness:

          Theirs is the language of the heavens, the power,
          The thought, the image, and the silent joy:
          Words are but under-agents in their souls.[11]

One could argue that Wordsworth himself exploits nature
only as a language for feeling; he projects or objectifies his
own emotions in the outward scene. But he believed that
it was especially in the language of nature that man could
know ultimate truths. These truths coexist both in the human mind and in the depth of things, but rarely (though
occasionally) become knowable in direct intuition. Instead,
they reveal themselves in the processes of imagination by
which the human mind weds itself to nature. They are expressed in the visible scene from two sources at the same
time, from the human mind and from the divine consciousness in and behind all things, the Nature in nature, so to

speak. And in turn these truths are reflected back to us in the landscape as we perceive it, thus becoming objects of cognition.

In comparison with the language of nature, words can be only spectres. They are inferior by almost any criterion that mattered to Wordsworth — immediacy of effect, distinctness, impressiveness, memorability, depth of connotation, and closeness to reality. On the other hand, truths expressed in the language of nature remain private and perishable. Only words can communicate these cognitions, and only words can give permanence to them. And the paramount value of what one has known becomes, of course, a motive for imparting it. Wordsworth feels that, like the Biblical prophets, each poet is granted his own "peculiar dower" or privilege to descry "Something unseen before." He would thus be influenced not only by love of fame, "That last infirmity of noble mind," as Milton says, but by gratitude and solemn obligation, when he hopes that "a work of mine,/ Proceeding from the depth of untaught things," may be "Enduring and creative" [12] — creative, that is, in the minds of readers for generations. Moreover, a poet may be impelled to write not only for the sake of other people, but for his own sake. I am not thinking of the vague mixture of habit, ambition, guilt, and readiness that we usually call a "creative drive" or "urge." The point is rather that certain moments or states of consciousness, mostly arising in boyhood and youth, seemed to Wordsworth sources, embodiments, and guarantees of his major beliefs. They were "the fountain light of all our day." Only by recording them in verse could he keep or recapture something of a vivid, immediate grip on them. For they are not permanent in memory. Even the ode on "Intimations of Immortality" implies that they can slip out of mind, if it also asserts, with a sort of chastened triumph, that they do not:

> O joy! that in our embers
> Is something that doth live,
> That nature yet remembers
> What was so fugitive.

No more than thirty-three years old, but already feeling the threat of time, Wordsworth can claim only that he yet remembers, with the background consciousness that he may forget. A less excited but more moving passage in the *Prelude* quietly discloses the naked truth of his feeling in these years. The recollections may perish. Poetry can go a little way to "enshrine" them. It is one of the plainest and most touching moments in Wordsworth:

> The days gone by
> Come back upon me from the dawn almost
> Of life: the hiding-places of my power
> Seem open; I approach, and then they close;
> I see by glimpses now; when age comes on,
> May scarcely see at all, and I would give,
> While yet we may, as far as words can give,
> A substance and a life to what I feel:
> I would enshrine the spirit of the past
> For future restoration.   (1805, XI, 334–343)

− 4 −

One finds, then, an almost impossible dilemma. To write poetry becomes imperative from public duty and private need. Yet words can hardly contain what one would have to put in them. We should not confuse Wordsworth's anxiety as he confronts the "sad incompetence of human speech" with the complaints or apologies most of us make — "I can't quite say what I mean." The fact may be only that we do not know what we mean. Or such remarks may be uttered as beadles of conversation, intended to prod hearers into wakefulness. Wordsworth can do the same thing —

> It was a grief, —
> Grief call it not, 'twas anything but that, —
> A conflict of sensations without name.[13]

Qualifying utterances of this sort need suggest no serious alarm that language is inadequate. But there was a far deeper distress.

Wordsworth's task, as he saw it, was to render into words, that is, into one medium, cognitions that had originally been either direct and unmediated, or fully mediated in another language. Hence his apologies have a special force and precise, curious implication: the "sad incompetence of *human speech*"; "aught that might be clothed/ In *human language*"; "It lies far hidden from the reach of *words*." [14] Here what was said earlier about the seductions and inadequacies of words again becomes relevant — their changing and indeterminate meanings, our possible failure to match them to our thoughts. But even if we escape these perils, we are still in shoal waters. To use words is a problem of translation. We strive, as I said, to put something already possessed and formed into another form. And how, doing this, can we help but change it? Here especially one sees the far-reaching implication of Wordsworth's (and Locke's) premise that words are separable from thoughts. If this is granted, perfect truth of expression is no longer possible. Moreover, if words inevitably distort, they also filter. So far as they can immediately incorporate states of mind, they do so only by leaving those states of mind less rich. There is an extended metaphor in Book VIII of the *Prelude* (ll.

561–576) that knots together some central persuasions of the romantic writers. For here Wordsworth associates the hazy and changing with life, the determinate and settled with death. Words — at least, completed verbal expression — are lined up on the side of death. He is describing his first impressions of London, and compares entering the city to passing from open day into a "huge cave." As one looks around, one "sees the vault/ Widening on all sides," the roof "That instantly unsettles and recedes," and "shapes and forms and tendencies to shape," that "shift and vanish, change and interchange," a "ferment silent and sublime." But as one's eyes grow accustomed, the ferment settles down, until the scene

> stands in perfect view
> Exposed, and lifeless as a written book.

The comparison almost exactly sums up his usual feeling about words. They must be adopted for the sake of revealing experience to the view of others (or of one's future self). They give a "visible shape," as he says elsewhere. But at the same time they determine experience to a particular and therefore dead physiognomy.

– 5 –

On some occasions, however, Wordsworth says almost exactly the opposite, proclaiming his faith in words and poetry. He does not refer solely to descriptive writing, in which, as I said, he always felt very sure of himself. Poetry, he also says at times, can communicate imaginative vision or knowledge, the intense and fleeting moments that, Wordsworth more often stresses, language cannot wholly grasp. In a sense, the about-face honors his feelings. When he asserts confidence, he is giving his heart in wonder to his great predecessors. Neither, when read closely, is Wordsworth necessarily inconsistent. There is a difference between communicating something and denoting it. Moreover, even if he were inconsistent, that need disturb no one. He was not writing a treatise. He was facing an acute difficulty year after year. From the standpoint of a critic or literary historian, the significant fact is that in Wordsworth the adequacy of language becomes a major focus of concern, a point to which he constantly recurs in varying moods of hope or misgiving.

In one passage of the *Prelude* (V, 594–605), Wordsworth exults that the "great Nature" in the works of "mighty Poets" can emulate, in some respects, the "living Nature" of woods and fields. It is true that words can never be as distinct and vivid to us as the language of nature. They are a different medium with independent and rival capabilities of their own. Indeed, their highest effectiveness chiefly depends on the fact that they are relatively indistinct. But they can sometimes be used in such a way that our response to the word becomes almost the same as our response to the thing:

> Visionary power
> Attends the motions of the viewless winds,
> Embodied in the mystery of words.

But only in poetry. For interpreting what lies behind Wordsworth's utterance at this point, one may say that words — a "mystery" or "transparent veil" — spread a faint haze across mental vision, and thus force our minds to work more actively. Poetry, of course, greatly intensifies the process by its resources of versification and by its looser and more varied syntax. Its intricate "turnings," as Wordsworth phrases it, can present things with something of the startling suddenness they may have when met at the rounding of a corner. In short, as we read the work of great poets "forms and substances" appear as they do in moments of heightened, imaginative perception of the natural world:

> Even forms and substances are circumfused
> By that transparent veil with light divine,
> And, through the turnings intricate of verse,
> Present themselves as objects recognized,
> In flashes, and with glory not their own.

For in essential matters a poet relies on suggestion. The language of poetry does not actually incarnate "thought," certainly not when the thought might be better described as immediate revelation. At such moments, words simply make gestures, pointing in the direction of the insights possessed by the poet. But that may be enough. Of course, almost all romantic poetry and thinking about poetry count heavily upon suggestive uses of language. But in Wordsworth they have a theoretical importance even greater, I think, than we usually keep in mind. We often express ourselves shabbily on these topics, talking about romantic poets as though they had a taste for suggestiveness, like a taste for oysters. It is like saying that modern poets make a hobby of symbolism — not false, but simply shallow, and what one might call a floating remark. Major writers do not work this way. The others, who aspire only to what Keats called the "commonplace crowd of the little famous," may soullessly imitate their contemporaries. For Wordsworth, however, suggestiveness was not a mere quality or spice of style. It was a sole means for communicating what most concerned him.

It follows that a reader must not be passive, not even merely vigilant. Returning again and again to this theme, Wordsworth pleads, growls, and thunders. The "mind is left at liberty, and even summoned, to act upon" the "thoughts and images" of a poem; after the genius of the poet has done its work, the reader must still exert a "corresponding energy." [15] Perhaps the most quaint and touching of these exhortations occurs in the *Prelude*. After describing the second of the famous "spots of time," Wordsworth says that the experience had a strong, subsequent influence on his habitual emotions. The psychological speculation is bold; Wordsworth does not — perhaps cannot — develop or clarify it. And then, suddenly, he turns in direct address to the "Friend," Coleridge, for whom he supposedly writes:

> Thou wilt not languish here, O Friend, for whom
> I travel in these dim uncertain ways
> Thou wilt assist me as a Pilgrim gone
> In quest of highest truth.   (1805, XI, 390–393)

Coleridge can be trusted to supply what Wordsworth elsewhere calls "the mind's/ Internal echo of the imperfect sound." [16] Such a mind, and such a friend, will hardly languish in the mere words one is able to set down. It is not simply that a "Pilgrim gone/ In quest of highest truth" deserves aid. He has, we remember, his "peculiar dower" and comes back from his quest with "Something unseen before." He introduces a "new element into the intellectual universe"; his "soul" makes a "conquest"; and it is precisely this novel, strange vision that must be communicated.

Is it to be supposed that the reader can make progress of this kind, like an Indian prince or general — stretched on his palanquin, and borne by his slaves? No; he is invigorated and inspirited by his leader, in order that he may exert himself.[17]

A poet, in other words, attempts to "call forth and bestow" what Wordsworth usually terms "power," that is, a power in the reader to go beyond what can be said in words, himself leaping the gap and arriving at the intuition in the poet's mind when he wrote. It is in this sense that a poem can be "Enduring and creative . . . A power like one of Nature's." [18] In fact, beyond mere physical survival in a book, it can be "enduring" only because it is "creative." Coleridge makes the point, with his streamy, thought-packed eloquence, when he says that Byron achieves "that one sole unfleeting music which is never of yesterday, but still remaining reproduces *itself*, and powers akin to itself in the minds of other men." [19]

No more than other romantic writers does Wordsworth spend much time speculating how the process of suggestion actually works. One might, of course, argue that a poem is evocative. That is, it taps and raises into consciousness what is already in the mind of the reader, or it returns to memory experience that the reader has forgotten. Wordsworth adopts this explanation on many occasions. In one example, after stressing that his great theme or "heroic argument" is the "might of souls" to intuit ultimate truths, or creatively to perceive them in the natural world, he mourns that "in the main" such moments cannot be described. And yet he is not "heartless"; for each man is a "memory to himself" and

> there's not a man
> That lives who hath not known his god-like hours.[20]

It is a generous thought, but it would explain only how one conveys such truths or feelings as of "the might of souls." It does not make clear how a poet communicates his particular "dower" or "conquest," his unique yet crucially important contribution to the "mighty scheme of Truth" in which all poets are connected. For what he must communicate, he says in the *Recluse* (ll. 686–690), is "shared by none" and yet "power and effort" can "impart" it. Suggestion, then, cannot be evocation as the term is ordinarily used. It communicates truths of which the reader had no inkling, experience to which his own personal life offers no approximation. Or, if this puts it too strongly, it is at least as valid as the opposite statement would be. Suggestion is a process in which the mind of the reader works creatively upon the poem. Any attempt to go further in speculating how — according to Wordsworth — suggestion might take place would involve us in the large subject of the romantic psychology of the imagination. Suffice it to say that by Wordsworth's premises the reader of a poem is or should be analogous to the mind of man confronting the natural world. He would not, I fear, have approved our modern criticism by minute analysis, which might be said to take up words in "disconnection, dead and spiritless." Perhaps the most important point, however, is simply that if Wordsworth could not trust to suggestive uses of language, he would find himself with a shrunk hope or motive for poetry.

– 6 –

Obviously one cannot begin to discuss any fundamental question in Wordsworth without at once raising others equally important. The preceding pages offer ample testimony. We began by thinking of Wordsworth's misgivings about form — not diction or versification, but form in the most inclusive sense as a structure of experience — and about language as a primary form. He fears he may be compelled to distort his immediate perceptions, and the result is a radical suspicion or even despair of poetry. But then, of course, one makes haste to qualify. The alarm was deep-seated and constantly stirring, but Wordsworth would hardly have been a poet unless he were optimistic about the special capacities of his art. So the suspicion of form at once involves such considerations as the function of poetry, the powers at its disposal, its inevitable limitations; and a great deal of Wordsworth's poetry would be relevant. Perhaps in a final attempt to deal with this large problem, we can confine ourselves to a single passage in Wordsworth, the dream at the start of Book V in the *Prelude*, where his hopes and fears flow into each other, inspiring what De Quincey called the "very *ne plus ultra* of sublimity." According to De Quincey, Wordsworth's lines were intended to "illustrate the eternity, and the independence of all social modes or fashions of existence, conceded to those two hemispheres, as it were, that compose the total world of human power — mathematics on the one hand, poetry on the other." [21] Since De Quincey, the passage has been interpreted in other ways or with more refined analysis. Whatever else might be said, the lines involve a symbolic account or summary of some of the main questions about any poem — its relation to the poet, to the reader, and especially to the object it strives to communicate.

Interpretation of these lines depends on recognizing a number of symbolic correspondences. Though they emerge only as one reads the passage with a remembrance of other lines and poems in Wordsworth, it may be helpful to state them at once in an unqualified way: the Arab is the poet; the shell is the poem; the dreamer is the audience; and the sea is the reality from which the poem comes and to which it leads. As the episode begins, the dreamer finds himself in a sandy desert, "all black and void." He feels "distress and fear," and his situation may project in narrative terms a dread of subjective isolation, of being lost in one's own mind, deprived of any stabilizing, health-infusing influence from without. At this point an Arab appears, mounted on a dromedary. As he is subsequently described, he is a typical romantic figure, a heroic explorer, "Bard and Sage," engaged on a perilous quest which may appear mad or Quixotic to the ordinary man. But to the dreamer he comes as a guide who may lead him out of the desert. He carries a stone and a shell, representing "two books," mathematics and poetry. Both of these books offer means of communicating with other persons and particularly with the creative genius that produced them, mathematics by wedding "soul to soul in purest bond/ Of reason," and poetry by its power to "soothe,/ Through every clime, the heart of human kind."

Here Wordsworth touches upon one obvious need and use of poetry. Poetry does not simply excite and order feeling. We acquire, as we read, a sympathy and relationship with the writer, or with the personality implied in the poem. We tend to overlook this in criticism today, but it often contributes a good deal to particular effects. More generally, that such a relationship exists is one of the reasons why poetry always offers — however much we deny it — an implicit reassurance or consolation.

As a symbol of poetry, the conch-shell is "resplendent" in color and "beautiful in shape," but Wordsworth especially builds on the common fancy that a shell retains the sound of the sea. When the dreamer puts it to his ear, he hears what Wordsworth, using the same figure in the *Excursion*, calls "Authentic tidings of invisible things" — not just the sea, in other words, but what it suggests as a major, recurrent symbol in Wordsworth's poetry. In summary, it is the being of God, vast, eternal, ceaselessly alive and moving. In moments of communion with God in nature, the earth itself becomes as a sea; its solid, distinct objects and forms seem alive, plastic, and undifferentiated, all reflecting one splendor of light as from a sheet of water. Hence there is a recurrent metaphor that speaks of the moment of revelation as a deluge,[22] both fearful and tremblingly desired. It sweeps over and destroys the ordinary contents of the mind, even obliterating the sense of an identity or self separate from the one Soul working through all things. Such moments are incommunicable, but poetry must somehow convey them. Accordingly, the shell "warns" the dreamer of the coming revelation. He hears

> A loud prophetic blast of harmony;
> An Ode, in passion uttered, which foretold
> Destruction to the children of the earth
> By deluge, now at hand.

After this threat or promise, implicit in any great ode, the dreamer still continues to follow the Arab-poet and so comes to the point of himself experiencing the overwhelming intuition. As he looks behind him, he sees a "bed of glittering light," and the Arab tells him it is "the waters of the deep/ Gathering upon us." Naturally fearing the onrushing waters, the dreamer pursues the Arab as he hurries "o'er the illimitable waste," but the Arab leaves him behind. Prophetic revelation cannot be put in words. A poet must finally abandon the reader, but he can leave him in a state of heightened imaginative power where he will intuit what was revealed to the poet.

The fear of the dreamer, then, is understandable. But there is also Wordsworth's own regret or even despair as he introduces and later reflects upon his narrative, as though the dream were somehow suggesting or embodying such emotions. He approaches the dream through a meditative passage, explaining that man may create "Things that aspire to unconquerable life," yet all human works "must perish." Even "poetry and geometric truth," endowed as they are

with "high privilege of lasting life," would be lost in some
universal cataclysm. The spirit of man is immortal, but there
is no equally deathless medium or "element" on which it
can "stamp" itself. These thoughts provide a surface interpretation for the events that follow in the dream. As a deluge
threatens the Quixotic Arab seeks to preserve the stone of
mathematics and the shell of poetry by burying them. But,
as I have suggested, Wordsworth's narrative hardly allows
us to stop at this point, and even as he introduces the dream
there are phrases suggesting a deeper, far more characteristic
alarm. For man seeks to "send abroad" his "spirit" or "immortal being," and yet he can only "lodge" it in what Wordsworth successively calls "garments," "adamantine holds," or
"shrines." There is an implied contrast between the spirit
and the shape in which it must be expressed, and this is true
even of an ode, for Wordsworth the least confining of poetic
shapes. The "shrines" are "frail," not merely because they
may perish, but because they cannot contain our immortal
being, or our oneness with Immortal Being, which we know
at moments and strive to communicate.

We are not departing, then, from Wordsworth's own feelings if we press his symbolism and explore the relations between the shell and the sea. The shell was shaped by the
sea, and may still evoke that vast, plastic being in which it
was once a living organism. But it is now simply a shell, a
beautiful but dead shape. If the Arab is himself a poet, there
is the plain implication that he can only obtain the shell
by taking it out of the sea. Thus as the deluge approaches,
the Arab himself flies before it. In order to preserve the
shell, he is hurrying to bury it. For a poet cannot write in
the moment of revelation. Just as the form can only be a
dead reminder of the immediate experience, the living moment of revelation, even if it could be put into words, would

shatter any form. At the end of the passage Wordsworth again compares a written poem to something itself inert and valueless, however precious the spirit it may contain. Thinking of the Arab on his quest, he feels that he too could go "Upon like errand."

> Oftentimes at least
> Me hath such strong entrancement overcome,
> When I have held a volume in my hand,
> Poor earthly casket of immortal verse,
> Shakespeare, or Milton, labourers divine.

Whether verse is represented as a casket or a shell, the spirit must be lodged in an enclosing shape in order to become immortal. There is, then, a peculiar balance of optimism and distress. Art may hold a permanent power of suggestion. It can communicate the immediate revelation to a responsive reader, but only when he goes beyond the work of art itself. For a poem does not embody the intuition it suggests. In the very act of composition a poet buries the living moment of insight, retaining only its dead box or shell. There is a genuine fear that form can become form only by killing experience, and perhaps a more scrupulous sincerity would prevent one from writing verse at all.

– 7 –

With respect to his attitude toward language, as in so many other ways, Wordsworth was a key figure in a historical development that has continued to our time. Certainly poets before Wordsworth had been led to question the powers of language. By the early eighteenth century, confidence had withered under the united suns of Locke and Newton, the one further supporting the Baconian attack on poetic uses of language, the other demonstrating the far more reaching grasp of a non-verbal language for the discovery of certain kinds of truth. But the first reaction of poetry had been to retreat. Poetry might not be adequate for the exact communication of major truths, but then that was not its purpose. There was no reason to doubt that poetry could carry out the modest functions reserved for it. But Wordsworth and his generation restored the art to its ancient sense of high purpose. It was only then that language revealed itself as a thwart obstacle, something not so much to be used as to get around.

Thus Wordsworth was the first major poet who faced the predicament of language in a distinctively modern way. And he began to devise expedients for meeting it. One sees already in him the straining away from regularities of grammar, syntax, and verbal meaning that characterize much of the poetry of our own day. He begins to warp and pack words, forcing us, for example, to accept the special meanings particular words may have for him. Or he uses key words — "nature," "sense," "spirit" — with a constant implication of all their possible meanings, a habit of speech that should not be described as ambiguous or equivocating, but as an attempt to match in language the organic depth of reality. And, like most later poets, he develops a personal language of recurrent images or symbols, a language that allows an otherwise impossible depth of association or meaning, and that forces us to read the whole of his work before we can master any part. Eliot's *Four Quartets* is possibly the apotheosis of this way of writing. In none of this, of course, does Wordsworth go so far as later poets. He may be said to heave against the regular and inherited forms of language, but our contemporary poets have often set out to smash them, hoping that some gleam of truth may strike through the broken pieces.

V

THE PSYCHOLOGY
OF BELIEF

SINCERITY BECOMES a poetic value only because it is first a moral virtue. It advances in esteem as certitude grows more difficult. It can be pleaded in compensation, as when a man without assured convictions assures us that his doubts are honest. This frame of mind is still wistful. It especially beset thinkers in the latter half of the nineteenth century. But one more step in what Keats optimistically called the "grand march of intellect" has taken us through the looking glass. Today there are not so many honest doubters. Advanced spirits are far more likely to think that doubt alone can be honest, and that they are not on the right path unless they feel lost. Their best hope is to remain undeceived till death, to go down in the dignity of bewilderment, eyes still open to the impenetrable vapors. "Wisdom," Santayana remarks, "is very old and therefore ironical," and it is indeed a refined irony if man's noblest instinct, his yearning toward truth, must end either in self-deception or a want of all conviction. As we look back to the nineteenth century we feel a special sympathy for those tired figures in whom conviction was blighted by honesty — Arnold, George Eliot, or Hardy. It is not surprising that in nineteenth-century literature the villains should so often be intellectuals, restless, emancipated, and analytic — persons, that is, who resemble their creators. For writers had the witness of their own diaries to tell them that the intellect is apt only to criticize, that the more sincere and scrupulous it is, the more it undermines old pieties, planting nothing in their place, and hence, by contrast, goodness is located in the instincts of humble, inarticulate persons. Neither is it surprising that the very writers who are most introspective should think with a striking independence and originality; their ideas are grounded in a fresh look at their actual experience. Of this temperament Rousseau is a prototype and Tolstoy the grand exponent, but in one way or another most major figures display similar traits. There is the free intellect abounding in theories and schemes, the crushing self-consciousness, and, at the same time, a yearning for the release of spontaneity and a deliberate intensification of feeling. But if the great figures of the nineteenth century might often see themselves as Hamlets sicklied o'er with the pale cast of thought, there was still a fundamental optimism. The cosmos was still thought to be rational. There was the hope that its order could be known, and strong emotion, for these heroic, questing spirits, seemed possible only in the company of an assured belief.

Wordsworth is fully representative. He, like Arnold and most thoughtful people, listened uneasily to the "long, withdrawing roar" of the sea of faith, and for a while he was carried out with it. But in the nineteenth century the habit of faith lingered forlorn when the faith receded. It may be that a militant sincerity can never be comfortable amid doubts, nor can it rest in what Keats called "fine isolated verisimilitudes" or random insights, not even in those isolated moments of vision that may seem to hold the answers we seek. Such moments compel assent, but Wordsworth's integrity leads him further. The revelation must be understood. Amid moral and metaphysical perplexities, our first responsibility, he assumes, is to commit ourselves to a belief or faith. But to speak of responsibility hardly captures Wordsworth's sense of urgency. The course of the French Revolution having temporarily shattered his convictions, he could testify that — for himself, at least — an assured belief was necessary to any fullness of life, even to the exercise of his poetic genius. Though far from a Baconian — their premises are opposite — he would have agreed with Bacon's diagnosis of the psychological results of mere scepticism. It may be "a fairer seeming way," said Bacon, "than arbitrary decisions . . . yet still when the human mind has once despaired of finding truth, its interest in all things grows fainter; and the result is that men turn aside to pleasant disputations and discourses and roam as it were from object to object." [1] With a similar insight, T. S. Eliot transforms the pleasant disputations and discourses into the tea-party of Prufrock, or the shadowy world of hollow men.

But Eliot merely projects an image of horror from a soul in crisis. *The Waste Land*, whatever we may say in appreciative enthusiasm, is not a faithful mirror of the world we dwell in. The truth is, as Wordsworth knew, that though the intellect may despair, a living being is never unprovided with convictions. They are implied in actions and responses. The task of sincerity is not so much to produce beliefs, as to discover those to which we are already committed, and to know that they are true. As for poetry, Wordsworth did not think it a special object of concern, set apart from other activities and interests, but a medium which allowed his deepest concerns to be pursued. Perhaps only in poetry, with the total involvement and connotative depth of language that it requires, could they be pursued to the end. The challenge or hope of sincerity was to be met in his art if anywhere. His account of the creative process might imply only that a poem embodies meaning or truth in an image or event

— a girl singing in a highland vale, a field of daffodils, a drowned body slowly rising from a lake — which the poet recollects or re-creates. As he composes, he may be flooded by a feeling of conviction; he does not necessarily emerge with a conviction that can be named. This might suffice for some poets, but it hardly satisfies all the purposes of life. Neither does it describe many of the poems Wordsworth actually set down. They present concrete experience, but go on to draw a meaning from it, a fact which explains both his extraordinary hold upon readers throughout the nineteenth century and the reaction at the end, when moral earnestness went out of fashion in literary circles. Yeats's view is representative. Wordsworth's "poetical experience" was of incomparable value, but he thought of it as an engine to be "yoked to his intellect. He is full of a sort of utilitarianism." This is the kind of pithy insight one learns to expect in Yeats. It describes Wordsworth exactly, though the implied evaluation need not be shared. Certainly Wordsworth thinks poetry should be utilitarian, if the term suggests an art that serves our practical, moral needs. He always remembered that a poem was to be read by a human being, and not, for example, by a critical machine, or by the departed spirits or supernatural beings Yeats sometimes invokes. Wordsworth's style is itself an assertion. It declares that some things matter more than art. It premises that "anxiety for Humanity" Keats generously praised in Wordsworth. A great poem, Wordsworth thinks, does its work not so much as a made object offering aesthetic satisfaction, and least of all as a brief escape, but as an example in living, an engagement of the whole being of the poet — his imagination, but also his conscience and intellect — in the whole of his experience.

It is this concern for the needs of life beyond the needs of art that purer, more rarified artists find so hard to forgive.

Thus Henry James, like his friend Turgenev, felt himself threatened in his deepest commitments by the majestic fact of Tolstoy, whose novels are an ocean of life, formless, vast, and teeming, and who later, in the search for religious truth, had "so monstrously forsworn" the exercise of his creative genius. In his later years, Wordsworth, too, found his poetic instincts at war with religious beliefs, and no one who knew him could doubt the outcome. But even in the poems of his young manhood it happens that the urge determining every part is to know the beliefs he holds and to state them in general terms. It is a matter of making beliefs available, of possessing them as inviolable maxims or guidelines.

—2—

It may be, however, that for many readers today Wordsworth's poetry will not have the special tone they associate with a sincere act of mind. The reason lies, of course, in Wordsworth's linking of sincerity with a strong, spontaneous emotion. His assumptions can be defended, and some relevant considerations have already been pointed out. Others will be suggested. But many of us may still be tempted to reflect that shallow vessels more readily overflow, and that our needs find their richer satisfaction in the extracts or deposits from a long simmering. A deluge of feeling certainly suggests that the speaker gives us his momentary mind, but evidences of tentativeness, of a commitment obtained after due inspection or self-consultation, are more likely to persuade us of a sincerity that leads to truth. For most of us are Baconians. Even when we take up ultimate questions, we are likely to think that just beliefs can be fetched only from acts of inference or induction. Without being recognized, this assumption inspires much contemporary criticism of Wordsworth. It appears to many readers that he had no adequate ground for his beliefs, and yet he seems triumphantly assured. Hence readers interpret the notes of exulting conviction as an effort to impose on himself, to overwhelm by emotion the uncertainties of his own mind and the defects of his argument. This criticism is not without value. It expresses an effect his poetry may have on sympathizers today. But it ignores Wordsworth's own premises. It is perhaps time to say plainly that Wordsworth does not attempt to persuade either himself or anyone else by argument. The reason is simple. Argument, in his opinion, should convince no one. If we equate intellectual honesty with logical inference and nothing else, we are shouldering an impossible burden. If we also think that our own beliefs have been derived from scrupulous acts of inference, we are fooling ourselves. The powerful demonstration of Wordsworth's honesty comes especially in the *Prelude*, where he does a job few would care to imitate. He tries, that is, to discover the actual sources of his beliefs, and, at the same time, to know what justifies them.

For in any struggle for belief some general questions are inevitably raised: How do we actually obtain our convictions? How do we assure ourselves that they are true? How can we trust the assurance? And the answers to these questions, once they are posed, must naturally be stated in discursive terms, the language of conscious understanding. Hence the present chapter attempts to reconstruct Wordsworth's theoretical psychology of belief, the loose scheme built up out of introspection with the mediating help of Coleridge. The subject may still have some importance generally. For though Wordsworth had no gift for systematic thought, he could muster an obstinacy and depth of reflection rarely to be matched. It also permits a more exact interpretation of Wordsworth's poetry from his own standpoint. Since he certainly wished to influence the convictions of his readers, the theoretical psychology of belief may help explain the poetic means of persuasion. Indeed, until we connect it with some general theory concerning the way beliefs actually come to us, the large question of the relation between our beliefs and our responses to imaginative literature cannot be fully discussed, though it has been much agitated in the last fifty years. We can, of course, ask ourselves whether or to what extent the beliefs we bring to a poem collide or agree with those expressed in it, and whether this influences our appreciation one way or another, but there is also the large question of the after-effect of a poem on our beliefs.

– 3 –

In one passage of the *Prelude* Wordsworth advises himself against an attempt to find the origin of belief. No man can know "the individual hour in which/ His habits were first sown." In fact, he asserts with leaden emphasis, in "words of Reason deeply weighed," that each "particular thought . . . Hath no beginning." [2] This utterance might well put a brake to further inquiry, except that it is only Wordsworth momentarily warning himself. He rolls right on. Not only does the *Prelude* speculate concerning sources of belief in general; it searches back in time to those events in which his own particular beliefs originated. He naturally says very little about beliefs received on authority — the large stock of assumptions inherited from the culture we live in and seldom questioned. This certainly is the source of most of our beliefs, but less so for the type of deeply personal and stubborn conviction Wordsworth attempts to

trace. The beliefs for which he accounts in the *Prelude* especially refer, of course, to Nature — its organic character, its
implication of a Divine Life, its formative influence on the
soul of man. But any attempt to set forth Wordsworth's
psychology of belief in a short space requires a more limited
theme, and in the eighth and subsequent books Wordsworth concentrates on one particular belief. "Love of Nature," he says, led him to a "Love of Man," and if the psychology of this peculiar process can be followed, it would
also apply to the beliefs about Nature itself which were of
even greater importance to him.

To call "love of Man" a belief may seem odd. But one of
Wordsworth's first assumptions is that beliefs are inseparably
twined with emotions. Anticipating a bit, one can say that
a belief not only derives from emotion — and is in a sense
emotion in a later stage of development — but that it also in
turn reinforces emotion and lends stability, so that "love of
Man" can also be said to depend upon beliefs concerning human nature. For, in this context, when Wordsworth speaks
of "love" he is thinking neither of Christian *caritas*, nor the
tenderness praised by the eighteenth-century and romantic
"benevolists." It is rather what one might call romantic hu-
manism, a veneration that wells up in the heart when one
thinks of man as sublime. And so Wordsworth celebrates
the grandeur of human fortitude, or the complexity and
depth of the mind. He thinks of the greatness of man's in-
satiable desire, tides of yearning no earthly experience can
contain, of the power of imagination as it transcends our sensory prison in knowledge of the infinite and eternal, and of
the presence of God in the soul. The resulting emotion is
summed up in a phrase — "reverence with love." He naturally assumes that it prompts humanitarian deeds, but on the
whole, and increasingly as he grew older, he seems to have

found it more difficult and more urgent to think highly of man than to be ready with comfort or help. Indeed, his love, he plainly says, embraces not so much the "punctual presence" — the phrase seems almost hostile when one keeps in mind that it refers to individual men as we know them from day to day in all the particularities of living. It is directed rather to the "spirit," to "the impersonated thought,/ The idea, or abstraction of the kind." [3] The poetry bears out this self-analysis. It keeps its noble watch, but still, as Coleridge said, he is a spectator *ab extra*, and if we think of love as a sharing and cherishing that goes out in joy to its objects, noticing and relishing their full actuality, the poetry simply does not seek human beings in this way. There are a few exceptions — "Michael," for example, or the tale of Margaret in the *Excursion* — but even poor Margaret seems a mere shade when compared to the final, vivid image of "spear-grass . . . By mist and silent rain-drops silvered o'er." In fact, as the narrator looks raptly at the grass, in the close of this story, the pathetic history of Margaret's life appears to him only as an "idle dream." The reader is supposed to quit the poem not with vibrant feelings of grief or protest, but with "meditative sympathies," and the concluding retreat from "uneasy thoughts" is notably assisted by converting the events of Margaret's life into abstractions — "sorrow and despair/ From ruin and from change." Throughout Wordsworth's poetry there is a striking difference between the presentation of natural objects, so vivid, concrete, and detailed, and the presentation of human beings, so often mere, stark abstractions. Nature was loved as a reality, man as an idea. As an inevitable by-product, love of man was a highly volatile emotion, likely to evaporate on a nearer view of men. In one of his letters, Keats expresses a temporary, anti-philanthropic mood:

Those whom I know already and who have grown as it were a part of myself I could not do without: but for the rest of Mankind they are as much a dream to me as Milton's Hierarchies.[4]

On the whole, it was only as men became a dream that Wordsworth was able to love.

That the love flows out to an idea of human nature does not, of course, belie Wordsworth's assumption that it is a valuable emotion. It is certainly preferable to an abstract hatred or indifference, not simply because it compels kindliness as a matter of will or principle, but because, like other forms of love, it still enhances life, gives a stir and motive. Moreover, to reverence an ideal image can lead to a sort of love for the people one meets — more enthusiastic, perhaps, than alert or discriminating — so long as we see them through a haze of preconceptions. That this happens is a commonplace of romantic literature, not to mention the lives of some of its writers. As Coleridge puts it, speaking in another connection, "Things take the signature of thought. The shapes of the recent dream become a mould for the objects in the distance, and these again give an outwardness and sensation of reality to the shapings of the dream." [5] But Wordsworth holds that only from a distance can one see things as they really are. "Pressed upon by objects over near," one becomes confused, and cannot behold a clear, essential form.

— 4 —

To go back to childhood experience and touch the origins of his beliefs presents Wordsworth with his greatest challenge. But however it may have been planted, once the sprig of reverence for man had begun to grow, it was propped and fertilized, Wordsworth thinks, by acts or processes of

mind that occurred in boyhood and college years. For one
thing, his attempts to write poetry had an important influence. At least until he was twenty-one years old, he says,
man was still subordinate to nature in his "affections and
regards." To this fact his early poetic exercises are, in his
opinion, sufficient testimony. They show little knowledge
of the actualities of human life, and little concern. Yet at the
same time, this first flapping of poetic wings helped jostle
him out of the heedless egotism of youth or the engrossment
with nature. For if he was not tempted to write of man's
life as it is, neither was he content with ungarnished description of natural things. The "busy Power" of "wilful
Fancy" would seek to add some charm not intrinsic to the
subject matter. In doing so, fancy turned itself "Instinctively
to human passions," and "burnished" natural objects by connecting them with episodes of exaggerated pathos or romantic wonder, mostly derived from books. For example, if he
noticed a foxglove, "Fancy loved to seat" a "vagrant mother"
beneath the plant. This poetry, though he now regards it as
deplorable, gave "the shapes of human life" a "new importance" to his mind. In other words, these crude attempts
encouraged a sympathetic interest; however shallow and
uninformed it might be at the start, it would gradually
rectify and deepen, the gothic sentiment of the early verse
evolving into the later tales of pathos with their quiet realism. [6]

But the sober contemplation of the actualities of man's
life can hardly by itself produce the reverence for human nature that Wordsworth prizes. A type of experience possibly
more decisive is the direct intuition of one's own nature,
provided that one contemplates what Wordsworth does in
himself. There was a time, he says, when the "pulse of Being
everywhere was felt." Individual objects kept their identity,

but he also apprehended the Divine Life working through each and incorporating all. Like stars, "the several frames of things" were discerned as separate, distinguishable through "every magnitude" of great and least, and yet were "half confounded in each other's blaze," the whole making up one "galaxy of life and joy." Then in this galaxy man, himself a star, "rose . . . to a loftier height"; and the intenser admiration is created by recognizing man's power of intuition, to which the insights just condensed in a metaphor bear witness. Of all visible natures, man is first in "capability of feeling"; he can be transported or "rapt away" by that contemplative ecstasy in which he intuits Being. And that he can do this is known immediately, by direct experience — "Man, inwardly contemplated, and present/ In my own being." In such self-intuition Wordsworth knows that man, more than any other mortal creature, is "instinct/ With Godhead," while also "by reason and by will" he acknowledges "dependency sublime." [7] In the *Essay on Epitaphs* Wordsworth makes a still more striking claim for self-intuition as the primary ground of knowledge in ultimate questions. We know that we are immortal, and yet "from the outward senses" we receive only "the impression of death." That is, we see people die; we do not see them live again. Our consciousness of immortality must derive from "communications with our internal Being, which are anterior to" all outward evidence of death. In this essay Wordsworth writes as a Christian believer, yet he adds that only because it "coincides" with the knowledge given in self-intuition has the Christian revelation a "power to affect us." [8] It is a version of a common theme of idealism since Plato, that we can only learn what in some sense we already know.

That a sojourn in London would nourish reverence or love for man seems wildly improbable, especially when the tourist is Wordsworth. The extended account of his first trip to London comes in *Prelude* VII. He shows himself to have been quite excited, but certainly he did not approve what he saw. In fact, the poetry voices frequent groans as his moral sensibilities are violated. "Foolishness and madness in parade" is his summing up of the city. Moreover, referring back to this visit in Book VIII, he again remembers all that he condemns and fears, and the language shows a genuine alarm, with its characteristic notes of safely abstract compassion (when he thinks of the "Debasement undergone by body or mind") or irritable contempt — "vulgar men about me, trivial forms . . . Mean shapes on every side." [9] But what he saw, he says, neither strangled nor even seriously threatened the faith he brought with him. Nothing could "induce belief" that he had been inspired with "vain conceits" or "walked about in dreams," and the final effect of London was the possession of "still more elevated views/ Of human nature." [10] As he explains this surprising result, Wordsworth offers a vivid, concrete instance and defense of the way we mainly notice what answers to our prior needs and wishes.

Wordsworth comes to London from a rural society in which, he thinks, men are very different. Hence what he sees of life in cities cannot be a complete index to human nature. But there were more fundamental grounds for reassurance. To draw conclusions about human nature only from observation would be foolish even if it were possible. For in the first place, since sensations do not equally press upon the mind — there is a process of unconscious selection — and since the mind that uses them gives sensations much of their content, no purely objective inference is possible. Secondly, even if it were possible, we also require certain beliefs simply because without them we cannot realize our fullest gift for life. Thirdly, we have the more direct knowledge given in self-intuition. Wordsworth rightly doubted the very possibility of sure inference, and particularly in matters of ultimate belief. Least of all would he hastily conclude anything from sights that were disagreeable to prior beliefs. The word "disagreeable" should be stressed. Wordsworth also records particular sights in London that supported his faith. Such occurrences gave him much satisfaction, but still there is a distinction to be made. It is one thing to infer from what Coleridge calls the "outward watchings of life," and quite another when we allow them to substantiate what we already know.

The imagination, Wordsworth plainly says, governs the "else too scrupulous march" of inference by subordinating it to the "heart's occasions." In other words, it is through the imagination that experience comes to us filtered or shaped in accordance with our vital needs, and the "modifying power" might ideally bar even the first impressions on which a threatening inference might be raised. Hence the central problem for Wordsworth is to explain how his youthful imagination was called forth in the city. He begins the self-analysis by describing his general state of mind at the time: "I sought not then/ Knowledge; but craved for power." He means, among other things, that he sought to identify himself with something sublime. When De Quincey (borrowing from Wordsworth, as he says) makes his well-known distinction between the literature of knowledge and the literature of power, he describes "power" at its height as "sympathy with the infinite," or at least a capacity for such sympathy exercised on subordinate objects that expand the mind. Accordingly Wordsworth speaks of the "amplitude of mind" by which he found a correspondent capaciousness around him. "Nothing had a circumscribed/ And narrow influence"; winged with "the strength and glory of our Youth," the mind soared over the "punctual presence" of individual men to discover something larger and more impressive, namely Man. [11] In London, that is, Wordsworth was able to protect his beliefs by contemplating Man as what, following Coleridge, we might call an idea. [12]

According to Coleridge, ideas are not simply images or abstractions, particulars or universals. At least, they are none of these things taken separately, for an idea coalesces them all. It is best described, to use Coleridge's own phrase, as "the universal in the individual," and it coexists in the mind and its object. It can be known transcendentally, and it also emerges to distinct consciousness through experience of its manifold realization in the concrete, though never, perhaps, without our transcendental knowledge as a ground. An instance is Shakespeare's supreme "heart-lore." The universal in each particular was "opened out to him . . . not as an abstraction of observation from a variety of men, but as the substance capable of endless modifications, of which his own personal existence was but one," and he used "*this one* as the eye that beheld the other." Moreover, an idea subsumes not only all its presentations, but also the whole response of the mind to them. [13] Wordsworth seldom employs the term in a strictly Coleridgean sense, and he also adopts synonyms Coleridge would deplore — "conception" or "abstraction." But "Nature," as Wordsworth usually handles the word, denotes an idea; it refers neither to particular items or scenes, nor to landscape generally, nor to a cluster of conceptions, but to all at the same time. And the passage on London in Book VIII is, among other things, a condensed account of the process by which an idea is awakened.

Seeking "power" in London, Wordsworth turns to the

huge scope of the city through space and time. Monuments and ruins, the "widely scattered wreck sublime/ Of vanished nations," speak to him, their suggestions deepened by historical information remembered from books. He has a feeling of the vivid, numberless lives played out,

> a sense
> Of what in the Great City had been done
> And suffered, and was doing, suffering, still.

Through all this — the countless, vanished lives, the intense passions that still make the "vast metropolis" their "chief living residence," the sense of history that throws the mind back in time and out in space to remote seas and continents — works and emerges the spirit or idea of Man, asserting itself through endless recesses of time and myriad varieties of life. As an idea it is sublime, the word "sublime" being used in the sense appropriated to it by aesthetic theory in the later eighteenth century; for it is an idea too great for the mind to grasp and therefore obscure, mysterious, awful. And from its inexhaustible manifestation, there is also the sense of overwhelming power. Hence London "was thronged with impregnations," and Man became an object of the imagination. As a result, the "human nature unto which I felt/ That I belonged," was "reverenced with love." For if in Book VII particular impressions of men in London seem to inspire a pained recoil, he now, in Book VIII, asserts that the imaginative idea of Man usurped his consciousness. "In this my joy," he adds, "in this my dignity/ Consisted." [14]

— 5 —

Wordsworth feels that these later processes — the reverence for Man rising in self-intuition, the idea of Man affirming itself in London — followed inevitably from decisive impressions of shepherds in childhood. Indeed, if one wished to be cranky, Book VIII of the *Prelude* could be described as a defense of prejudice. Throughout this retrospect that ranges up to the early adult years (before the shocks that followed the French Revolution), Wordsworth never shows himself questioning his prepossessions or deciding to believe one thing rather than another. His usual metaphor, in referring to the development of belief, is of steady advance on a path. The direction has been left, he feels, to the "gracious Guide," Nature, by which — or whom — he was "led to knowledge"; and it is only in looking back that the path can be traced. When man — the shepherd — first appeared as a distinct object to be contemplated, he was a "stranger in my path" (for in childhood, family and friends had been mere extensions from himself). When later he rejoiced in the French Revolution, he was still moving on the "self-same path"; for this ardent upsurge seemed to substantiate his faith in human nature. Under the joint shock of the reign of terror and the English war against France, there was a "turn of sentiment" for the first time in his life. Having been disappointed, he tried to start over, building his beliefs with stones of inference. But such reasonings were "false/ From their beginnings"; for he had "turned aside/ From Nature's way," the word "way" suggesting both a path and also a right or natural process in forming belief.[15] Alternative metaphors present Nature training or instructing him. In almost every relevant passage, Wordsworth uses a passive construction, making himself the object of Nature's influence.

If one asks how early encounters with shepherds could determine even his response to London, the answer seems to be that there is a continuity of emotion. Because of certain vivid occurrences in childhood, the

> human form
> To me became an index of delight
> Of grace and honour, power and worthiness; [16]

and this feeling for man persists, both assimilating and determining later experience, finally becoming a conscious belief.
It is important to remember that neither Wordsworth's first
nor subsequent admiration for man directs itself primarily
to moral qualities. He certainly thinks himself fortunate that
in the lake district he was surrounded by "something of a
better life," and he dwells on the virtues of local shepherds,
their independence, faithfulness, courage, and endurance.
But, to repeat, the passion of reverence kindles less from
moments when man is virtuous than when he appears sublime, when there is an initial awe and check before greatness,
and then an expansion of the mind as it identifies with its
mighty object. If he wants to account for his later beliefs
about man, it is this profound awe and wonder that he must
trace to its sources in experience, just as his mature idea of
nature has its roots in earliest infancy and in the haunting
moments described in Books I and II of the *Prelude*. There
were the episodes of snaring woodcocks at night, when
among "the solitary hills" he seemed to hear "low breathings" coming after him, and then the times when he clam-
bered among the high rocks, "shouldering the naked crag"
as the "loud dry wind" seemed to blow through him, declaring some "strange utterance." Then after a brief paean to
Nature, there is the famous boat-stealing episode: as he
rowed, a huge peak suddenly rose behind him in the night
and seemed to pursue him, the experience leaving him with
a sense of "unknown modes of being." As the passages ac-
cumulate, they suggest an increasingly sophisticated awareness — the difference between the concrete, vaguely animal
or monstrous "low breathings" and the far more conceptu-

alized "unknown modes of being" — of something in nature
beyond the mere visible scene. If we accept Wordsworth's
story, then, such events awakened a haunting sense of numinous presence, and the poetry that renders such experience
certainly predisposes the reader in interpretating what comes
later. For the same sense of things is suggestively alive,
though usually less explicit, in all other recollections of
boyhood — in the "alien sound" from the "far distant hills"
amid the tumult of ice skating, or the "gleams of moon-
light from the sea" as the young riders race along the shore.
Analogous moments in Book VIII are presented with far
less elaboration, but the method is the same. Wordsworth
seeks to find and render those decisive passages in experience
which were the origin and feeding source of his later reverence for man.

The poetry, it seems to me, notices four such moments,
though only three remain in the final text. The earliest —
"while yet a very Child" — took place upon "a day of exhalations . . . mists and steam-like fog." Wordsworth was
going "Along a narrow Valley" when suddenly

> aloft above my head,
> Emerging from the silvery vapours, lo!
> A Shepherd and his Dog! in open day:
> Girt round with mists they stood.[17]

It is easy to see why these lines were later omitted. Though
Wordsworth asserts that this sight was beheld "with joy and
love," there is little in the actual description to substantiate
or explain these emotions. Nevertheless, there is sufficient
indication that something very impressive was occurring,
not only from the context introducing these lines, but also
from the tremendous emphasis put on the phrase, "A Shepherd and his Dog." Unless we take this as mere anticlimax,

it suggests that the scene holds some unexpressed symbolic value for Wordsworth. Moreover, a reader familiar with Wordsworth understands that, however unsuccessfully, the poetry here renders a moment of "vision." It describes, that is, a moment when some permanent truth was enshrined in a token or image and revealed to the imagination. The mind of the beholder has cooperated to give this scene its value, but the outward circumstances are also necessary. They rouse and influence the mind, so that the "truth," or its incarnation in this particular symbol, emerges from both the mind and the observed object. But there is also the special peculiarity of Wordsworth's system that cannot be ignored, though it strands even the most nimble sympathizers. Nature, he feels, not only permits, but also — he often implies — arranges such symbolisms. It is this line of thought that produces criteria by which one can tell, in doubtful cases, whether or not Wordsworth refers to what he would interpret as a moment of imaginative vision.

The passage at hand shows most of the usual characteristics of such experience. In the first place, these episodes often unfold a similar sequence of events. A typical, composite example would present Wordsworth alone on a path or moorland, perhaps at night, preoccupied with his thoughts or simply with finding his way. There would be a hush in the air and probably a hypnotic murmur of water in the distance. Suddenly he is startled. There is a flash of light, perhaps, from an opening in clouds or vapor; he looks up, and something is revealed in the visible scene before him. In the second place, there is the special function or role assigned to mists; for mists in nature are analogous to the imagination. The comparison becomes explicit in many places, notably in the great passage already cited that follows the episode of crossing the Alps — imagination

rose from the mind's abyss
Like an unfathered vapour that enwraps,
At once, some lonely traveler.   (VI, 594–596)

In general, mists are exhalations from some unknown source;
they both hide and transfigure the world of sense. Their
mere presence suggests that something is about to be dis-
closed, that a veil is about to break, and when they part, they
isolate what is seen in some unfamiliar, timeless realm —
"Girt round with mists they stood." Referring back to the
famous passage in Book VI, one can say that when mists
surround the traveler on his path, the "light of sense" has
gone out, and that when they open there is a "flash that has
revealed/ The invisible world." Moreover, we saw that when
a poet successfully renders the vision granted to him, language becomes a "transparent veil" or dissolving mist and
the poem itself a sort of winding path for the reader: he
proceeds through "the turnings intricate of verse" and before his imagination things present themselves "in flashes."

Even if the first encounters with shepherds did not resemble other memorable passages in the *Prelude,* one would still
have to interpret them in terms of Wordsworth's theoretical
psychology of imaginative vision. What Wordsworth says
about the growth of his mind is too often discussed as an
exposition of Hartlean associationism — "Trot Trot on the
beaten road of Hartley," as Coleridge said in another connection. At best this view oversimplifies. There is, of course,
a residue of associationist theory, particularly in the thought
that when two objects are present at the same time, and one
of them evokes intense emotion, the emotion will also suf-
fuse the other, which, thereafter, will continue to rouse the
same emotion when encountered by itself. "Shepherds were
the men who pleased me first," Wordsworth says, because
they could be viewed as items in a natural scene, or, as he

puts it, he looked "At Man through objects that were great and fair." He is also capable of saying that natural objects become more dear because of the "ordinary interests of man,/ Which they embosom," but in either case the "two principles of joy," Nature and Man, were associatively linked.[18] But when Wordsworth urges that love of man began with early impressions of shepherds, his psychological scheme simply cannot be mere associationism. The reason is obvious. If the psychology were associationist, Wordsworth's account would not be credible. Perhaps it is not credible by any theory, but certainly in his childhood Wordsworth saw men other than shepherds and shepherds in countless, diverse circumstances. Hence no theory that tends to make the mind a mere product of all its experience can account for the decisive importance of a few particular moments. One requires, instead, a psychology showing that the mind unconsciously determines what will help to determine it. At the same time, it is also necessary to show why reverence for man cannot be originated in cities. Hence one must fall back on the peculiarly balanced theory of the imagination by which Wordsworth holds that the mind works both upon and from external objects. It selects and partly shapes what it notices, but it also takes suggestions from without. Cities, Wordsworth thinks, would not provide sights to influence the mind of a child in the desired direction.

The decisive encounters with shepherds retained in the final text (*Prel.*, VIII, 262–279) are presented in rapid summary. Yet like the analogous passages in Book I (where Wordsworth retraces the experiences that produced his conviction of a Divine Presence in nature), as these three episodes succeed each other, they imply an increasingly conscious awareness. Once again, they begin with an event rendered as it might be interpreted by a child:

> When up the lonely brooks on rainy days
> Angling I went, or trod the trackless hills
> By mists bewildered, suddenly mine eyes
> Have glanced upon him distant a few steps,
> In size a giant, stalking through thick fog,
> His sheep like Greenland bears.

Here the image is relatively naïve — giants and polar bears from boyish tales of wonder. There is no attempt to name the child's feelings, no word to condense the meaning of the scene, and, if I can trust my ear, the sound and movement of those last two lines reflect this unsophisticated sense of things. Another type of encounter is introduced immediately:

> or, as he stepped
> Beyond the boundary line of some hill-shadow,
> His form hath flashed upon me, glorified
> By the deep radiance of the setting sun.

In these two episodes nature by its agents of mist and light had obviously endowed the shepherd with his size or glory. In the final scene, however, the impression of man is less conditioned by natural powers. He appears more as a being sublime in his own right:

> Or him have I descried in distant sky,
> A solitary object and sublime,
> Above all height! like an aerial cross
> Stationed alone upon a spiry rock
> Of the Chartreuse, for worship.

Thus, Wordsworth goes on, in such experience

> was man
> Ennobled outwardly before my sight,
> And thus my heart was early introduced
> To an unconscious love and reverence
> Of human nature.

– 6 –

Summarizing Wordsworth's thinking about the origins of belief, one can stress two assumptions. In the first place, to repeat, belief cannot be derived from inference. Besides the reasons already mentioned, Wordsworth remembers what is sometimes hushed up in the decencies of theory, namely that we must act and time is short. He would heartily endorse Newman's remark in the *Grammar of Assent*: "Life is not long enough for a religion of inferences; we shall never have done beginning if we determine to begin with proof." In the second place, belief comes, and must come, before extensive knowledge or information about its object. The shepherds he saw in a visionary way were, after all, men "With the most common." They suffered "From vice and folly, wretchedness and fear." But the child was scarcely aware of this. Before his "inexperienced eyes" men were "purified" and removed "to a distance that was fit." That this was so answered the needs of his own moral development — for otherwise "How could the innocent heart bear up and live?" It also, however, enabled him to receive at once the essential truth with respect to human nature. And it is altogether necessary, if we are to end by possessing a truth, that it should be received at the start. For Wordsworth knows that though beliefs are awakened in experience, they are also the ground on which experience takes place. He grants, of course, that what we observe may gradually transform belief, but he holds that the process usually works in reverse, that what we believe determines what we observe. A "fact" is not an isolated reality to be dealt with, but an interpretation that has already been made when we acknowledge it as a fact. Information, then, is acquired and incorporated mainly on the basis of prior beliefs. "So we all of us in some degree/ Are led to knowledge," though in this context "knowledge" is a term with a stretch. It means extensive information, but it also means true knowledge or "genuine insight." As a child, Wordsworth says, he had been "turned toward the truth," began with a "prepossession," an "advantage," and a

> defence
> Against the weight of meanness, selfish cares,
> Coarse manners, vulgar passions, that beat in
> On all sides from the ordinary world
> In which we traffic.[19]

In all of this, needless to say, Wordsworth opposes the scientific method eighteenth-century thinkers had too often applied everywhere, even in religion. But in this long, meditative autobiography, he attempts to show not only that beliefs must be given at the start, but also how they were given to him. He thinks mainly of belief as a development from emotion, and the emotions that predispose him were first created in moments of vision, moments so impressive that they determined his subsequent feelings and convictions. If one asks why they were vivid and memorable, the answer must be put in terms simultaneously objective and subjective; for the imagination resolves "into one great faculty/ Of being bodily eye and spiritual need." To some extent, the outward circumstances of the vision — the suddenness, the startling guise of the thing seen — may account for its compelling power. But in countless random excitements we perceive novel aspects of things without finding them especially significant. The moment of vision also fulfills needs of the heart. It manifests a truth that dwells both within the mind and without, and it does so in what can be described as a symbolism — "The excellence, pure function, and best power/ Both of the object seen, and eye that

sees." The symbol engages feeling at once and abides in recollection to be read or interpreted. Reflecting back, Wordsworth can state a meaning. But the meaning, though it can
be put abstractly, lives for the mind only by a continual flow-
ing back into the experience that awakened it. Such episodes,
or "spots of time," as Wordsworth calls them, seldom occur
as one grows older, but their memory stands exempt from
time, a fountain or feeding source to which one can always
return. So it is in hope, at any rate. We saw that Wordsworth fears lest even the recollection of such vivid awaken-
ings may slip from his grasp. Hence he will turn to poetry
as a means of giving them permanence. It is an impossible
task; such experience cannot be wholly mediated in language. But so far as words can give "Substance and life,"
he will enshrine "the spirit of the Past/ For future restoration" — for the heartfelt re-experiencing of the truths im-
plicated in such episodes.[20]

— 7 —

If any one moral emerges from the last few chapters, it
is that an ideal of sincerity, if pursued too remorselessly, can
be devastating. Once it has been invoked, the eye fixes upon
the self. We begin to go round in a circle — am I honest in
what I say? do I actually believe it? do I know it is true?
can I put the truth in words? — the mind turning over like
a dry pump. In this labyrinth of scrupulosity one can even
become bored and listless. Yet how, except by stark oblivion
or outright insincerity, can one help but ask such questions?
An answer, I think, emerges throughout Wordsworth's poetry, in what he says in argument and in what he does. For
the anxieties of sincerity arise mainly when we attempt to
state what we believe. It seldom occurs to us to deny or
doubt whatever stands before us in the concrete, or as an

image in the strongholds of memory. Here our credence is automatic. We do not ask what we believe, or whether it is true. Hence the uncanny stress Wordsworth gives to verbs of emotion or sensory apprehension. They are signs of exultation, of possessing a knowledge that seems undeniable. In the *Excursion*, the Wanderer had been taught religious truths as a boy:

> The mystery, the life which cannot die;
> But in the mountains did he *feel* his faith;
>
> . . . .
>
>   there his spirit shaped
> Her prospects, nor did he believe — he *saw*.
>
>   (I, 225–232)

There is always the possibility that we may be wrong. We could be the victim of some deception or illusion, and must finally live by probabilities, which is what makes acute paranoia so difficult to cure. On the other hand, where we are genuinely committed, we do not accept our belief as merely probable. We never conceive that it may be changed. And though convictions of this kind may still be stated abstractly, they usually refer to something known in the concrete. It is this fact which offers a means of by-passing the roadblock set up by an ideal of sincerity. To turn back to the concrete, to dwell on it, to lose the thought of self in the object contemplated, is to restore again the feeling of conviction that dissolves in an attempt to state what we believe. This, of course, is what Wordsworth does in his poetry, and the mere fact that to write poetry more or less compels one to present things concretely may make it an important help. One can add that if the formal requirements of poetry, which Wordsworth pares to a minimum, can complicate the pursuit of sincerity, they can also become a valuable distraction.

But poetry to Wordsworth was a total act of mind. Concrete experience, after all, does not interpret itself. To know what it assures us of, we must use language discursively, with the result that we are forced to make or recognize conscious commitments. When this happens, the fatal question is likely to arise: how can we assure ourselves that our belief is true? Wordsworth, of course, does not raise the question as a subject for theoretical speculation. He remains autobiographical, and exhibits a temporary tumble into doubt and then a process by which heightened certitude was achieved. In doing so, however, he naturally develops or implies premises that can be stated. The question could be divided in two: how, as a matter of psychology, do we in fact come to an assurance? what, as a matter of philosophy, makes the assurance legitimate? But nothing in Wordsworth suggests the distinction. He would, I think, assume that when our common human nature compels us to believe, that belief must be "legitimate" in the only sense in which the term can be useful. At least, one can find no further warrant.

For Wordsworth takes for granted that there are no objective tests or criteria by which the truth of a belief can be guaranteed. Just as processes of induction and logical demonstration do not originate belief, they cannot confirm it, except in matters largely irrelevant to our moral and religious concerns. Wordsworth's faith in man, which staggered during the later stages of the French Revolution, finally reasserted itself when he went off to live with his sister in the country, where political passions gave way to other interests, and where he could again contemplate and misunderstand English rustics. Perhaps any rooted belief is likely to sprout again when no longer seriously challenged. But the restoration came after a psychological crisis, and the crisis was itself caused partly by an attempt to use Baconian — or Godwinian — methods. He would, he had thought, seek "evidence" for his beliefs. He would adopt "One guide, the light of circumstances, flashed/ Upon an independent intellect." If we credit Wordsworth's statement, the youthful hope and effort put forth were heroic:

> So I fared,
> Dragging all precepts, judgments, maxims, creeds,
> Like culprits to the bar.

Yet it was a mere thrashing around — "now believing,/ Now disbelieving; endlessly perplexed" — that ended in destroying "All feeling of conviction." In bitterness of heart he told himself that man has

> in no concerns of his a test
> Of good and evil; knows not what to fear
> Or hope for, what to covet or to shun.[21]

And if the state of mind was temporary, it taught him that inductive methods hold no promise of conviction. Newman, making a somewhat similar point in the *Grammar of Assent* — that by itself the mind can obtain "no ultimate test of truth" — feels, with Pascal, that it indicates our need of revelation. There may be an analogy in the *Prelude*. Wordsworth never doubts that his own moments of vision have the authority of revelation, but if one wonders how he could be so sure, one confronts the same difficulties that have helped to perplex or shatter Christian faith since his time. For a belief that some particular event constitutes a revelation cannot stand on external criteria or evidence. "Evidences of Christianity," sighs Coleridge at the end of *Aids to Reflection*, "I am weary of the word"; whatever rests on evidence can be toppled by other evidence, or, supposing we can agree to argue from the same set of facts, alternative hypotheses can always be brought forward.

If we have any hope that the truth of a belief can be assured, the criteria must be subjective. That is, they must refer to the way in which belief is entertained. Wordsworth mainly stresses that a belief is likely to be true to the extent that it is accompanied by a strong feeling of conviction. To trust a feeling of conviction need not be the mere resort to *de gustibus* that it might seem — though perhaps not so far from it as Wordsworth might wish. We are thinking of conviction as it takes place in an aware, widely experienced, and honest human being. Moreover, we should try to keep in mind how it actually feels to be convinced. To say that doubt implies self-division or inward strife is a tautology, but it may be meaningful to put it the other way round, reminding ourselves that conviction is "fraught with peace." "Believe me, Southey!" says Coleridge, "a metaphysical Solution, that does not instantly *tell* you something in the Heart, is grievously to be suspected as apocry[p]hal." [22] In a poetic or ideally gifted mind, such synthesis or harmony grows organically and involves the whole past and present life of the individual, his experiences, feelings, and thoughts, to the extent that they are relevant. But the mind of a poet, Wordsworth also asserts, does not differ in kind from that of other men, but only in degree.

Putting it another way, one might stress that both objective and subjective elements must be reconciled in a belief. It rises out of experience, yet it also fulfills a pressing claim of the psyche. Either our antecedent interest in a belief or the outward evidence in its favor would to Wordsworth be a reason for crediting it. But they may conflict. When, however, a particular belief answers to both need and evidence we feel an inward peace or harmony, which can, in turn, be taken as a practical and immediate warrant for the belief. That Wordsworth grants the desirability of outward evidence is not a concession to inductive method. It indicates only that his idealism was not mad, and that he was striving to become open to the whole testimony of experience. If a belief is true, it will be substantiated. This does not mean, to repeat, that belief has the nature of an unprejudiced hypothesis. It still seeks out what will provide verification, opposing a protective screen or filter against anything else. But at the same time, a belief that ran counter to all concrete evidence would not be very satisfying to a rational being, and that a belief can be substantiated is immensely reassuring. Moreover, after a cannonade of hostile evidence, a faith that recovers its ground becomes even more deeply entrenched.

In speaking of an antecedent necessity for belief, the romantics did not refer only to our general hope for a religion or philosophy that gives meaning to life. We may be compelled to certain particular beliefs simply because we are men. Some convictions, in other words, may be elements or inevitable products of human nature, as a flower inheres in a seed, and these must be true. They are analogous to instincts in animals. As Coleridge puts it, "The bull-calf butts with smooth and unarmed brow." In every *"ingrafted word* of promise, Nature is found true to her word; and is it in her noblest creature that she tells her first lie?" [23] The trouble comes in deciding just which beliefs are ingrafted in human nature. Here again the criteria may be objective or subjective. The conviction of personal immortality may be taken as an example. If it is indeed a faith of men everywhere and in every age, we can presume, with Coleridge, that it is planted in human nature. Or we may find by introspection that even our most spontaneous emotions presuppose it. Without the "sense of immortality," Wordsworth says, there could be no love, no joy, no "wish to be remembered after we had passed away from a world in which each man had moved about like a shadow." [24] In the act of introspection Wordsworth would, of course, try to distinguish between beliefs that seem necessary to all men, and those required only by a particular individual or group — perhaps from accidents of temperament or situation. Wordsworth's desire to think of man as sublime is, I think, mainly an instance of a desperate need arising from a personal struggle. The reverence it fostered could serve as a defense or check against his own strongly aggressive and hostile instincts. That a belief has a vital function in one's personal life is certainly a motive for crediting it, but not a reason.

— 7 —

We have in Wordsworth, then, what should probably be called an organic view of belief. He shows early impressions or emotions persisting through subsequent experience, selectively assimilating whatever can nourish them, finally evolving into a clear and rational understanding. "Have you children," says Coleridge,

or have you lived among children, and do you not know, that in all things, in food, in medicine, in all their doings and abstainings they must believe in order to acquire a reason for their belief? . . . in spiritual concernments to believe and to understand are not diverse things, but the same thing in different periods of its growth. Belief is the seed, received into the will, of which the understanding or knowledge is the flower, and the thing believed is the fruit. [25]

One point, however, Wordsworth was led to make far more clearly than Coleridge. Both agree that in all stages of their growth the assents by which we live are felt to be unconditional. At no time do we suppose that greater assurance could be required or obtained. Yet in this long review of his own development, Wordsworth also finds that his confidence or trust has vastly deepened. It is, perhaps, like being in love; for love, when it deserves the name, always supposes itself entire and perfect, yet it persists only by growing. Faith intensifies, according to Wordsworth, with our increasingly distinct understanding of it. Such mental grasp results from trial in the welter of experience and from self-analysis. It also involves an accompanying consciousness of reasons for the belief. Reasons would include almost everything mentioned hitherto — the origins of the belief in moments of revelation, the appertaining needs it fulfills, the amount of feeling invested, the witness and test of concrete experience — and also what might more usually be called reason, that is, a sense that the belief is consistent with others to which one feels equally pledged. Wordsworth explains his temporary upset after the French Revolution by saying that though he "had oft revolved" and deeply felt his belief, it was not yet "thoroughly understood." For in the first outgoing of a child's heart,

> we love, not knowing that we love,
> And feel, not knowing whence our feeling comes.[26]

However accurately Wordsworth describes a process of belief that may work itself out in us, this toil of introspection leads where we might not wish to go. It appears that virtually any belief that happened to seed itself might take hold and flourish, especially, perhaps, in Wordsworth's mind, of which, said Coleridge, the soil was "a deep, rich, dark mould, on a deep stratum of tenacious clay." Among the stately trees that came up, there was, Coleridge often suspected, a clump of giant weed, namely the beliefs Wordsworth once summed up — in a phrase he later deplored — by declaring himself "A worshipper of Nature." "O dearest William!" cried

Coleridge to his journal after one argument in 1803, "Would Ray, or Durham [naturalist divines], have spoken of God as you spoke of Nature?" And years later, near the end of the *Aids to Reflection*, Coleridge animadverted on those "who feel it more in harmony with their indefinite sensations

> To worship Nature in the hill and valley,
> Not knowing what they love."

This, he rightly thought, was the case with an increasing shoal of persons in his time, and, though Coleridge never admits it, Wordsworth's poetry was serving as a sacred text of this new religion. Had he been pressed, Coleridge would, I think — certainly with inward reluctance and misgiving — have described Wordsworth's nature faith as mysticism, which was no word of compliment:

When a man refers to inward feelings and experiences, of which mankind at large are not conscious, as evidences of the truth of any opinion — such a man I call a Mystic: and the grounding of any theory or belief on accidents and anomalies of individual sensations or fancies . . . I name Mysticism.[27]

Yet what Coleridge terms "anomalies of individual sensations" are for Wordsworth those moments in time which are so imperious and indelible. Coleridge, of course, pleads for a faith based on inward feelings of which all men are conscious. That there are any such may be doubted, and, in the end, it is hard not to feel that Wordsworth — far more clumsy in definition, confused and contradictory as he is when compared to his friend — may have accomplished something as valuable as Coleridge's brilliant attempt to give a subjective ground for Christian faith. For, maybe because he was writing poetry, Wordsworth manages to remain more concrete and faithful in showing how belief originates and develops in us.

Here we touch one of the high regions on which he survives the flood of time. One may not share many of his beliefs, or even grant them the favor of a serious consideration. Yet poetry has no more honest witness to the way in which the mind actually maneuvers in the field of experience.

VI

WORDSWORTH
AND HIS AUDIENCE

NEOCLASSIC poetry almost always reflects a strong sense of an audience. That is, the poet shows himself addressing someone else, either a particular individual or the general public, and the verse is controlled by an implied social situation. But an altogether different convention governs most romantic and later poetry. The poet is usually assumed to be uttering an internal monologue. In this respect Wordsworth occupies a borderland between neoclassic art and high romanticism. Often his poetry, like that of Blake, Shelley, or Keats, seems oblivious of listeners, and this is especially true when he rises to a mood of transport. At other times, he can resemble neoclassic writers, showing a delicate sensitivity to the probable responses of a cultured public. But neither the tone of prophecy nor the acknowledgment of social proprieties is his characteristic stance. He writes as though he were speaking to close friends or to domestic companions. If one asks why Wordsworth caught this tone or mode, any answer one attempts must keep in mind the influence on him of contemporary taste, the particular circumstances of his career — he was neglected or decried for years by the general public, while extolled by a few readers — and also the sometimes extraordinary daring and originality of his poems. But whatever the reasons behind it, he writes a talking poetry — as opposed to something more internal, more rapt, or (as in Byron) more oratorical — and the themes and manner of this talk could seem very intimate. This effect of intimacy, to which even garrulity or awkwardness may contribute, was long an important reason for his hold upon readers, and it still works a waning magic today.

Throughout the nineteenth and early twentieth centuries, to be labeled a Wordsworthian suggested something more than that one admired and studied his poetry. It was not quite analogous to being a Keatsian or a Shakespearean. Enthusiastic readers were likely to be disciples, or at least they would feel an almost personal relationship with him. The lure of this could lead captive one of the finest tastes among English critics. "I am a Wordsworthian," Arnold announces. "I can read with pleasure and edification *Peter Bell*, and the whole series of *Ecclesiastical Sonnets*, and the address to Mr. Wilkinson's spade, and even the Thanksgiving Ode." [1] Though Arnold had known Wordsworth personally, and had his tongue a little in his cheek, and was in fact making a selection to disengage Wordsworth's better work from the inferior mass, the remark is still revealing. Wordsworth can create an audience to which his poetry will appeal even when it is bad poetry. To many readers, says de Selincourt with unreserved sentimentality, Wordsworth is "not a poet only, but a friend; and among our friends the most trivial admissions are often welcomed because, in their very triviality, they seem to bring us nearer to the object of our love." [2] James Russell Lowell, though a president of the Wordsworth Society, was not a friend of this sort, and therefore poses the issue in a different way. Wordsworth, he says, sometimes reminds us of "local histories in the undue relative importance given to trivial matters. He was the historian of Wordsworthshire." [3] Local histories, however, are not written for the book-of-the-month club. To think what type of audience they presuppose suggests at once the unusual degree of sympathy and biographical interest sometimes required and created by Wordsworth's poetry.

But if the poetry may appeal by its intimacy, pulling the reader toward something analogous to a close, personal relationship, this is not true without qualification. There is also a strong infusion of what usually would be interpreted as a public manner. So far as Wordsworth was actually writing for family or private friends, the oratory and didacticism in his verse reflect a not very pleasing aspect of his character. But he naturally sought a wider public, and if we choose to think in terms of literary history rather than biography, we can explain the tone of his poetry as the result of colliding influences. The note of intimacy was relatively novel in the poetry of the early 1800's, but Wordsworth can hardly be viewed as an innovator. He shares this stance with the *avant garde* of his generation. A strong, immediate source was Rousseau's *Confessions*, and Wordsworth's poetry — the *Prelude* especially — could be interpreted as a verse equivalent to the prose confessions and familiar essays of the age. One thinks particularly of the essays of Lamb or Hazlitt, which themselves often read like pages torn from an ampler confession modeled on Rousseau. But sharing at least a family resemblance with these writers, Wordsworth also shows the tug of a traditional poetic rôle — that is, poetry should be public utterance with a didactic purpose.

There were, then, two desires not easily to be reconciled. Like Rousseau, Wordsworth says many times that he writes "to give vent to my own mind," and he even declares that were he a rich man he would not publish. Yet he also proclaims that "Every great Poet is a Teacher: I wish either to be considered as a Teacher, or as nothing." [4] That this hope could be fulfilled while preserving an intimate manner seems unlikely. In talking to our friends, most of us do not strive to improve their moral character, least of all in an open and admitted way; and perhaps we should not have many friends if we did. There is a tone in his verse that may obstruct appreciation. The intimacy he offers will not be to everyone's taste. When we read the confessions of Rousseau or of other romantic writers, we usually enjoy a sense of fellow-feeling. The author does not appear less guilty and foolish than we. Wordsworth's poetry most emphatically does not leave this pleasant impression. It confesses only the author's virtues. It may or may not be true that (to cite Grosart's remark again) "the closer one gets to the man, the greater he proves," but Wordsworth certainly hoped we would feel this way — or, more precisely, he hoped that the poetry would create this feeling in us. He wanted to arouse admiration for himself; he considered that the emotion would be salutary for his readers. In other words, his poetry accomplishes its didactic function by displaying the poet as a moral or spiritual example. He allows us to come near so that we may esteem and emulate. At times, he even lists his own virtues: "pure in heart," "content/ With my own modest pleasures," "removed/ From little enmities and low desires." [5] One should add, however, that there was not much vanity in these assertions. Such traits of character were not achieved by him but given through the kindness of Nature. Nevertheless, like other romantic poets, Wordsworth presents himself as a sort of hero, a hero we can know on an intimate footing. At least a sense of familiarity with reverence more or less was the particular attitude to the poet that his verse aroused in some readers. To such readers — the youthful De Quincey or John Wilson are examples — this was a main source of attraction. It was not the intimacy by itself that caught them, nor solely the sense of greatness, but the union of the two emotions. It appeared that Wordsworth lived more or less as we all do, and yet vividly, happily; he seemed to possess some inward source of strength.

– 2 –

We can start by asking just what audience Wordsworth had in mind, a subject he often discussed. *Peter Bell* opens with an idyllic scene in which Wordsworth depicts the sort of hearers he would like, and the relation he would like to have with them. To summarize the passage may make his actual dilemma a little clearer. The poet is among friends, persons who feel an active concern — "a thousand fears" — for him. Such an audience will take a keener interest in the story from their sympathy with the speaker. Among these friends, he has an acknowledged rôle: he is their poet and they have gathered to hear him. He can number his whole audience, nine persons in all, and is acquainted with each person individually. Thus he feels sure that this is a suitable occasion for the simple syntax and colloquial diction with which he wishes to experiment. The point is the ease and security provided by this ideal audience — because it is well disposed and also because it is known.

Through most of his greater years Wordsworth was not sure whom he was addressing. The leading facts were that the poems did not sell and the influential journals, with some exceptions, remained indifferent or hostile. Hence Wordsworth was soon convinced that the general public would not welcome his verse, and yet he was naturally not satisfied to write solely for a few familiars. One inevitably wonders to whom, then, one can speak. Wordsworth consoled himself with various answers which, collected together, seem to exhaust all conceivable possibilities. He is writing for posterity, for serious students of poetry, or for "human nature." Some of these suggestions are merely defensive. Certainly Wordsworth would like to be read by serious students of poetry, but he did not direct himself to any specially trained or elite group. When he urges that "an *accurate* taste in poetry . . . is an *acquired* talent," he intends merely to plant a suggestion that he may himself be a better judge than his readers. In fact, many years later he adds that those who have long "applied to the consideration" of poetry "the best power of their understandings" may hold opinions "the most erroneous and perverse." [6] In practice, then, to say that you are writing for the best judges is simply to appoint as a judge whoever happens to like your poetry. To assert that one writes for posterity is equally senseless except as a statement of hope. It would naturally have to be an "improving posterity," as Wordsworth puts it, but since one knows nothing about future generations, they can hardly be an audience. The state of mind is neatly parodied by Charles Lamb: "When my last sonnet was rejected, I exclaimed, 'Damn the age; I will write for Antiquity.' " [7]

Wordsworth also made the peculiar claim that he was speaking to human nature, that is, to a permanent and universal character that abides in all of us, underlying traits compelled by changing social manners. But if we take Wordsworth's claim as anything more than self-praise, it appears that in order to address human nature, one requires a rather clear notion of what it is. Wordsworth, as we saw, falls back on primitivism. It turns out that human nature best displays itself in his rustic neighbors. As long as he could believe — or even half believe — this, he might have a visible and present audience. For a while, at least, he tried to direct some of his poems to such persons and naturally rejected criticism from other quarters. A man, he tells John Wilson,

must have lived "among cottages and fields, and among children . . . before his judgment upon *The Idiot Boy* would
be in any way decisive with me."[8] Years later he remarked
that he had composed some of his poems in the hope that
they might circulate as halfpenny ballads. And he recited
his verses to all comers, whatever their class or educational
status. There is old Mrs. Knott—no rustic, but no critic
either—who was favored with a reading from the *Excursion*, a reading apparently chanted or boomed; for "She could
not hear his loud voice; but understood the story very well
when her Niece read it." On another occasion Dorothy remarks, "We have our Haircutter below stairs, William is
reading the Leech-gatherer to him."[9] These attempts are inconsistent with the premise that an accurate taste is an acquired talent, but there was something far more alarming.
Human nature, as located in cottage-dwellers, proved to be
quite as unresponsive as the general public: "Well you see
. . . there's pomes and pomes, and Wudsworth's was not for
sec as us."[10]

— 3 —

Confronted with this widespread rebuff, Wordsworth
struggled for years to understand and explain it. He was far
from meek or humble. When he thought of reviews and
their readers, he had in his early years no trouble accounting
for their reaction on grounds favorable to himself. His solic-
itations were sober and virtuous. That they were not accepted proves the public is debauched, and the seducers are
known. First they were Pope and his crew, with their "extravagant and absurd diction," and then "frantic novels,
sickly and stupid German Tragedies, and deluges of idle and
extravagant stories in verse."[11] Later he would especially
note the "fiend-like" fascination of Byron, to which he him-

self was immune. Accustomed to such trash, readers have become frivolous and vain. They have no capacity to appreciate earnestness, and, moreover, they seek in poetry a support for their self-love. For the personifications and circumlocutions of Pope's style are cold imitations of a way of speaking that earlier poets actually fell into when excited by strong passion. Upon an unthinking reader such devices still impress "a notion of the peculiarity and exaltation of the Poet's character," and they inflate his "self-love by bringing him nearer to a sympathy with that character." [12] Worst of all, readers go to poetry to nourish their class pride. There are, of course, countless open statements of class consciousness in eighteenth-century literature — for example, Gray's *Elegy* — but Wordsworth largely ignores these to notice more insidious temptations. David Hartley had already suggested that snobbery is one of the sources of our pleasure in the arts generally. Wordsworth thinks the versification and diction of neoclassic poetry cater to social pride by their artifice. A reader must learn to enjoy them, and thus the poetry reminds him of his own acquired cultivation. There is also the threat of an even subtler corruption — not solely from Augustan poetry but from the literature of the age generally. That art should focus on what is universal in human nature was a commonplace of eighteenth-century criticism. But Wordsworth keeps in mind that differences produced by social class are just as local or accidental as those of geography or historical period. In other words, he connects the critical doctrine with values that are directly moral and political. Novels, plays, and poems that portray "manners and character produced by times and circumstances" are, in fact, emphasizing what divides men from each other. They feed a dangerous sense of superiority (or inferiority) based on chance acquirements, so that a difference in dress or accent may be felt to imply a difference in soul. As he puts it in the *Prelude*, such books

> set forth
> Extrinsic differences, the outward marks
> Whereby society has parted man
> From man,

while they forget that "we have all of us one human heart." Wordsworth tries to reveal "those points of human nature in which all men resemble each other." [13] To this purpose lyric poetry, he feels, is uniquely directed by its formal requirements. Simply because of its little space and intense mood, it must concentrate on essentials.

In his early years, then, Wordsworth blames his troubles almost entirely on the faults of his readers, and particularly on their pride and selfishness. One might say that he had composed his verse in distaste of the public and found a further reason for distaste in the reception he encountered. The style and subjects of the *Lyrical Ballads* are designed to ensure an attraction independent of changing fashions, but they are also deliberately calculated to offend and correct the feelings of the sort of person who usually reads poetry — that is, members of the middle and upper classes. In other words, both his attitude to the public, and, at least in his opinion, the attitude of the public to his work, should be explained in connection with his still liberal politics. To show and urge how all men are alike may be consistent with any political faith. Wordsworth prided himself on it even when he was sunk in Toryism. On the other hand, the approach can easily involve an implicit questioning of the social order, and this subversive tendency seemed to emerge in the *Lyrical Ballads*. It bristled even in the primitivism, the use of lower-class or rustic persons to exemplify human nature. At least to his own satisfaction, Wordsworth proves that the "maternal passion" is the same in Betty Foy with her idiot child as it is in a fine lady. Adopting a line from Langhorne's *Country Justice*, one can say that Wordsworth "felt as Man, and dropp'd a human Tear." That Langhorne is himself describing a "pitying Robber" may also remind us that there was ample, immediate precedent for this theme in Wordsworth — the sense of solidarity with the Man in even the most wretched and outcast of men — though Wordsworth is much less sentimental than most eighteenth-century humanitarians. Since the radical tendency would not escape readers of his poetry, Wordsworth may have had some color of justice in attributing their lukewarm response to prejudice. They were refusing to admit that the one human nature we all share should lead to a universal sympathy.

But some readers and critics attacked Wordsworth on his own ground. His portrayals were too minute and particular, and his feelings were idiosyncratic rather than normative. Wordsworth increasingly saw the force of these complaints, but did not therefore disvalue his poetry. Instead, he learned to justify it in other terms. In the initial stages (roughly 1802–1807) of this gradually shifting argument, he is likely to say something like this: the feelings he renders are permanent and universal in human nature, but they will seem odd to most readers since, in cultivated and urban individuals, truly natural responses have usually been supplanted by false refinement and affectation. Hence it is not enough "to delineate merely such feelings as all men *do* sympathise with," least of all if we mean by men

Gentlemen, persons of fortune, professional men, ladies, persons who can afford to buy . . . books of half-a-guinea price, hot-pressed, and printed upon superfine paper.

A true poet must restore the sensibility of his readers, rectifying and revivifying in them a way of feeling that is "more sane, pure, and permanent, in short more consonant to nature." [14]

By 1807, Wordsworth pursues a rather different road in vindicating his poetry, which has also changed. He no longer stresses (and he naturally does not disavow) that his work turns our eyes toward norms of feeling constant in all men. He now says that his poetry is personal and edifying. It is personal in the sense that it issues from his own private life and expresses his own emotions. Still, however, there is the tendency — it persisted throughout his life — to "attach to the approbation" of his verses, as Crabb Robinson delicately phrases it, a "connection with moral worth which others may deem the effect of vanity." [15] For Wordsworth now urges more than ever that his way of life and the emotions it fosters are exemplary. His poetry offers a habit of feeling that all men ought to share, but from which most readers are barred —

merely think of the pure absolute honest ignorance, in which all worldlings of every rank and situation must be enveloped, with respect to the thoughts, feelings, and images, on which the life of my Poems depends.

As he goes on, he treats Lady Beaumont to a vigorous harangue:

The things which I have taken, whether from within or without, — what have they to do with routs, dinners, morning calls, hurry from door to door, from street to street, on foot or in Carriage; with Mr. Pitt or Mr. Fox, Mr. Paul or Sir Francis Burdett, the Westminster Election or the Borough of Honiton; in a word . . . what have they to do with endless talking about things nobody cares anything for except as far as their own vanity is concerned, and this with persons they care nothing for but as their vanity or *selfishness* is concerned; what have they to do (to say all at once) with a life without love? [16]

The implication is clear. In order to appreciate his poetry, one must at least be capable of entering into the feelings it expresses. Persons who live "in the broad light of the world" have no experience that would provide even the ground for such a participation. In such remarks one sees Wordsworth's theory of poetry shifting. He is moving away from the neo-classic view that art mirrors and appeals to a universal human nature, and toward a more romantic and modern view. The reader must be able to identify himself with the poet, who speaks mainly out of his personal life and feelings.

In the final stage of this development, Wordsworth recognizes that the sensibility recorded in his poetry is unique, or at least strongly individual. To be sure, he had always felt this —

> Possessions have I that are solely mine,
> Something within that yet is shared by none —; [17]

the *Prelude* was studded with utterances in this vein. But a long time passed before Wordsworth emphasized it to account for his troubles with the public. His most extended and thoughtful discussion of these difficulties occurs in the Supplementary Essay published with the Preface of 1815. The essay is decidedly immodest; it intends to prove that any great and original writer will not be popular in his lifetime. It begins by analyzing the reading public into various classes or types of person — the "young, who in nothing can escape delusion," tired business men "unbending their minds with verse," and so on. The undeniable conclusion is that only a very few individuals in any age can be reliable critics. Most readers prefer an inferior order of verse. As Wordsworth puts it, "what a small quantity of brain is necessary to procure a considerable stock of admiration!" He demonstrates this fact by a tendentious review of literary history, and then attempts to explain it. A great poet's struggle for recognition does not consist mainly in "overcoming the prejudices of false refinement" or "divesting the reader" of his pride and vanity. Now, in 1815, the point is that the sensibility of a major poet is always original: "Of genius, in the fine arts, the only infallible sign is the widening the sphere of human sensibility . . . Genius is the introduction of a new element into the intellectual universe." It follows that a poet has the "task of *creating* the taste by which he is to be enjoyed," a remark Wordsworth never tired of echoing from Coleridge.[18] In other words, the poetry of genius confronts the reader with perceptions and emotions so unfamiliar that he may not even apprehend them. Writing to Catherine Clarkson in 1814 of the *Excursion*, Wordsworth says that as she reads it the "impediments" she may encounter resemble those that can block appreciation of the ode on "Intimations of Immortality":

This poem rests entirely upon two recollections of childhood; one that of a splendour in the objects of sense which is passed away; and the other an indisposition to bend to the law of death, as applying to our own particular case. A reader who has not a vivid recollection of these feelings having existed in his mind in childhood cannot understand that poem.

In the *Excursion*, he goes on, there are many images in which natural objects — he is thinking of mountain scenery — are used as suggestive analogies of "Immortality and Infinity."

If a person has not been in the way of receiving these images, it is not likely that he can form such an adequate conception of them as will bring him into vivid sympathy with the Poet.[19]

If such sympathy does not exist, it may come in time. The reader may encounter objects or undergo experiences that enable him to understand the poet, and also the poetry will gradually modify the sensibility of those who study it. They will, for example, begin to view mountains, valleys, rivers, clouds and what not with Wordsworthian eyes. When this happens, they will come to the poetry with the most vivid sympathy conceivable. But before readers can themselves fall into such habits of feeling, the poetry must show the way, communicating ideas and possibilities of response that may at first be utterly alien. To do this, it must, as we saw, suggest to the imagination. It must rouse and rely upon an "auxiliary impulse" or "co-operating *power*" in the reader that will permit him to see and feel with the poet. "To create taste is to call forth and bestow power . . . and *there* lies the true difficulty." [20]

– 4 –

Wordsworth could at least expect, however, that his poems would appeal immediately to his private friends. There was a desperate personal urgency in this expectation. He had to have a sense of sympathetic hearers simply in order to write — or, rather, to write as he desired. We do not fully appreciate his courage unless we understand that he carried on not only against neglect or reproach, but against the drag of his own deep misgivings. While he defended his technical innovations, he too felt that they were questionable. He justified the singularity of his associations or feelings (for example, the affectionate interest in mad people), but he had qualms in doing so. The faiths he most cherished — that Nature is benign and even tenderly conscious of Man, or that Man should be regarded with love and awe — were as doubtful as they were necessary to him. Even in the retired vale of

Grasmere, it was hard to preserve them. Since his confidence was so precarious, he would not read censorious notices of his poems ("You cannot scower a spot of this kind out of your mind"), and, much to the annoyance of his domestic circle, he banned the leading journals from his house — "he despises their want of principle so much." When he did come upon hostile appraisals, his insecurity leapt out in a harsh, moralistic scorn of their authors ("a miserable maggot crawled out of the dead carcass of the Edinburgh review").[21] Again, he had the sort of friend that reports unfavorable comment, and these items invariably provoked lengthy explanation, defense, and contempt. Catherine Clarkson wrote to tell him the dispraise of a Miss Patty Smith. Wordsworth — in a letter already cited — replied at once. Miss Smith had questioned his religious orthodoxy:

She talks of my being a worshiper of Nature. A passionate expression, uttered incautiously in the poem upon the Wye ["Tintern Abbey"], has led her into this mistake; she, reading in cold-heartedness, and substituting the letter for the spirit.

As for the *Excursion*, she has misunderstood it, partly because her own religious views are no doubt shallow. But if, reading the *Excursion*, she does not feel for the plight of Ellen, Wordsworth can only "thank Heaven" Miss Smith is not a person "I am forced daily to converse with." As for her "notion of poetical imagery," it is "probably taken from . . . *Gertrude of Wyoming*."[22] Other examples are a letter of seven pages in the printed text to Lady Beaumont on Mrs. Fermor, who, though generally sympathetic, had objected to two sonnets; to Sir George Beaumont against a friend of Beaumont's who had noticed a fault in "Daffodils" ("my Poems must be more nearly looked at before they can give rise to any remarks of much value"); seven pages from the thirty-two-year-old poet defending "The Idiot Boy" in reply to John Wilson, an admiring youth of seventeen at the time.[23]

But the most severe shock came when his own particular friends failed to sympathize. He revenged himself in protracted abuse. Charles Lamb, who confided to Manning that the *Lyrical Ballads* "are but drowsy performances," did not, of course, suggest this to Wordsworth. But acknowledging receipt of the second edition, he incautiously remarked that nothing in it had moved him so much as some poems in the earlier publication. In reply, he received the joint letter from Wordsworth and Coleridge that he calls his "northern castigation" — "four sweating pages" in which, among other things, Wordsworth "was compelled to wish my range of sensibility was more extended."[24] Yet Lamb failed again when he was allowed to read the *White Doe of Rylstone* in manuscript, which proved, as Wordsworth explained to Coleridge, that "Lamb has not a reasoning mind, therefore cannot have a comprehensive mind, and, least of all, has he an imaginative one." Hapless Sara Hutchinson found the speech of the leech-gatherer tedious in an early draft of "Resolution and Independence." "Everything is tedious," Wordsworth exclaims, "when one does not read with the feelings of the Author." Then, more in sorrow than anger, her lapse of sympathy is transformed into moral blindness, Wordsworth relentlessly concluding "I will talk more with you on this when we meet."[25] And when Coleridge published his famous review in the *Biographia Literaria* (1817), which, though highly laudatory, admitted that Wordsworth had defects, Lamb was "sure Mr. Wordsworth will never speak to Mr. Coleridge again." They met at dinner a few weeks later, and Crabb Robinson was "for the first time in my life not pleased with Wordsworth." His manner towards Coleridge "was cold and scornful." [26] These letters and comments are the more striking in that they often include assurances that "my ears are stone-dead to this idle buzz, and my flesh as insensible as iron to these petty stings" of criticism." [27] Needless to say, we are seldom so alarmed by censure unless it focuses misgivings we share and suppress.

– 5 –

It seems likely, then, that if Wordsworth had any particular audience in mind as he composed, it would be his family and friends plus a few enthusiasts in the reading public. If one tried to ignore biographical information, looking only to the poetry and asking what sort of audience it presupposes, one would come to a similar conclusion, though it would be more tentative and qualified. As a matter of fact, Wordsworth's poems frequently name the circumstances in which they are supposed to be uttered or the persons addressed. Many of the lyrics are apostrophes. Wordsworth was ready to buttonhole almost any object or abstraction — birds, the moon, flowers of various kinds, garden tools, sleep, duty. "To the Cuckoo" is an example. The bird is addressed repeatedly, and since no other hearer is suggested, and since the cuckoo naturally makes no response to the poet, he is alone with his thoughts. Throughout Wordsworth's poetry, an apostrophe usually signals precisely this. It tells us that we are about to enter the privacy of a man with himself, and in his essay on "The Three Voices of Poetry," Eliot remarks that "part of the enjoyment" of such verse lies in "*overhearing* words which are not addressed to us." In fact, John Stuart Mill makes this the basis for distinguishing poetry from eloquence: "Eloquence is *heard*, poetry is *over*heard. Eloquence supposes an audience" to be courted or influenced; "The peculiarity of poetry appears to us to lie in the poet's utter unconsciousness of a listener." [28] Among the English poets Mill especially responded to Wordsworth and Shelley, and his remark suggests one of the chief attractions he found in them. The relish was partially compensatory, both in Mill and in other Victorians. A culture increasingly reticent, in which even domestic life was governed by shyness and strict formalities, would naturally turn to poetry for the intimate self-revelation it seems to convey.

Often the poems show Wordsworth speaking to his wife, his children, his sister, or other familiars. For to address loved ones is like talking to yourself in the important respect that they are relatively permissive — this was true at least of Wordsworth's circle. As an audience, they would not inhibit or control the poetry in any way, and they would also bring to bear a protective sympathy. The hope is plainly stated at the start of the *Prelude*. Wordsworth never approved of this long autobiographical poem, "a thing unprecedented in literary history that a man should talk so much about himself." [29] Later on, he explained it as a vestibule in which he showed his credentials for a vast didactic work, the *Recluse*, he planned to write. But the defense was retrospective and the *Recluse* significantly unfinished. In the first book of the *Prelude*, he offers a different apology. Among other things, he reminds himself and his readers that the poem is written for Coleridge. This situation makes it both easy and appropriate for Wordsworth to be as self-concerned, discursive, and confessional as he may wish. A friend will desire to learn "how the heart was framed/ Of him thou lovest," and hence will not think that he has "lengthened out/ With fond and feeble tongue a tedious tale." He can even venture to speak of that occasion of drunkenness — the only one in his life — when at college he "poured out/ Libations" to the memory of Milton; for the friend will "forgive the weakness of that hour." Moreover, Coleridge shelters his home-bred beliefs from the harsher scrutiny an unloving audience might induce. He even shares the opinion that Nature had fed Wordsworth's "lofty speculations," so that this peculiar doctrine can be voiced "unapprehensive of contempt." [30] Like the habit of apostrophe, this choice of a friend as audience gives the reader the fascinating and, as Eliot points out, enjoyable rôle of an eavesdropper. But the final version of the *Prelude* only twice mentions Coleridge by name, while it repeatedly (48 times) calls the listener a "dear Friend." There is a temptation offered to the reader. He may substitute himself for the person addressed, applying the caressing remarks to himself and accepting Wordsworth's encouragement to suspend "Harsh judgments" and become "prompt/ In sympathy." [31]

Even when Wordsworth does not present himself apostrophizing some object or concept, or speaking to some particular individual, his poetry still preserves the habit of direct address with an implied intimacy. The famous lyric on "The Solitary Reaper" is an example. In the first line — "Behold her, single in the field" — one assumes that, at the very moment he notices the Highland girl, the poet speaks to a companion. (It is significant for understanding what poetic effects Wordsworth sought that, though he had seen many solitary reapers on his Scotch tour, the particular experience the poem describes was not his own. It was suggested by a sentence in Thomas Wilkinson's *Tour in Scotland*, though Wordsworth writes it up as his own and, moreover, as voiced spontaneously.) The exclamations repeated in the first stanza — "Stop here!" "O listen!" — draw the reader into an experience immediately taking place. To say this is, of course, to bring out responses which ordinarily and rightly do not come to conscious notice, and would be naïve if they did. But at the theater we all to some degree resemble Partridge in *Tom Jones,* and in a similar way naïve assumptions of various kinds always lurk as an element in our total response to literature. The later line in the poem — "Will no one tell me what she sings?" — simply sustains the sense of participation established at the beginning. It tends to create an illusion that the reader is present as the poet speaks, and potentially able to reply. Something of the same kind occurs in most of Wordsworth's poems — "Daffodils" or "Michael," for example. The effect is always to pull the reader toward a rather intimate relationship; the poet would not speak as he does except to familiar associates.

For when we are colloquial, personal, direct, and self-analytic, it can be assumed that, if we are talking to others, they would probably be close friends. But any judgment that a style is colloquial depends on the anticipations of the reader, that is, on the norms of speech to which he is accustomed and the tones he expects of poetry. To us, for example, the *Excursion* may seem preachy. To Charles Lamb it was the "noblest conversational poem I ever read," or so he told Wordsworth.[32] But the "natural" or colloquial aspects of Wordsworth were quickly seized and carried further by younger poets — Leigh Hunt or Keats, not to mention *Don Juan.* To our generation, used to hearing

> An aged man is but a paltry thing
> A tattered coat upon a stick,

or

> Earth's the right place for love:
> I don't know where it's likely to go better,[33]

Wordsworth will not sound refreshingly colloquial. He has moments, needless to say. Sometimes a natural order of

monosyllabic words in short clauses will suggest Robert
Frost:

> Our walk was far among the ancient trees:
> There was no road, nor any woodman's path.

But the poetry at once shocks our ears with an obese Latin-
ism ("umbrage"), and then decays, from our point of view,
into a typically amplifying syntax:

> But a thick umbrage — checking the wild growth
> Of weed and sapling, along soft green turf
> Beneath the branches — of itself had made
> A track.

Similarly, there is often an idiom soaked in personality:

> She was a woman of a stirring life,
> Whose heart was in her house;

there is sometimes a casual ease that still works its magic —
Michael's boy herding sheep, "Something between a hind-
rance and a help"; there is the occasionally grotesque or
child-like way of putting things.[34] But there is also a constant periphrasis and a habitual sententious abstraction. Certainly Wordsworth and his generation transformed literary
history by developing a more plain and simple speech. But
we cannot suppose his verse continues to work the same
revolutionary emancipation. If we still feel a certain intimacy, it is not because we hear much colloquial ease.

   We are, I think, tugged into intimacy mainly by the subject matter — deeply personal histories such as "Nutting,"
"To a Cuckoo," "Tintern Abbey," and so on — and by the
nobly direct way in which Wordsworth utters his feelings.
"I speak bare truth," he says in the *Prelude*, "as if to thee
alone in private talk." [35] There still is — though we are now

more accustomed to it — something astonishing and deeply attractive in a poet who will keep the same tone of open, explicit seriousness whether he is meditating on human life generally —

> man grows old, and dwindles, and decays;
> And countless generations of mankind
> Depart; and leave no vestige where they trod —

or on the extinction of the Venetian republic, or, in the passage already cited, disclosing his own private fears:

> the hiding-places of man's power
> Open; I would approach them, but they close.
> I see by glimpses now; when age comes on,
> May scarcely see at all.[36]

Wordsworth inherited this poetry of statement from the verse essays and descriptive-meditative works of the eighteenth century, but these poems dealt with interests and sentiments widely shared. Incorporating a similar directness of approach with a new source of interest, namely himself, Wordsworth helped to develop a type of poetry which, though far from unknown in earlier periods, has spread and flourished in the last hundred years. As examples one can cite Tennyson's *In Memoriam* or most of Arnold's lyrics. Even Eliot, despite earlier resolutions (which Arnold also made) to work in an "objective" way, finally becomes personal and meditative in portions of *Ash Wednesday* and the *Four Quartets*. In fact, Yeats speaks for many poets of our time when he resolves to cast off the coat of glittering poetic embroidery that may conceal the heart: "there's more enterprise in walking naked."

To cite Tennyson, Arnold, or Eliot as examples may suggest that we usually find the poet in the brooding pose of

Rodin's "Thinker." There is a more active, lyric expression, also characteristic of Wordsworth, in which direct, personal speech achieves the highest intensity. The verse still remains straightforward and declarative, but the poet now seems to cry out at a moment of aroused feeling, and the effect of such poems comes partly from what seems a headlong encounter with passion. I do not have in mind the vague, unrooted wailing that characterizes one side of romanticism (Shelley's "O world! O life! O time!" for example), but a poetry that embodies whatever circumstances give rise to the emotion. Such verse strikes with the weight of immediate experience and the shock of intimacy, when intimacy transcends all the polite reticences of merely social behaviour and confronts us with unreserved joy or grief. Some brief quotations may illustrate:

> Surprised by joy — impatient as the Wind
> I turned to share the transport — Oh! with whom
> But Thee, deep buried in the silent tomb.

. . . .

> I wake and feel the fell of dark, not day.
> What hours, O what black hours we have spent
> This night!

. . . .

> What shall I do with this absurdity —
> O heart, O troubled heart — this caricature,
> Decrepit age that has been tied to me.[37]

Despite the obvious differences in these poems by Wordsworth, Hopkins, and Yeats, the manner is essentially the same. It is "the articulate voice of life," to borrow a phrase from Wordsworth, and its power is immense.

– 6 –

In most lyrics, after all, a poet seems more to resemble a hermit crab. He crawls into a usable shell, as Tennyson did when he incorporated his emotions on the death of Hallam with the myth of Ulysses. Of course, the figure of the shell refers not simply to an imagined character, but also to narrative, symbol, dominant metaphor, circumstance treated descriptively, or similar expressive means. When Wordsworth speaks of the imagination, he often has in mind precisely this process of incorporating subjective feeling with a concrete image, though insofar as the word describes how poetry is or should be written, he limits the theory to the extent that he supposes the heart can find its partner for the expressive dance only among natural objects. He argues that such union is creative discovery or revelation, and that the individual mind and the outer world of nature glide almost automatically towards this harmony, neither party offering much resistance. But in poetry generally, and more especially in that of Wordsworth, relations between the expressive object and the personal emotions of the writer are seldom so agreeable. The most unvexed cooperation usually seems to occur when the object appears to take the lead, summoning from the poet whatever feelings are appropriate to its own character, he offering merely his craft and a dog-like fidelity. This, however, Wordsworth does not do, and, indeed, to say, as Hazlitt said of Shakespeare, that it is possible "only to think of anything in order to become that thing, with all the circumstances belonging to it," is to speak in terms merely theoretical or comparative; no work of art was ever composed in complete self-abnegation. If the object has a partially independent being, and so can make demands of the artist, his own personal emotions always assert themselves to some degree, and the act of composition involves a continuing tension, whether conscious or not, between what the artist is urged and the object permits him to say. It is not simply that the object may bend or qualify; it may also be an impassable barrier. For example, "Ulysses" gives, as Tennyson said, his own "feeling about the need of going forward, and braving the struggle of life," but it does not suggest his sense of religious faith attacked or even the simple, stricken grief which were also responses to Hallam's death. One obvious reason is that the myth of Ulysses offers no scope for such emotions, and this may help to explain why *In Memoriam* escapes to the bleak freedom of direct, personal speech.

In Memoriam is only one witness to the fact that such brooding directness often implies conflict or at least deep uneasiness in the poet himself. For if he actively seeks to ease his own distress, he will try to contemplate his inner life in a language of statement. We can illustrate the point by referring to analytic psychology. Therapy may begin by recalling dreams, but the aim is to interpret them. The method itself rests on the more general fact that most people cannot understand, or cannot feel secure in their understanding and deal with a problem, until meaning has been expressed to the reason, that is, in plain, declarative terms. Hence Wordsworth may re-create personal experiences felt to have been especially significant, in the process capturing all the vitality and suggestion of the great moments in the *Prelude*, but, to repeat, he returns to direct statement as soon as he feels compelled to interpret what he so vividly remembers. He cannot be merely suggestive and concrete. Although it is encouraged by the example of immediate predecessors, what drives Wordsworth to write a poetry of statement is often the urgent need to control and clarify his own mind and feelings.

To suggest that an artist, in creating, may work out his own psychological therapy has become so commonplace as to be almost meaningless. Yet in the case of Wordsworth, there is reason to suppose that the therapeutic effort was relatively more direct and urgent, and that it had a powerful influence on the style and form of his poetry. The thought may offend some readers, persons who think of Wordsworth as a model of serenity and health in a frenetic world. This idealization, however, obscures much. If Crabb Robinson may be believed, Wordsworth once remarked, "I have no need of a Redeemer," but his readers, however sympathetic, ought not to agree with him. The mind, he habitually says, is an abyss; it can become disordered and ungovernable, like the primordial chaos Milton refers to in *Paradise Lost,* over which the creative power of God "dove-like sat'st brooding." Domesticating the Miltonic sublime in his typical way, Wordsworth trusted that the mind might be made a nest, or both nest and "duteous . . . mother dove" who "Sits brooding" in the nest, patiently incubating poems. Perhaps he finally attained this tranquil productiveness, but the greater poetry came first, the poetry in which he seeks to explore and quiet his own mind. The *Prelude,* especially the 1805 version, might be described as a continuing self-analysis, with Coleridge as the passive auditor. Like many of Wordsworth's poems, it is particularly concerned with formative experience in childhood. Hence Wordsworth offers a liberal opportunity and warrant for the tendency, swelling through the last thirty years, to discuss him as a psychoanalytic case history, and to assume that his genius was rooted in his complexes. The point of view has at least the virtue of generating a certain fellow-feeling. A reader may take a more sympathetic interest in a Wordsworth who, like himself, wrestles with personal conflicts, than in Wordsworth the sage.

But at best the psychoanalytic approach involves much guess and gratuitous assumption. ("A blight never does good to a tree," Blake reminds us, and "if a blight kill not a tree but it still bear fruit, let none say that the fruit was in consequence of the blight.") Perhaps without adding to the vanity of long-distance analysis that leads one critic to say that Wordsworth felt guilty about deserting Annette Vallon, another that he shuddered away from an incestuous attraction to his sister, a third that he unconsciously feared he had killed his father, and so forth, we can simply take it for granted that, composing out loud on long, ruminative walks, he was often engaged in protecting his own psychological peace against whatever threats were pressing at the moment.

Indeed, the fact is obvious in his greater lyrics. They show that when pressed by anxiety Wordsworth, like many people, resorted to self-examination. He would attempt to isolate and explain the cause of his distress, and then to mitigate it still more by viewing it in perspective. This or a closely analogous process is enacted in such poems as "Tintern Abbey," "Resolution and Independence," "Intimations of Immortality," the "Ode to Duty," and "Peele Castle." These poems are haunted with a sense of change, of a turning that has taken place in his inner life. There is a fear that something has been lost — "Whither is fled the visionary gleam?" — or simply, as in "Resolution and Independence," a sudden alarm for the future. In any case, to repeat, he finds his inward composure shattered, and strives to manage the threat by giving it objective statement, so that he can stand aside and assess it. He is especially prone to what one might call a self-inventory or stock-taking: in all these poems past states of mind are summarized and compared to present feelings. During this process the grip of anxiety is further weakened as Wordsworth finds some ground of reassurance: "I'll think of the Leech-gatherer on the lonely moor"; "I only have relinquished one delight"; "Not without hope we suffer and we mourn."

Of course, many of Wordsworth's greater poems have no intimate or important reference to his own personal history. One thinks immediately of "Michael" or the story of Margaret in the *Excursion* (though some readers will infer Wordsworth's remorse behind every mention of an abandoned mother). But on the other hand, at times his poems only appear to be about persons other than himself. They are veiled autobiography, and rise out of the same needs as the *Prelude* and the poems just mentioned. An obvious example is the life-story of the Wanderer told in the first book of the *Excursion*. In fact, the mask he puts on simply allows Wordsworth greater freedom to rearrange his own past for the sake of explaining or confirming his present mind. And autobiographical references may be present even where one would least expect. As an example, we can think for a moment of the *White Doe of Rylstone* (1807), a romance in which the central character is a woman, the action and Elizabethan setting utterly remote from anything in Wordsworth's personal life. Yet the more vital portion of this poem, the spiritual history of Emily, may project his own emotions at the sudden death of his brother in 1805, and then, in what one might call anticipatory or unfulfilled autobiography, go on to chart the path he would wish to follow. After her first anguish at the death of her father and brothers, Emily displays a proud, stoic defiance ("Her soul doth in itself stand fast"), that is very like Wordsworth's own response to grief ("But welcome fortitude") in the "Elegiac Stanzas" of 1805. But the gentle companionship of the white doe gradually frees Emily from the chains of mere stoicism, what Wordsworth finely calls the "self-reliance of despair," and she achieves a religious tranquillity. The poem, to quote from Wordsworth's explanation to Coleridge, describes an "ascent of love" to "heights of heavenly serenity." My thought is not, of course, that it directly incorporates Wordsworth's experience, but merely that it refers to the shock of his own grief and works it out according to a wishful pattern, Wordsworth accomplishing through Emily what he could scarcely achieve in his own person. But most of the poem is devoted to the doings of Emily's father and brothers. As Coleridge (speaking of an earlier version) tactfully put it, this portion is "*comparatively* very heavy." In 1836, long after the poem had been published, Wordsworth told Mr. Justice Coleridge that he would again revise it; for "from anxiety to 'get on' with the more important parts" when he was writing it, "imperfection had crept in" to the "mere business parts." The phrase "mere business parts" exposes the source of the trouble. It is the attitude of a writer not interested in his character or plot, but only in exploiting them for some ulterior purpose. A poetry used to manage personal distress is rarely able to show much outgoing interest in other human beings.

— 7 —

Inward and personal as it is, a spirit of declamation also breathes through Wordsworth's poetry. This particular tone can easily be explained by the grip of the literary past on him; but it also mirrors his relations with his intimate circle, where he was an oracle. He learned from Coleridge, of course; he took suggestions from many people; his family and friends were mostly persons of firm character, not easily subdued. Yet such were the force and the need of his temperament that he dominated them all, and their independent flings and teasings occurred within a settled and accepted reverence. Old age that frequently hardens character into caricature did not spare Wordsworth. One is often astonished by the smug self-approval of his later years. Mrs. Alaric Watts tells an instance. The poet "asked me what I thought the finest elegiac composition in the language." It was an ominous question. When she "diffidently suggested 'Lycidas,' " he replied, "You are not far wrong. It may, I think, be affirmed that Milton's 'Lycidas' and my 'Laodamia' are twin Immortals."[38] But if Wordsworth became an increasingly jealous deity to his household, already in 1800 Thomas Poole had accused Coleridge of "prostration in regard to Wordsworth," and in 1803 Coleridge, having been neglected by his friend during an illness, could not help noticing Wordsworth's "Self-involution": "I saw him . . . living wholly among *Devotees* — having every the minutest Thing, almost his very Eating & Drinking, done for him by his Sister, or Wife — & I trembled, lest a Film should rise, and thicken on his moral Eye."[39] When Wordsworth's political affections shifted to the Tory party, the devotees shifted with him, becoming even more rabid, if that was possible. The atmosphere of the household can be briefly summed up in a couple of anecdotes. The first is told by Haydon, and has doubtless become trebly picturesque by passing through his exaggerative imagination:

Laodamia, one of Wordsworth's finest things, his wife persuaded him had too *lenient a fate* for loving her Husband *so absurdly* — at her persuasion he corrected the conclusion . . . While Wordsworth repeated this ["Laodamia"] in his chaunting tone, his wife sat by the Fire quite abstracted, moaning out the burthen of the line, like a distant echo. I never saw such a complete instance of devotion, of adoration.[40]

Sara Coleridge tells that when both Wordsworth and his

wife were quite old, Mrs. Wordsworth wished to observe a day of fasting appointed by the church on account of the Irish famine. "Oh, *don't* be so *foolish*, Mary," said her husband. There was no further discussion. Mrs. Wordsworth gave up what she had "set her heart upon.[41]

Wordsworth remarks in one of his Prefaces that a poet must establish a "dominion over the spirits of readers by which they are to be humbled and humanised." It is a very odd thought. Perhaps it never occurred to any other poet. It may tell more about himself than Wordsworth intended, like Tolstoy's statement — noticed by Orwell — that we naturally yearn to slap people who disagree with us. But the word "dominion" is appropriate for describing the hold Wordsworth obtained on many readers as well as on his family. His domestic sway was reflected in his style, which in turn humbled or prostrated those who were susceptible of it. Yet the influence of his home authority on his style is hard to exemplify, mainly because it crops out in traits that can be explained in more obvious ways. It lends, one might say, an additional bold righteousness of tone. It was a psychological ground or support for his declarative vocabulary and complexly rolling sentences. Wordsworth maintains "the high dogmatic Eloquence, the oracular [tone] of impassioned Blank Verse" that delighted Coleridge, who also thought "Poetry without egotism comparatively uninteresting." [42] It can be felt, for example, in one of the tributes to Coleridge, then absent in Malta:

> But thou art with us, with us in the past,
> The present, with us in the times to come.
> There is no grief, no sorrow, no despair,
> No languor, no dejection, no dismay,
> No absence scarcely can there be, for those
> Who love as we do.[43]

Such verse is noble, generous, large-minded, simply because the language is so direct and the syntax so controlled, suggesting strong emotion deliberately uttered. There is no adverse criticism in adding that this is not quite the way one usually speaks to intimate friends, even in verse, even, perhaps, when offering reassurances of this kind. Or, for one more example, the poetry sometimes falls into gruff, almost childlike explosions of the sort his family heard quite frequently. In "The Old Cumberland Beggar" Wordsworth suddenly attacks government by utilitarian principles:

> But deem not this Man useless — Statesmen! ye
> Who are so restless in your wisdom, ye
> Who have a broom still ready in your hands
> To rid the world of nuisances;

and there is the peremptory Wordsworthian snort in "The Tables Turned": "Books! 'tis a dull and endless strife" ("Oh, *don't* be so *foolish*, Mary!")

The point is that a thoroughgoing Wordsworthian must sometimes be willing to accept domination. To read "Tintern Abbey" with the highest relish demands a submission to the onrush, a willingness to be invaded — "Mr. Wordsworth is never interrupted," Mary Wordsworth is said to have cautioned Keats when in conversation the younger poet attempted to break in on a monologue.[44] Yet to lay undue stress on this aspect of Wordsworth's verse would distort our sense of it; the quietly meditative and informal aspects are just as important.

It is perhaps appropriate, in conclusion, to attempt a general formula, to state, so far as one can, how the reader relates himself to this poetry. In part, of course, as Wordsworth watches his own mind he helps us to understand ourselves. Like any great artist, he makes us conscious of emotions we have felt but scarcely noticed, thus reclaiming some lost theme of our own sensibility. But art also changes our sensibility, not by retrieving what has been lost, but by granting a direct enlargement. We are touching on a major function of poetry that is often ignored at the present time, though nineteenth-century criticism, taking its directions mainly from Wordsworth, used to put it first. For poetry is not just aesthetic pattern, an experience conscious, massive, integrated, and complete. If it were only that, it would still be much more than a mere ornament or flickering enhancement of living. It would still effect a direct moral relevance, breeding a salutary dissatisfaction with somnambulism and incoherence. It would lead us to strive for aesthetic quality in all our activities, in each separately and in all as one. But poetry also offers knowledge of another human being, of the poet who, by his skilled workmanshp, will express himself, or one side of himself, exactly and completely. Thus Wordsworth, in the intimacy of private meditation and conversation, confronts us with a person different from ourselves. The experience is bewildering and a little painful. The same difficulty recurs, of course, with almost all poetry, perhaps all art. We are dipped in an alien sensibility, though not to the same degree when it is a matter of "what oft was thought, but ne'er so well expressed." But if we wish to enjoy romantic poetry, it especially requires that we give something of ourselves to the poet. Wordsworth and his generation were consciously aware of the process of identification in our approach to literature, and they exploited it. On the whole, poetry today is equally intimate, or more so, and the effect is always, as Wordsworth says, to widen "the sphere of human sensibility."

VII

RESOURCES OF STYLE
AND EXPRESSION: I

A GOOD minor poet has a limited set of verbal habits. From one poem to another his style is marked, predictable, and each poem may achieve the unerring grace that comes more readily when one has only a few notes. Moreover, the homogeneity of his style imposes or results from a relatively fixed subject matter or mood. The larger figures always approach that myriad-mindedness of which the great English example is Shakespeare, and hence their style will also be various and flexible. Using a rather mechanical image, one can say that the mature style of a major poet — Pope, Yeats, Eliot, Tennyson — develops by acquiring, perfecting, and blending together different poetic styles. He has his own distinctive manner, of course, but he can also speak in conspicuously diverse ways. But this consummate variety usually comes at the end of a long career. Wordsworth achieved it very quickly. By 1798 he can chat in minute observation of a hill of moss:

> Ah me! what lovely tints are there
> Of olive green and scarlet bright,
> In spikes, in branches, and in stars,
> Green, red, and pearly white!

and then, approximately six weeks later, hold forth in the sublime generalities of "Tintern Abbey":

> A motion and a spirit, that impels
> All thinking things, all objects of all thought,
> And rolls through all things.[1]

Separated by so short a time, these styles are differentiated to a degree remarkable in any poet, much more so in a man twenty-eight years old. Yet each samples a large mass of poetry. For many years Wordsworth could still manage voices so diverse.

Like everyone else, a writer learns to express himself by imitating. He does not, however, catch merely his technique from other writers. In art, a mode is also a mood. Forms cannot be adopted without something of the feelings and attitudes we associate with them, and yet we can only imitate where we potentially share. Hence a man discovers himself by his choice of models; the range of his sympathies shows in the diversity of influences that can affect him. With the possible exception of the twenty years Milton gave to prose, English poetry suffered its chief loss in the early death of Keats. One can guess something of his potential scope from the fact that he could apprentice himself to writers so different as Leigh Hunt, Milton, and Dryden. Wordsworth also responded to diverse influences and developed his poetic resources by rapidly assimilating them. For example, the meditative poems of the later eighteenth century helped release his grave language of statement. Ballads would have encouraged the verse of artless simplicity. And, of course, there was always the example of Milton fostering a style that makes utmost demands on the reader. For like Milton, Wordsworth could think in labyrinthine sentences that seem indifferent to the average limits of intellectual grasp.

He began, as every young poet does, with exercises in the verse fashionable at the time. His first published works — *An Evening Walk* and *Descriptive Sketches*, both printed in

1793 — are in the eighteenth-century genre of loco-descriptive poetry in heroic couplets. *Guilt and Sorrow*, written between 1791 and 1794, agitates feelings of social protest in two realistic narratives, faintly connected and told in Spenserian stanzas — a form also modish at the time. The poem has fine passages and the additional honor of first suggesting to Coleridge his distinction between fancy and imagination. Though in later years Wordsworth, according to Charles Lamb, did "not see much difficulty in writing like Shakespeare, if he had a mind to try it," *The Borderers* (1796–1797) was his only attempt in drama. It shows considerable power, but suffers, like much romantic drama, by being stuffed with reminiscences from great plays back to the Greeks, as though high moments from Beethoven, Mozart, Handel, and Bach were spliced together in a symphony. By 1798 Wordsworth had stepped into his great decade. His stylistic development shows him triumphantly passing a first test posed to any aspiring artist. He was able, that is, to control or change his style in accordance with deliberately conceived intentions. The ability stayed with him to the end. It could result in poems that stand at stylistic extremes, but the extremes could also be united in a speech flexibly alive to the slightest shifts of mood or attitude.

— 2 —

One stylistic extreme appears in one of the two poems called "To a Butterfly":

> Stay near me — do not take thy flight!
> A little longer stay in sight!
> Much converse do I find in thee,
> Historian of my infancy!
> Float near me; do not yet depart!
> Dead times revive in thee:

Thou bringest, gay creature as thou art!
A solemn image to my heart,
My father's family!

Oh! pleasant, pleasant were the days,
The time, when, in our childish plays,
My sister Emmeline and I
Together chased the butterfly!
A very hunter did I rush
Upon the prey: — with leaps and springs
I followed on from brake to bush;
But she, God love her! feared to brush
The dust from off its wings.

The poem is obviously far from the pomp and weighty emotion that come especially in Wordsworth's blank verse. It
creates an impression of utter simplicity, almost of artlessness. For one thing, it strives for no taut intensity through
devices of sound or rhythm. Also, the diction is entirely unpretentious. Simple, short words follow each other in the
order of common speech. If, with Keats, one looks upon
fine phrases like a lover, the poem will be a disappointment.
The language seems transparent; it does not compete for our
attention as a thing to be admired in its own right. The syntax or arrangement of thought is equally artless and exclamatory. It presents no difficulty; it is marked by surprising, almost inert repetitions ("Stay near me — do not take thy
flight!/ A little longer stay in sight"), and in the first stanza
the thought eddies back upon itself ("Float near me; do not
yet depart"). Moreover, this exclamatory style leads to para-
taxis — placing statements one after another without grammatical connectives to name how they relate to each other —
and this is common in Wordsworth's poems in shorter meters. Only the final clause of the poem begins with a con-
junction, used to emphasize the contrast between the speak-

er and his sister. What especially strikes one as loose and informal is the refusal to use syntax to underscore meanings. For example, the close of the first stanza distinguishes the butterfly, a "gay creature" in itself, from the "solemn image" it evokes in the poet. The contrast should be felt and functional in our response to the poem, and yet it is not marked in the syntax as it would have been in an Augustan poem, perhaps by antithetical balance within a line.

Poetry such as "To a Butterfly" could not hold a high station in anyone's hierarchy of English verse. But the poem is not a failure, and it succeeds because it is unpretentious. It arouses no expectations that it will not satisfy. Beyond this, there is a recognition of just proportions. The speaker, after all, is an older man recalling his childhood. He is both indulgent and amused, an attitude suggested by the potentially mock-heroic contrast between the slightness of the objective fact (chasing a butterfly) and the child's weighty emotions ("a very hunter"). In other words, this conscious blend of playfulness, earnestness, and sentimentality conveys what one feels to be a proper attitude toward the subject. The tribute to Emmeline (or Dorothy) is serious, and yet along the scale of human values Wordsworth does not assign an undeservedly high place to delicate and tender sympathies such as hers. One general point is that, in contrast to our usual view of Wordsworth, the poem suggests something of a sense of humor. At least one can say that it shows a saving tact, an ability to avoid bathos, and in his later years Wordsworth could sometimes write what one can only call a poetry of wit.

−3−

That Wordsworth had any gift or relish for humor is solemnly denied. Sara Coleridge, who knew him well in his later years, speaks of "Mr. Wordsworth's utter want of all sense of the humorous,"[2] and subsequent critics mostly agree. A few jokes are recorded — all feeble. One day he met a tramp who asked, "Sir, have you seen my wife?" Wordsworth replied, "My good man, I did not even know you were married." This exchange seems to have amused Wordsworth very much. In a story told by Joseph Severn, conversation turned on the vegetarianism of Shelley, Haydon, and some others. If, said Wordsworth, "by chance or good luck they ever met with a caterpillar" in their vegetables, "they thanked their stars for the delicious morsel of animal food." These anecdotes certainly do not belie Sara Coleridge's remark. On the other hand, many Wordsworthians seem themselves not to have been notably endowed with a sense of humor. Or if it existed, it was retracted in approaching Wordsworth, since his poetry was read as a sacred text. Hence, if he had a sense of humor, his disciples might not have noticed it. Less sympathetic readers discover abundant sources for laughter in his poetry, but they are amused at his expense, or so they think. Perhaps inspired by an inevitable wish to contribute novel insights, some critics have lately tended to emphasize that there is deliberate comedy in his work.[3] Even if the tendency is pushed too far, it may still be a valuable corrective; for it can open our eyes to nuances in poems often read as mere strenuous earnestness.

No one would argue that the humor of things comes first in Wordsworth's vision. But there were habits of mind that, had they not been impeded by a scrupulous sense of justice, could have resulted in comic poems. He had little potential knack for the controlled wit of Pope that depends on analytic distinctions, but he might have written farce or satire on the lines of Cowper or Burns, perhaps nearer to Burns than Cowper, since it would have been rough, obvious, lighthearted, and high-spirited. "The Waggoner" is an example. Jollity is not, of course, identical with humor, but when it is present it exerts a qualifying influence; it should prevent us from mistaking frisky exaggeration for sober doctrine. There are poems that have often been misread in this way. Examples are "Expostulation and Reply" or "The Tables Turned" with its notorious stanza:

> One impulse from a vernal wood
> May teach you more of man,
> Of moral evil and of good,
> Than all the sages can.

Before clubbing Wordsworth for this silly thought, we should read it in context. It is not offered as a distillation of earnest reflection, a credo to which the speaker commits himself with religious finality. Instead, it comes as part of a dramatic "scene," as Wordsworth calls it, a dispute in which both parties are excited and off balance. We do not expect sobriety of thought from a man who begins "Up! up! my Friend, and quit your books;/ Or surely you'll grow double." The tone of spontaneity and humorous exaggeration partially masks the paradoxes that follow and softens the extreme assertions. Perhaps this one example will suffice to illustrate the general point, namely that disciples who gulp at Wordsworth and readers who reject his propositions can both be mistaken in the same way. For both parties tend to isolate his doctrine from its setting in poetry, reading him as a preacher even when he is not preaching.

As one potentially comic resource, Wordsworth possessed a habit of picturesque illustration by means of a bizarre image. For example, in Book III of the *Prelude* he contrasts the frivolous Cambridge of his experience with his imagination of students in the medieval university:

> When, in forlorn and naked chambers cooped
> And crowded, o'er the ponderous books they hung
> Like caterpillars eating out their way
> In silence, or with keen devouring noise.   (ll. 452–456)

Or earlier in the same book he compares his idle but moderately happy life at college

> To a floating island, an amphibious spot
> Unsound, of spongy texture, yet withal
> Not wanting a fair face of water weeds.   (ll. 336–338)

Any reader of the *Prelude* will remember many such elaborate and far-fetched metaphors. Often the image is so unexpected that one feels sure the comedy was not intended. The point is only that such metaphors frequently occurred to him and could be deliberately exploited for comic effects, as, for example, they are in "A Poet's Epitaph." The poem testifies to comic skills and a potential playfulness in Wordsworth that should be kept in mind. One would not make excessive claims. To perceive shadings of humor in Wordsworth will not cause major revaluations, leading us to enjoy poems ignored in the past. The gain is rather in finding that some poems always admired are more complex and also better than we have supposed.

– 4 –

For the most part a sense of humor shows itself in Wordsworth not by anything that makes one laugh, but by a sophisticated self-awareness that qualifies some poems. William Blake, for example, utterly lacked it. It is the capacity that enables a man to take himself seriously — there was nothing of J. Alfred Prufrock in Wordsworth — and yet, at the same time, to look at himself from without. After all, Wordsworth was born fourteen years before the death of Johnson. His early poems often quote or paraphrase Pope. He was strongly influenced by eighteenth-century literature, and on the whole this literature tended to laugh at enthusiasm, not because enthusiasm is inherently ridiculous, but because it is often blind and crude. It may lack self-knowledge, and it may not be alert to the implications a statement will have for other people. Wordsworth shows a residue of these attitudes more than we usually acknowledge; for too often we expect of him only a tone of simple earnestness.

"Nutting," for example, tells of an episode in Wordsworth's childhood when he went out to gather hazel nuts. He came upon a quiet grove and despoiled it with "merciless ravage." The general themes of the poem are the large concerns of the first two books of the *Prelude*: the recognition dawning in such experience of nature as animate and haunted by a spiritual presence; the strengthening in the child of a consciousness of self, based on a heightened awareness of existences independent of the self and utterly different; the fearful discovery of egoistic drives in himself or human nature and the concomitant birth of conscience and a sense of moral responsibility. In view of this, the opening lines of the poem are deceptive. They prepare for nothing of such momentous consequence. The poem begins in a mood of nostalgic release, an older man looking back to his childhood and remembering "One of those heavenly days that cannot die." As he pictures himself in childhood, he is amused by the "quaint" figure he recollects. His appearance would have been odd, with the "huge" sack over his shoulders, the nutting crook, and the miscellaneous items of clothing — "proud disguise of cast-off weeds." But more than that he is playfully conscious of a disproportion in the child's feelings. The child intends no more than to gather nuts, but "in the eagerness of boyish hope" he goes "sallying forth" as if on a military expedition; his clothing is an "accoutrement." There is, then, a double consciousness, so to speak, in the opening lines. It gradually disappears, and through most of the poem we share only the point of view of the child. But at the start Wordsworth communicates both the eagerness of the child and the amusement of an older person contemplating it.

This is not simply Wordsworth speaking as an adult. It is better described as the voice of adulthood; for it implies in Wordsworth a recognition of the way persons other than himself would have viewed this child. To put it another way, Wordsworth has made a concession to our social consciousness. In effect he is saying, "I know that there is something potentially ludicrous in this poem; for it gives weighty meanings to a very slight episode or quirk of feeling." He is maintaining a rather complicated attitude, including in a unified expression both the ordinary and the uniquely personal significance of this experience. It is partly for this reason that the last three lines are a mistake:

> Then, dearest Maiden, move along these shades
> In gentleness of heart; with gentle hand
> Touch — for there is a spirit in the woods.

Until these lines, the speaker's attitude is equivocal, a fact that contributes to the poetic success. The child has ravaged the hazel bower, but to call it a "ravishment" expresses mainly the weightiness of the child's feeling, his thrilled fascination and sense of guilt. The reader can accept this order of values because he need not suppose the mature Wordsworth has pledged his judgment to it. But the last three lines state an explicit proposition in general terms, and because the proposition, thus put, cannot be accepted, the expression becomes sentimental. The conclusion of "Nutting," then, can be compared with "The Tables Turned." In the former poem, we were not compelled to take doctrine at its face value. At the end of "Nutting," the reverse occurs, and it is only one of many similar instances where Wordsworth interferes with a poetic success. For he was not concerned solely for poetry, or rather, as I said, there was an imperious temptation to find a moral in his experience and to state it.

Nevertheless, the start of "Nutting" is also characteristic. The beautiful poem "To a Cuckoo" is another, more complex example. It shows Wordsworth regarding the doings of his own imagination in a highly self-conscious way. Here again are some of the large themes of Wordsworth's most significant poetry: the action of the imagination in converting a sensory impression into a symbolism; the fear that his imaginative power is failing; the effort to find in himself a continuing, unchanged identity, linking his adult self to his childhood; the sense of the natural world implicating an invisible, numinous being. Hearing the cry of the cuckoo, the grown man thinks of the "golden time" of childhood, when the voice of the unseen bird, ubiquitous and disembodied, suggested a spiritual presence behind the common appearance of things. The sense of this could make the familiar world "visionary," and lead the child on a quest: "To seek thee did I often rove . . . And thou wert still a hope, a love," something "longed for" but "never seen." And as the older man listens to the cry of the bird, he finds that it still releases his imaginative power. For feelings of loss or deprivement stir uneasily behind this poem. They explain the intensity of Wordsworth's joy as he finds himself unchanged from childhood, still possessing the same visionary sense of things:

> O blessèd Bird! the earth we pace
> Again appears to be

> An unsubstantial, faery place;
> That is fit home for Thee!

But the poem differs from most of Wordsworth's weightier utterances. For ordinarily when Wordsworth's poetry creates a symbolism, it does not distinguish between the reality, the thing observed or experienced, and the use of it as a way of talking about something else. Daffodils — in the well-known poem that begins "I wandered lonely as a cloud" — do not simply stand for a nature inspirited with the joy of Being; they are what they represent. To use Coleridge's phrase, the symbol is "consubstantial with the reality" of which it is the conductor. But in "To the Cuckoo" Wordsworth knows that the bird is not itself to be identified with a spiritual presence that informs the natural world. As he listens to the cry of the cuckoo he does not commune with an ultimate mystery, but only with a suggestive analogy that quickens the imagination. Because he keeps this in mind his tone of voice is far less weighted than it might otherwise be. Hence it is appropriate to use the jingling stanzas and tripping verse, which would themselves block the highest seriousness. As Walter Pater recognized, this "quaint gaiety of metre" often accompanies a "mysticism" that is "half-playful."

− 5 −

It also happened, however, that a self-correcting sense of humor would fail him utterly. The results are blind absurdities as grotesque as anything in English poetry. He richly deserves that an anthology of lapses by major poets should be entitled after one of his sonnets, *The Stuffed Owl*. Ever since the *Poems* of 1807, Wordsworth's freaks of bathos have been maliciously enjoyed. Yet there was also a tendency, reinforced by Matthew Arnold, to think that these lapses were unrelated to his greaer verse, as though there were two Wordsworths, the inspired poet and the dud, somehow wrapped in the same skin. James Russell Lowell summed it up in 1876:

There are Jeremiah and his scribe Baruch. If the prophet cease from dictating, the amanuensis, rather than be idle, employs his pen in jotting down some anecdotes of his master, how he one day went out and saw an old woman, and the next day did *not*, and so came home and dictated some verses on this ominous phenomenon, and how another day he saw a cow. . . Presently the real prophet takes up the word again and speaks as one divinely inspired, the Voice of a higher and invisible power.[4]

As one example of a triviality sonorously uttered Lowell picks (after Jeffrey) from the *Excursion*,

> List! I heard,
> From yon huge breast of rock a solemn bleat;
> Sent forth as if it were the Mountain's voice,[5]

a passage which perhaps inspired J. K. Stephen's well-known parody on the two voices. Lowell also notices a climatic moment in the tale of Peter Bell and the ass:

> *Now* — like a tempest shattered bark,
> That overwhelmed and prostrate lies,
> And in a moment to the verge
> Is lifted of a foaming surge —
> Full suddenly the Ass doth rise!

Yet these and other lines always held up for ridicule emerge from precisely the same habits of mind that also result in Wordsworth's greatly original and liberating work.

There are passages in poems no one questions that might be thought to show an emotion similarly in excess of its occasion. In "Tintern Abbey" Wordsworth speaks of his boy-

hood gladness, "When like a roe/ I bounded o'er the mountains." The lines are obviously sincere, but the phrasing may
seem too energetic and the picture grotesque. The poem
goes on to say that he has lost this first delight:

> That time is past,
> And all its aching joys are now no more,
> And all its dizzy raptures. Not for this
> Faint I, nor mourn nor murmur.

Here the language sounds a little like Satan's great speech
in hell, in the first book of *Paradise Lost*: "not for those . . .
do I repent or change." But is it thus heroic to bear up under
the dwindling of youthful vividness and passion? Or one
might cite the closing lines, where Wordsworth addresses his
sister:

> Nor wilt thou then forget
> That after many wanderings, many years
> Of absence, these steep woods and lofty cliffs,
> And this green pastoral landscape, were to me
> More dear, both for themselves and for thy sake.

Again the tone and phrasing — "after many wanderings,
many years/ Of absence" — might seem more appropriate
in the mouth of Odysseus returning to Ithaca than in Wordsworth coming back as a tourist to a particular river valley.
The point is not that these lines are unsuccessful. Far from it.
But — to repeat — they show in his greatest poetry the same
tendencies that could also lead him into grotesque failures. Something similar might be said of the poem to Hartley
Coleridge, a six-year-old as the title tells us. The opening
lines are,

> O Thou! whose fancies from afar are brought;
> Who of thy words dost make a mock apparel;

and the reader may be surprised. Is it, one may ask, reasonable to speak to or of a child in this inflated language of momentous apostrophe and rhetorically accumulating clauses? Even Coleridge boggled at the seventh stanza of "Intimations of Immortality," where a child is addressed as "best Philosopher." Similar questions could come to mind almost everywhere in Wordsworth, posed not only by moments of climax but by the common impulse of his poetry. For example, in the middle of "The Green Linnet" Wordsworth suddenly exclaims, "Thou, Linnet! in thy green array," and again the word "Linnet" — that commonplace bird — must somehow sustain and justify the emotions collected in "Thou".

Yet most of the lines cited above are less startling in their contexts. That is to say, with most readers Wordsworth usually obtains the sort of participation he requires. But with some readers he succeeds even in lines often deplored. There is, for example, a striking testimonial from Crabb Robinson in a letter written in 1802, before he had met Wordsworth and become a friend:

Wordsworth has the Art — the characteristick Art of Genius — of doing much with simple means. His repetition of simple phrases, and his dwelling on simple but touching Incidents, his Skill in drawing the deepest moral, and tenderest interest out of trifles evince a great Master, a Talent truely Shakespearean, for instance in Goody Blake —

> And fiercely by the Arm he took her,
> And by the Arm he held her fast.
> And fiercely by the Arm he shook her,
> And cried I've caught you then at last.

how cunning this delay! this dwelling on so slight a Circumstance.[6]

Robinson's critical powers were not contemptible. He was a gossip and busybody, but well-read and among the first to welcome the *avant-garde* poetry of his great contemporaries. To me these lines seem far from Shakespearean, but the lesson is that with Wordsworth, more perhaps than with most poets, praise of his artistry is likely to depend on a vivid receptivity for the vision of things that sways his emotions. There may be a wide consensus that one passage or another falls into anticlimax. But such judgments can hardly be taken as unshakably pure and objective. With the exception of a few extreme verses, the critical harmony testifying that Wordsworth stumbles into bathos becomes discordant in selecting instances. His poetry teeters constantly on the edge of collapse, and it takes only a slight shift or disengagement of sympathy to disintegrate his effects, a fact that explains why he is so easy and tempting to parody.

On the side of technique, then, romantic poetry can often be described as imposing traditional signals of serious and impassioned emotion — for example, rhetorical accumulation of clauses, Miltonic diction and syntax, *genres* such as the irregular ode — upon a subject matter that formerly seemed unworthy of such elevation. This habit was simply one expression of a more general fact. The romantics were compelled to reorder the system of values they inherited. By and large, this reordering displays itself in two ways, as their poetry splits into a concern with the homely themes of common life or a search for metaphysical truth. The romantics of the first generation — Coleridge, Southey, Wordsworth, Lamb — dwelt on the daily stuff of human existence in a way for which there was no precedent. Many Augustan poets might have been willing to handle tales similar to that of Michael, or of Margaret in the first book of the *Excursion*. But they could not have managed these stories with Wordsworth's serious pathos, neither condescending nor sentimental, and without a tinge of satire. Perhaps they would have approved it, but they had no ability to make us feel that the "ordinary sorrow of man's life" matters as it does in Wordsworth, and the same thing is true of the quiet revelation of domestic happiness in these writers.

In the second place, the romantics were confronted anew with man's ontological needs. Yearning for clues to the ultimate reality, Wordsworth fell back upon moments of personal experience that seemed imperious revelations, sources of a faith if only the "strange utterance" could be interpreted. Thus the poems that tell of such experience necessarily confer an extraordinary importance upon objects or events that might seem commonplace to anyone else. What Wordsworth says in the Preface to the *Lyrical Ballads* holds for all his greater poetry: "the feeling therein developed gives importance to the action and situation, and not the action and situation to the feeling." Virtually all literature since Wordsworth shares the same approach. It readily flowers into bathos and unintended burlesque; for when the milieu offers no consensus, who is to say what value should be attached to things and experiences? A writer has no guide but himself, and may often fall into what others will think an emotion disproportionate to its object. But the same approach also permits what is always claimed for Wordsworth and his contemporaries, that they revealed a new world, or a new freshness and significance in the familiar.

– 6 –

Any attempt to offer a general account of Wordsworth's style must obviously by-pass numerous exceptions. There is, however, a large group of poems that can hardly be overlooked, even though they may be thought not characteristic.

For the main habit of Wordsworth's mind was ample reflection, and the next chapter concentrates on his meditative stride. But in many of the shorter poems, some of them Wordsworth's most widely known lyrics, there is very little overt meditation. Some random moment of experience is picked up, stripped of clogging detail, and, as it might seem, merely described. These poems do not go on to interpret themselves in discursive language. Their tone is deceptively casual. They can easily be read in too shallow a way. To Wordsworth's contemporaries, these lyrics — which include the "Lucy" poems and a good many of the flower pieces and bird watchings — often seemed trivial, pointless, or namby-pamby. They could hardly have thought anything else. They naturally would not study a new poet with the same attention we give to a classic of our literature. They had not read the *Prelude*, and so lacked the background familiarity it provides. Most of all, they were not used to a poetry conceived as these lyrics are. For like many modern poems — or like those of Blake and the longer poems of Shelley — they are written in a half-private language of imagery. It is a language a poet often unconsciously develops over a period of time. Associations cluster around images until the images become symbolic, both for himself and for readers saturated in his work. Using this language, Wordsworth can be entirely concrete and yet expressive in ultimate concerns. And poems that can appear utterly simple may present moments of revelation as significant, though far less emphatically phrased, as any in the *Prelude*. As examples, we can dwell on "I Wandered Lonely as a Cloud," "The Solitary Reaper," and "Stepping Westward."

"I wandered lonely as a cloud" begins with a contrast — Wordsworth alone, detached, wandering, and the flowers together as a crowd dancing.

> I wandered lonely as a cloud
> That floats on high o'er vales and hills,
> When all at once I saw a crowd,
> A host, of golden daffodils;
> Beside the lake, beneath the trees,
> Fluttering and dancing in the breeze.

As a suggestion to be picked up later, we can note that this cloud that floats is apparently not strongly touched by the blowing breeze. And then comes the astonishing metaphor:

> Continuous as the stars that shine
> And twinkle on the milky way,
> They stretched in never-ending line
> Along the margin of a bay.

It is an odd association — flowers seen in daylight with stars at night, or the milky way with the margin of a lake. It points not so much to the visual scene as to the emotional reverberations it sets off, feelings of sublimity and infinitude that are totally unexpected by the reader, and that may, at first, seem strangely inappropriate to this scene of lake and flowers. But the poem at once returns to visual description —

> Ten thousand saw I at a glance,
> Tossing their heads in sprightly dance —

and the third stanza opens on the same note:

> The waves beside them danced; but they
> Out-did the sparkling waves in glee.

Like the daffodils, the waves on the lake are excited by the wind, and throughout Wordsworth's poetry the wind or breeze is a loaded image. He speaks of the wind as a ubiquitous presence that fills or moves natural things, or with which they commune. Putting it more directly than

Wordsworth does, one may say that the breeze is a figure
for the breath of God. But to call it a figure of speech scarcely
conveys the immediacy of Wordsworth's vision. To convert
a literal fact into a symbolism is a very common process of
mind. With Wordsworth, however, one feels that the symbolic becomes literal; it is almost as though to watch daffodils fluttering in the wind were actually to see them touched
by the Divine Life. Then, too, one remembers that in Wordsworth "life" is virtually synonymous with "motion." One
might almost say that in their motions the waves and flowers
express the Divine Life that blows through them. It is not
inappropriate to recall the passage already cited from "Tintern Abbey," where Wordsworth speaks of

> A motion and a spirit, that impels
> All thinking things, all objects of all thought,
> And rolls through all things.

As much as thoughts of a crowd, colors and dancing, these
deeper associations or habitual symbols explain why Wordsworth immediately attributes joy and glee to the waves and
the daffodils. The Divine Being that rolls through all things
is a principle of joy. For all creatures other, perhaps, than
man, to be is a blind delight — "The pleasure which there
is in life itself," Wordsworth phrases it in "Michael" — and
he will sometimes interpret any least motion as an upwell-
ing or expression of it. In "Lines Written in Early Spring,"
he saw

> The budding twigs spread out their fan,
> To catch the breezy air;
> And I must think, do all I can,
> That there was pleasure there.

And as the green linnet, in the poem of that name, flits and
darts about "In joy of voice and pinion," it too becomes both

a visible manifestation and rather unexpected image of the
One Life pervading everything. It is

> A Life, a Presence like the Air,
> Scattering thy gladness without care,
> Too blest with any one to pair;
> Thyself thy own enjoyment.

Preoccupied with ambitions, vanities, domestic attachments,
fears and responsibilities, adult human beings lost touch with
the Life that binds all things in glee, though to possess the
"sentiment of Being" would be our most intense happiness,
keener than any love or hope. And, of course, even for human beings life is still joy fundamentally, but with trivial
gains and cares we overlay this primary emotion. In moments of heightened imaginative power the grown man
may still apprehend in natural things the "quickening soul"
that works through all — "I saw one life, and felt that it
was joy" [7] — and as he senses their joy he feels the same
primary happiness dawning once again in himself. The
classic statement of this occurs in "Intimations of Immortality" —

> Ye blessèd Creatures, I have heard the call
> Ye to each other make; I see
> The heavens laugh with you in your jubilee;
> My heart is at your festival,
> My head hath its coronal,
> The fulness of your bliss, I feel — I feel it all —

but the same thing happens at the end of the poem on daffodils. Or rather, Wordsworth here says that such sudden
moments, when we know the life of nature, return in memory, and that they have a continuing power to reawaken in
us the same sense of the happiness of being, which is also the
happiness of Being.

At the moment when he actually came upon the daffodils, Wordsworth had "little thought" or understanding of what he saw and felt. But in contrast to the first stanza, he now feels himself to be no longer alone. He is with the flowers (in their "company") and knows something of their joy ("A poet could not but be gay").

> The waves beside them danced; but they
> Out-did the sparkling waves in glee:
> A poet could not but be gay,
> In such a jocund company:
> I gazed — and gazed — but little thought
> What wealth the show to me had brought.

The word "show" may even suggest that this vision was especially staged for him. Such an implication would be altogether in keeping with Wordsworth's sense of a ministering Nature.

To the last stanza Coleridge voiced strong objections. It exemplified, he thought, the sort of lapse in Wordsworth that we already noticed: "*mental* bombast . . . a disproportion of thought to the circumstance and occasion."

It is a well-known fact, that bright colors in motion both make and leave the strongest impressions on the eye. . . . [They] may become the link of association in recalling the feelings and images that had accompanied the original impression. But if we describe this in such lines, as

> For oft, when on my couch I lie
> In vacant or in pensive mood,
> They flash upon that inward eye
> Which is the bliss of solitude!

in what words shall we describe the joy of retrospection, when the images and virtuous actions of a whole well-spent life, pass before that conscience which is indeed the *inward* eye: which is indeed '*the bliss of solitude?*' [8]

To think of the conscience is surely an intrusion. The poem has nothing to do with the conscience. Coleridge goes on: "We seem to sink most abruptly, not to say burlesquely, and almost as in a *medly*," from these lines to

> And then my heart with pleasure fills,
> And dances with the daffodils.

But perhaps what flashes upon the "inward eye" is not so much "bright colors in motion," or pleasurable feelings connected with the scene, as a symbolic event that speaks to Wordsworth of the union of all things in a bond of joy. If so, we do not "sink most abruptly" to the last two lines, but encounter the most drastic kind of understatement. The poem asserts that the vision abides and returns upon the mind in that sudden "flash" Wordsworth habitually associates with a moment of revelation. Recollecting the event after it has become symbolic, Wordsworth is something more than "gay." Now at last the heart "dances with the daffodils."

Though it presents a much darker vision of things, "The Solitary Reaper" equally articulates fixed associations. In a valley of the Scotch Highlands, Wordsworth looks at a girl working in a field:

> Alone she cuts and binds the grain,
> And sings a melancholy strain;
> O listen! for the Vale profound
> Is overflowing with the sound.

As in "I Wandered Lonely as a Cloud," he embodies his feelings in a comparison, a double one this time. The girl is like a nightingale singing from an oasis "Among Arabian sands"; or

> A voice so thrilling ne'er was heard
> In spring-time from the Cuckoo-bird,

> Breaking the silence of the seas
> Among the farthest Hebrides.

In both metaphors a bleak vastness — the desert or the sea — surrounds the island or oasis. The Highland valley would be set amid uplands similarly gaunt and inhospitable. Throughout Wordsworth's poetry there is a contrast between bowers, nooks, coverts, or valleys — places where man is sheltered and protected — and moorlands, ocean, mountain summits, and the like, where man finds himself exposed, a homeless wanderer. In nooks and bowers, of course, we are happy; such retreats are often pictured as a sort of paradise. But there is also the desolate landscape of "visionary dreariness" — the exposed place where man confronts a world that is not protective, not necessarily made for his happiness. In these passages the cosmos is seen to be vast, inscrutable, indifferent, and potentially threatening. It is alive with storms, with the "loud, dry wind" that blows with a "strange utterance," with mists that advance in menacing and "indisputable shapes." Such images are also part of Wordsworth's symbolic language. In one passage he says that the unsheltered place is "bare to the eye of heaven," a terrifying image if one thinks about it.[9] It is the wanderer, Wordsworth often feels, the man who exposes himself, or is exposed, who comes face to face with the ultimate nature of things.

As he listens to the song of the Highland girl, Wordsworth cannot tell what her "theme" may be. But that is of little importance. What matters is that she sings. As with the sight of daffodils ("I gazed — and gazed — but little thought"), Wordsworth simply looks and hears: "I saw her singing at her work . . . I listened." And then he must quit the valley, but something has been caught from this encounter:

> The music in my heart I bore,
> Long after it was heard no more.

For out of a few images insistently repeated — the girl reaping, the song, the valley and the bleak space around it — Wordsworth has created a symbolic event, revealing a truth of human life. Engaged in common tasks man can fill his familiar world with his own music, keeping back the vast silence. But no communion of joy now links man with nature, or the Life that informs it. The Highland girl is in every way "Alone." The cosmos remains unanswering.

"The Solitary Reaper" ends with Wordsworth walking "up the hill," leaving the valley behind him. In the *Prelude* he tells that many a time some road that "crossed/ The naked summit of a far-off hill" seemed

> like an invitation into space
> Boundless, or guide into eternity.

It could symbolize the beckoning, felt everywhere in romantic poetry, to confront the ultimate nature of things.

> Yes, something of the grandeur which invests
> The mariner who sails the roaring sea
> Through storm and darkness, early in my mind
> Surrounded, too, the wanderers of the earth.
>   (XIII, 147–155)

As a symbolic figure, the wanderer is alone. Other human beings do not understand or sympathize in his quest. But in "Stepping Westward," there is a phrase of greeting — "*What, you are stepping westward*." The phrase has for Wordsworth the feel of "something without place or bound." To be greeted this way is to be understood; it weaves a "human sweetness" through the

> thought
> Of travelling through the world that lay
> Before me in my endless way.

"Stepping Westward" is not one of Wordsworth's best efforts, but no poem more clearly illustrates the trait of his genius already seen in the two previous poems, how out of commonplace incident he will evoke something alien and visionary. He and Dorothy were in Scotland. Once at sunset they met "two neatly dressed women, without hats, who had probably been taking their Sunday evening's walk." [10] But the poem has little to do with a Sunday evening or two women "without hats." The speaker is in a "strange Land" — Scotland, of course, but something more. He is "far from home," as Wordsworth literally was, but the phrase is more deeply suggestive. There is even the statement that he has no "home or shelter." The greeting comes to him from some feminine figure "walking by her native lake," someone who lives in this strange land. Perhaps there is not only a "human sweetness" in the greeting but encouragement from a source less natural and familiar. We can recall that the old leech-gatherer is

> like a man from some far region sent,
> To give me human strength by apt admonishment.

In "Stepping Westward" the glowing sky in front seems to "lead him on"; the greeting

> seemed to give me spiritual right
> To travel through that region bright;

and

> stepping westward seemed to be
> A kind of *heavenly* destiny.

So far as "Stepping Westward" contrasts with "The Solitary Reaper" or "I Wandered Lonely as a Cloud," it does so partly by speaking of our heavenly destiny. But "heavenly" has no Christian meaning in this poem. Except for its more emotional overtones, it might be translated as "skyey"; for, catching up the yearning so typical of romantic poetry, it refers only to vague regions of brightness toward which man is endlessly stepping.

VIII

RESOURCES OF STYLE
AND EXPRESSION: II

ANYONE EAGER to locate works of art within a *genre* would find Wordsworth unusually baffling and messy. In fact, unless one employs rather nebulous categories, his poems can seldom be assigned to any *genre* whatsoever. There is an influence from ballads in many of them, but they are almost never true to the form, being much too reflective. The title *Lyrical Ballads* at once implies a blurring of types. He tried his hand at the irregular ode or false Pindaric, but not very often, and he also hoped that "Tintern Abbey" might be considered an ode, the fact again suggesting that a rigid separation of *genres* was not uppermost in his mind. And what label can one attach to poems such as "Nutting" or "There Was a Boy," not to mention the *Prelude*? Perhaps the most one can say is that his longer poems issue from what he called a "composite order," the descriptive-meditative verse of the later eighteenth century. Indeed, this type of verse especially suits and characterizes the poetry of sincerity. As a tradition continuing from the eighteenth century to our own day, it links poets otherwise so diverse as Thomas Warton and T. S. Eliot.

In any completed process of meditation, one can ordinarily distinguish several stages. At the start, one may be at some place — a country churchyard, a deserted village, Tintern Abbey overlooking the Wye valley, or Dover Beach —

or attention fixes itself upon some object or memory. Then, of course, one thinks about it. The mind goes on a journey, wandering from the present object and returning to it, maybe recalling similar objects or instances, or comparing the thing observed with the self. Finally there is a moment of discovery. Some new insight dawns, or some old truth is recaptured with clarity and force. The point is that a poetic enactment of this process will require diverse talents, for description or narration and also for discursive abstraction. We have seen that Wordsworth can write poems in which his meditative voice is scarcely heard, and he can also compose pieces that are almost entirely abstract reflection or summary — for example, the "Ode to Duty" or the "Character of the Happy Warrior." But especially in the *Prelude* one finds a constant, wonderfully effective transition from concrete vignette to sustained comment and exposition, the latter rising out of the vignette and interpreting it. But what particularly characterizes Wordsworth is not these two acts of mind, or the alternation between them, which would be found in any number of poets, but the quality of these acts considered separately, and the way in which they are joined. For the descriptive passages are seldom far from symbolism. The expository passages lack the quiet gait we usually associate with meditation, being much more impassioned. And in the movement from one to another, Wordsworth can seem peculiarly inevitable.

— 2 —

For an example of Wordsworth's expository or meditative verse, we can turn to "Tintern Abbey." Immediately after the opening lines describing the Wye valley, there is a typical movement of impassioned generalization, express-

ing what he owes, he says, to the "beauteous forms" of
nature.

> These beauteous forms,
> Through a long absence, have not been to me
> As is a landscape to a blind man's eye:
> But oft, in lonely rooms, and 'mid the din
> Of towns and cities, I have owed to them
> In hours of weariness, sensations sweet,
> Felt in the blood, and felt along the heart;
> And passing even into my purer mind,
> With tranquil restoration: — feelings too
> Of unremembered pleasure: such, perhaps,
> As have no slight or trivial influence
> On that best portion of a good man's life,
> His little, nameless, unremembered acts
> Of kindness and of love. Nor less, I trust,
> To them I may have owed another gift,
> Of aspect more sublime; that blessed mood
> In which the burthen of the mystery,
> In which the heavy and the weary weight
> Of all this unintelligible world,
> Is lightened: — that serene and blessed mood,
> In which the affections gently lead us on, —
> Until, the breath of this corporeal frame
> And even the motion of our human blood
> Almost suspended, we are laid asleep
> In body, and become a living soul:
> While with an eye made quiet by the power
> Of harmony, and the deep power of joy,
> We see into the life of things.

The vocabulary exploited in this passage is "pure" in
Wordsworth's sense: it would serve either for poetry or for
prose (exceptions are the word "oft," the inversion of "sensations sweet," the periphrasis of "corporeal frame"). But

this is hardly the simple, colloquial diction we saw in "To a Butterfly." Instead, it is much more abstract, polysyllabic, orotund, and, in short, successfully dignified and emphatic. The abstraction ranges from the extreme of "beauteous forms" to the mere generality of a phrase such as "towns and cities"; and, as Josephine Miles points out,[1] this steady flow of general terms typifies Wordsworth's poetry more than is usually realized. It has often been noticed that when the poetry begins to parade in its stately way, abstract nouns tend to come in pairs or larger clusters —

> of genius, power,
> Creation and divinity itself
> I have been speaking.[2]

The passage from "Tintern Abbey" illustrates a common Wordsworthian variation in which nouns are coupled by the preposition "of." The tendency to construct phrases in this way was a legacy to Wordsworth from the generalizing habits of Augustan verse. But in Augustan poetry such phrases are likely to have a slightly different formula. An example is the genitival-conjunctive phrase where we have adjective-noun-of-adjective-noun, as in Johnson's great line, "The secret ambush of a specious prayer"; and the adjectives define the particular variety of the general kind to which the noun refers. Such a line compels analytic discriminations, and hence makes an intellectual appeal. By lopping off the adjectives and leaving the nouns in their naked dignity — "power of harmony" — Wordsworth evokes responses more immediately emotional, often at the cost of vagueness. In the passage at hand the nouns are joined according to a recurrent, loose pattern. One of the pair may offer a rather vague abstraction: mystery, harmony, power. But its partner serves to link it with a sensation, image, or feeling: "din of towns," "burthen of the mystery," "power of joy." In such phrases we find Wordsworth converting an abstract, conceptual discourse into poetry.

The passage also shows a pronounced reliance on polysyllables — "weariness," "restoration," "unremembered," "unintelligible" — and these words stand as massive blocks in the middle of the line: "feelings too/Of unremembered pleasure"; "the heavy and the weary weight/Of all this unintelligible world." Since as we read we cannot scurry over words so large and heavy, they arrest us to realize and feel. And to mention that Wordsworth can also put things in a somewhat orotund way need not imply that the emphasis does not succeed. It is merely that when he speaks, for example, of a "gift/Of aspect more sublime," the phrasing is not very direct or natural. Similar locutions are "the breath of this corporeal frame," and the negative affirmation — a persistent habit of Wordsworth's — that occurs in the phrase "no slight or trivial influence."

Yet this elevated, polysyllabic diction changes at key points in the passage. At moments especially evoking intense response, the poetry may resort to a different language — simple, sometimes naïve, sometimes understated and suggestive:

> that best portion of a good man's life,
> His little, nameless, unremembered acts
> Of kindness and of love.

The phrase "a good man's life" is homely, peculiarly Wordsworthian. And nothing could be put more simply than "acts of kindness and of love." Wordsworth manages such phrases so that, without being ostentatious, they lend a sort of sweetness to this lofty discourse. Toward the end of the passage there is the statement that sensations from natural objects lead to an almost mystical trance: "we are laid asleep/In body, and become a living soul." The simple phrase, "a living soul," acquires through understatement a depth of suggestion. It is not merely that with our bodily sensations stilled or unnoticed we are conscious only of our souls: we are dead souls most of the time. Or there is the close of the passage:

> While with an eye made quiet by the power
> Of harmony, and the deep power of joy,
> We see into the life of things,

where the last phrase comes in the plainest language, "the life of things."

The syntactical structure of the passage immediately reflects the way Wordsworth's mind usually moves. For it is obvious that he thought freely in blank verse. These are not what Coleridge described as "rhyme-less or rather rhyme-craving" pentameters, the timid and self-conscious blank verse often found in Augustan poetry. In the first place, then, the lines from "Tintern Abbey" display a basic orderliness. Since this is a passage of meditative summary, Wordsworth names in succession various effects he owes to communion with nature: "sensations sweet," "tranquil restoration," "acts/Of kindness and of love," and finally a "blessed mood" in which "We see into the life of things." In the second place, however, there is an urge to amplify by interpolation and apposition, and the amplification is so constant and extreme that it becomes difficult to keep in mind the main threads of discourse. There is a conflict, then, between the need to order and the equally pressing need to explain what is being ordered, and the conflict produces a recurrent syntactical movement in the passage. To give meaning to his propositions, Wordsworth must at once extend and develop

them in subordinate clauses. Then, however, he breaks off
and takes a new grip on the main grammar of the sentence,
repeating virtually the same words (for example, "that
blessed mood . . . that serene and blessed mood") and thus
emphasizing the fundamental objects of his thought. Yet
each repetition also serves as the basis for another expansion.
The pattern, then, can be described as a recurrence to key
ideas or phrases, each return bearing an added freight of
meaning and leading to a new amplification.

Wordsworth's blank verse is seldom so complexly articulated as it is in these lines. But the passage is still characteristic, showing syntactical habits that control even verse so
apparently unpretentious as "Michael." If one rewrites these
sentences from "Tintern Abbey" with the deletion of modifying phrases, parentheses, and subordinate clauses, one
ends with something like this: "But I have owed to the
forms of nature sensations and feelings. To them I may
have owed another gift, a particular mood." The purpose of
this travesty is to highlight some key facts. It shows that the
few ribs or main supports of the thought are joined together in a very clear way, that at bottom there is a simple,
repetitious structure not very remote from conversational
speech. But along this thread Wordsworth coils twenty-
eight lines, though only two sentences. In doing so, he relies
mainly on three syntactical forms: suspension, subordination,
and apposition. The suspension — the intervention of extended modifiers between the main grammatical elements
— is extreme. To a hasty reading the grammar might appear
broken, and a constant and prolonged suspension, as in this
passage, demands considerable attention in the reader.

It often happens that the main business of Wordsworth's
sentences is accomplished in subordinate clauses following
from predicate objects. As Donald Davie remarks,[3] this

generally characterizes the syntax of romantic poetry. It should, I think, be correlated with the premise of spontaneity. Before the act of expression, the poet has not mastered and laid out his ideas, but instead the poetry enacts a process in which his mind suddenly comes upon them. Thus Wordsworth's speech can seem both spontaneous and inevitable. The habit of suspension binds the elements of the sentence in an urgent forward movement — one keeps going because one expects the next major element in the grammar of the sentence — while the intervening subordinate clauses amplify in unpredictable ways. They suggest a free expansion of thought almost breaking away from the powerful dominance of an orderly mind. Finally, the impression of spontaneity is further strengthened by an extraordinary reliance on apposition. This is typical of Wordsworth. He keeps it up through long passages. It is a means of arresting the step from one major statement to the next until the thought is fully expressed in some necessary phase. Often the appositional phrases come as successive diverse approaches to some central meaning or emotion to which language cannot pierce. Apposition is not characteristic of Augustan verse, nor of any poetry that speaks common opinion.

– 3 –

Yet I have treated this passage too much as though it were merely sober discourse. Every reader must find that it is much more, that the drive behind it is not so much to state and distinguish as to create emotions, and emotions not remembered, but alive and immediate. For example, the three lines that come to a climax with "We see into the life of things" refer to past experience, but have the tone of a mystical joy known in the present moment. We have, then, a poetry that looks like exposition — is exposition — yet also works to a different purpose. F. R. Leavis goes so far as to say that though Wordsworth seems to set forth an argument, the poetry will not let us concentrate upon it. He is speaking of the *Prelude* and means no adverse criticism; Wordsworth succeeds because he compels the sort of attention he requires, and excludes other sorts.[4] Leavis finds, I suppose, that because the verse can look like systematic explanation, it beguiles the reader. It makes him feel that the claims of reason have been satisfied, thus rendering him more susceptible to the feelings Wordsworth expresses. To explain Wordsworth in this way shows that one is alive to the emotional thrust of the verse. It may be preferred to reading his poetry as though it were only a presentation of ideas. But it is too simple.

In the *Prelude* Wordsworth certainly attempts to persuade us of certain general truths, or what he believes as such. They are proclaimed in moments of direct statement. He also explains what he means at considerable length, giving reasons for thinking and feeling as he does. These expository passages are difficult. It is easy to see how they might be thought to give only the illusion of an argument. The difficulty is partly that Wordsworth is seldom minded to

> level down the truth
> To certain general notions, for the sake
> Of being understood at once.   (XIII, 212–214)

There is also his complicated syntax. But what mainly accounts for the impression of Leavis and others is that Wordsworth's expository passages have a habit of ellipsis. The omissions may have been necessary; had he stated his ideas with the careful, step-by-step development that makes for immediate clarity, many passages would have been sluggish poetry. But even if Wordsworth had been totally heedless of poetic effect, his expository moments might still have been elliptical. His poetry does not differ much in this particular respect from his prose. Moreover, his tendency to ellipsis is easily explained, at least in speculation. He was trying to compose spontaneously, and in such circumstances most people will leave out steps when the train of thought is a habitual one. Also, Wordsworth had not in his daily life the sort of contradiction that disciplines a man to explain himself more fully. In other words, his mode of argument or discourse suggests once again that he had in mind an audience of intimates or sympathizers. But if one studies his poetry until one knows his mind, one follows his expository passages and finds them sufficiently meaningful. It is also true, however, that he does not attempt to persuade mainly by argument or explanation. He knew that the head must be captured through the heart, and so, because he wants to influence our beliefs, he makes a direct and powerful attack on our emotions.

Immediately after the famous episodes in Book I of the *Prelude*, where Wordsworth tells of snaring woodcocks at night, of climbing the "perilous ridge" until he felt himself almost suspended by the strong wind, and of rowing out on the quiet lake when suddenly the mountain seemed to rise up behind him, he soars into a mood of exulting religious conviction; it comes in an apostrophe that begins "Wisdom and Spirit of the universe!" In each of these three experiences he had seemed to encounter a Presence in or behind the things of the natural world. Though it expresses intense feeling, the apostrophe that follows also contributes to Wordsworth's argument or exposition; it describes in general terms what formative effect such experience had on him and tries to account for this effect.

> Wisdom and Spirit of the universe!
> Thou Soul that art the eternity of thought,
> That givest to forms and images a breath
> And everlasting motion, not in vain

> By day or star-light thus from my first dawn
> Of childhood didst thou intertwine for me
> The passions that build up our human soul;
> Not with the mean and vulgar works of man,
> But with high objects, with enduring things —
> With life and nature, purifying thus
> The elements of feeling and of thought,
> And sanctifying, by such discipline,
> Both pain and fear, until we recognize
> A grandeur in the beatings of the heart.   (I, 401–414)

The expository content of this passage is not hard to grasp — not, at least, the major statements. The difficulty comes rather in seeing how or why Wordsworth moves from one major statement to the next; the main point in paraphrasing is to fill in these transitions. The passage says that there is a Wisdom, Spirit, or Soul that everlastingly pervades the forms of nature, and that this Spirit chose the poet as an object of special care ("for me"), deliberately educating or disciplining his character. The human nature with which we are born comprises (is built up by) an aggregation of diverse passions, including such passions as pain and fear. These — pain and fear — are usually unredeemed in the sense that they do not contribute to our moral or religious life, but instead reduce us to a jelly of self-solicitude. But in the process by which Wordsworth's particular character was formed, all of the passions were integrated with each other, and they were also purified and sanctified. For from his earliest infancy his passions were called forth in response to sublime and enduring objects in the natural world. Because in childhood his feelings were not directed to fleeting, trivial, and selfish aims — rivalry in school, for example, which Wordsworth thought pernicious — but rather to objects that are themselves great, his adult nature will respond and aspire only to whatever is similarly lofty and permanent. In other words, the massive forms of nature are the source of his adult integrity, high-mindedness, and religious ardor; for he will seek only what reproduces the feelings of awe and sublimity first given to him in the natural milieu of his childhood. As a result of such formative discipline he has learned to "recognize/A grandeur in the beatings of the heart." The word "recognize" is important. The point is that by communion with the natural world our emotional being purifies itself until we can know its core or essence — our aspiration toward the infinite and eternal.

As a statement of doctrine in metaphysics or psychology, this apostrophe may be thought vague, or unconvincing, or both. But certainly it is charged with discursive thinking far more than most poetry. And one can add that this passage acquires a greater precision of statement when it is read with the boat stealing and previous episodes in mind. In fact, many of the key words refer directly back to those episodes. For example, that the "Wisdom and Spirit" gives

                    to forms and images a breath
        And everlasting motion

is not just a vague way of saying that all things are animated by the Divine Life. "Forms," "breath," and "motion" are words picked up from what comes before. After taking a woodcock from the snare of someone else, the child

                    heard among the solitary hills
        Low breathings coming after me, and sounds
        Of undistinguishable motion.

When he climbed the ridge, "Shouldering the naked crag,"

                    the sky seemed not a sky
        Of earth — and with what motion moved the clouds!

When at night he took the boat and rowed out into the lake, the mountain seemed to loom up and pursue him with "measured motion like a living thing," and for many days afterward,

> huge and mighty forms, that do not live
> Like living men, moved slowly through my mind
> By day, and were a trouble to my dreams.

In this apostrophe, then, Wordsworth actually says that the "Wisdom and Spirit of the universe" gave natural objects that particular breath and motion — the "low breathings" and "measured motion like a living thing" — by which his character was formatively disciplined.

Yet, at the same time, the passage makes a naked appeal to our feelings. The first two lines are a good example:

> Wisdom and Spirit of the universe!
> Thou Soul that art the eternity of thought.

These invocations emerge from a background of clear thinking. Educated readers in Wordsworth's day would have understood that "Wisdom" and "eternity" are appellations issuing from the faculty of reason (hence the "eternity of" or known by "thought") that knows God in his attributes, while "Spirit" and "Soul" speak of a vital Presence intuited by the imagination, so that each line may be said to combine two ways of knowing. But from one point of view, it could be urged that these opening lines simply weave together nouns — "Wisdom," "Spirit," "Soul," "eternity" — that, together with the Biblical forms of the verb and the pronoun "Thou," establish a tone of religious inspiration and prophecy. Wordsworth's readers would have encountered very similar tones of voice in other writers. The point is that when a man speaks in this voice, one is not accustomed to quibble over what he says. With this in mind one can argue that in this passage Wordsworth, though he is himself thinking, relies mainly on a purely poetic or rhetorical means for securing assent. Another example comes in the two lines that somehow equate "high objects" and "enduring things" with "life and nature." "High objects" would have an outrageous effect as a phrase in merely expository writing. For in this context, to speak of "high objects" and "enduring things" is to pun; the phrases refer to mountains, and especially to the mountain Wordsworth has just called to mind in the passage about stealing the boat. With this mountain his "passions" were deeply "intertwined." And since it seemed to stride after him across the lake, the mountain can certainly be described as "life" as well as "nature." To associate "life and nature" with the vast bleakness of mountains is characteristic of Wordsworth and altogether strange. Partly because it does convey into us peculiar associations such as these, or the vision of things they embody, Wordsworth's poetry — like all poetry that matters — goes beyond anything that expository writing can manage.

— 4 —

In discussing Wordsworth's poetic resources, we began by pointing out that he can speak in very diverse styles. At one extreme, the language tends to be simple, colloquial, and concrete. At the other extreme, it becomes abstract, polysyllabic, complexly articulated, copious, and even pleonastic. We also said that, in general, his poetry displays two distinct activities of mind: there is description, observation, or narration and, secondly, reflection or meditation. Now, however, we can add that the more homely language is usually associated with descriptive or narrative writing, while Wordsworth's elevated style is reserved for the overt inter-

pretation of concrete experience in the poetry of meditation
or abstract doctrine. Moreover, the verse that tells a story
or incident is usually rather quiet in feeling, or at least
poems mainly in this mode and language tend to under-
state their themes, or to express them indirectly, or to be
qualified by a sense of potential comedy. In any case, Wordsworth's outpourings of direct, extremely powerful emotion
come in passages of argument and summary — not, in other
words, when he presents experience, but when he interprets
it. The fact is worth dwelling on; one would, of course,
usually expect the reverse to be true. But this — the immense
passion in meditation — is one of the most obvious and individual features of Wordsworth's poetry. It means that by
the time he was writing poetry, Wordsworth's strongest
emotion — at least the strongest he could express in poetry
— occurred in the statement of belief or doctrine.

Because his meditative writing differs so markedly in tone
and language from the quiet pulse of his descriptive or narrative verse, the shift from one mode to the other can seem
far more sudden and drastic than in most reflective poets.
Much of the drama of Wordsworth's verse arises in these
transitions. As a characteristic example we can take up the
passage cited before from Book VI of the *Prelude* (ll. 562–
608), where Wordsworth recounts the experience of crossing the Alps on his youthful walking tour. It begins in a
relaxed, circumstantial way. Wordsworth and Jones, his
companion, had been traveling with a band of mule-drivers
who could serve as guides. They all stopped for lunch; the
mule-drivers finished quickly and hurried on, but Wordsworth and his friend loitered awhile. Resuming their journey, the two then

> paced the beaten downward way that led
> Right to a rough stream's edge,

and ascended a hill on the other side of the stream. Soon they realized they were lost, but they met a peasant, who told them they must retrace their steps, and

> that our future course, all plain to sight,
> Was downwards, with the current of that stream.

And so the narrative continues in quiet pace, colloquial ("all plain to sight"), effortless, and simple. They were sorry to hear that they must walk back and down,

> For still we had hopes that pointed to the clouds,

and questioned the peasant over again, gradually realizing with regret that they had crossed the Alps.

And then, suddenly, comes the dramatic shift of tone, as the meaning of this regret breaks upon Wordsworth's mind and he launches into an impassioned statement of faith. With this change of tone, the mighty abstract nouns ("imagination," "power," "incompetence") are unfurled, the phrasing becomes orotund ("human speech") and the verse picks up its relentless forward surge in the complex syntax of suspension ("imagination . . . rose") and apposition:

> Imagination — here the Power so called
> Through sad incompetence of human speech,
> That awful Power rose from the mind's abyss.

And the passage that follows is typical. On the one hand, it is complex exposition — in fact, it is a key passage for understanding Wordsworth's psychology of the imagination — and yet there is a massive weight of utterance and feeling. Imagination, he says, rose

> Like an unfathered vapour that enwraps,
> At once, some lonely traveller. I was lost;
> Halted without an effort to break through;

> But to my conscious soul I now can say —
> 'I recognise thy glory': in such strength
> Of usurpation, when the light of sense
> Goes out, but with a flash that has revealed
> The invisible world, doth greatness make abode,
> There harbours.

The emotion has gradually been changing through these lines. After the surge of the opening, the verse becomes strongly end-stopped, and, for Wordsworth, relatively abrupt and broken. And then, as he begins to find words for the meanings he has discovered, the long, Wordsworthian stride resumes; the climactic, unqualified statement of faith begins to come forward. It is put with the verbal practices that usually characterize Wordsworth's *credos* — the insistent repetition, the procession of abstract nouns, the profusion of adverbs that seem not so much to qualify as to sweep away qualifications (only, never, evermore), the uncanny stress on the verb "is" that becomes absolute affirmation in Wordsworth.

> Our destiny, our being's heart and home,
> Is with infinitude, and only there;
> With hope it is, hope that can never die,
> Effort, and expectation, and desire,
> And something evermore about to be.

This whole passage of meditation, as Wordsworth interprets and explains the vivid regret he experienced on hearing that he had crossed the Alps, might be described as a brief drama of the mind coming upon a truth. It shows insight or self-intuition developing first as a sudden feeling or inexpressible consciousness ("I was lost;/Halted") and gradually transforming itself into a belief that can be proclaimed.

At his best, Matthew Arnold remarks, Wordsworth is

inevitable, as inevitable as Nature herself. Arnold means, I suppose, that in Wordsworth's poetry one sometimes feels a peculiarly close linkage or appropriateness of parts to each other, referring by "parts" to diction, versification, theme, feeling, and whatever other elements we usually abstract for the sake of critical discussion. But more particularly, Arnold must have sensed a continuity in the sequence of thought and feeling, a movement of ideas, associations, moods, and demeanors that seemed so natural or probable it could be called inevitable. In this episode from Book VI of the *Prelude* the continuity flows across and binds together the narrative and reflective passages, despite the extreme and arresting change of tone from one to the other. In other words, this poetry seems spontaneous and unpredictable, while (in contrast, for example, to Byron's *Don Juan*, which is certainly unpredictable) it also builds in a massive, sustained way.

If one hopes to account for this impression of inevitability, one cannot find that any logical or psychological necessity governs the expression. That man's destiny and essential nature lie in hope, aspiration, and striving toward the infinite is not always suggested by a reluctance to walk down mountains. The reflection may be appropriate to the experience, but hardly seems more or less natural or probable than any number of other reflections. But between the narrative and expository passages, there is a system of echoings or cross-references that work almost surreptitiously, like magnets, to pull the passages together. We noticed the same thing in the lines discussed earlier that begin "Wisdom and Spirit of the universe," where words such as "breath" and "motion" refer back to previous uses in narrative passages, and where the phrase "high objects" was a covert allusion to a mountain. Here in Book VI one might almost say that the narrative passage embodies in symbolic terms what comes as explicit statement immediately afterwards. When Wordsworth and his friend resumed their hike after lunch and came to a mountain stream, the hill on the other side "held forth/Conspicuous invitation to ascend." The beckoning, in other words, is up; or, as the later passage puts it, "Our destiny . . . Is with infinitude." The travelers "clomb with eagerness." They were loth to "descend," to take the "plain" course, "the beaten downward way," which is the way of most people, or rather the way life forces upon us, though the romantic hero resists, will not consent to it — "For still we had hopes that pointed to the clouds." And then, too, just as the narrative passage tinges a concrete experience toward symbolism, the expository passage turns into metaphor what had been literal in the previous passage. The mind is a traveler lost in mountains (amid vapors and abysses) just as Wordsworth was in the Alps. The whole passage in Book VI of the *Prelude* is as characteristic of Wordsworth's better poetry as any that could be found. One might say that where a modern poet would probably implicate the meaning in an image, and a renaissance or neoclassic poet would illustrate the meaning by an image, Wordsworth employs both symbolic and discursive modes of thought, using them to complement each other. If one sought a formula, one could perhaps suggest that his verse enacts a process of discovering the meaning in the image.

– 5 –

And yet the movement of Wordsworth's poetry is far more subtle than anything we have been able to suggest hitherto. It is true that there are characteristically the large wheelings from one mode of poetry to another, with dra-

matic shifts of emotion and style. But there is also an un-
ceasing process of very delicate modulation that accounts,
more than anything else, for the sense of a living voice still
communicated by the poetry to many readers. In fact, one
of the important reasons for dwelling on diverse styles in
Wordsworth was to establish sets of association or expectation, to present magnified images of diverse ways of writing, hoping thereby to respond more precisely to the common texture of his verse. For as we observed in "Tintern
Abbey" — it could have been mentioned in every poem
discussed — when Wordsworth exploits one set of verbal
resources he does not entirely exclude others. More frequently than it splits into sharply differentiated styles
Wordworth's poetry takes what might be called a middle
ground, a stance from which it can move in any direction.
As an example, we can take some stanzas from "Resolution
and Independence"; for, as Coleridge says, this "fine poem
is *especially* characteristic." Wordsworth is describing the
old leech-gatherer as he first saw him.

> Such seemed this Man, not all alive nor dead,
> Nor all asleep — in his extreme old age:
> His body was bent double, feet and head
> Coming together in life's pilgrimage;
> As if some dire constraint of pain, or rage
> Of sickness felt by him in times long past,
> A more than human weight upon his frame had cast.
>
> Himself he propped, limbs, body, and pale face,
> Upon a long grey staff of shaven wood:
> And, still as I drew near with gentle pace,
> Upon the margin of that moorish flood
> Motionless as a cloud the old Man stood,
> That heareth not the loud winds when they call;
> And moveth all together, if it move at all.

This is Wordsworth's middle style, neither artless nor elevated. The passage begins by faintly recalling the syntax of weighty iteration and amplification ("Not all alive nor ... Nor"), but at once becomes more quiet and colloquially relaxed. There is a moment of literal, almost uncouth, observation, where Wordsworth describes the old man as a child might — "His body was bent double, feet and head/ Coming together." But at once the poetry is far from childlike in the suggestive polysyllable (pilgrimage) and the paired nouns — "constraint of pain," "rage/Of sickness" — that brood so impressively over the general lot of man. Then this is softened by the colloquial phrase, "times long past," and the next stanza opens in homely awkwardness — "Himself he propped." There is a line uniting Wordsworth's gifts for natural phrasing and descriptive exactitude — "a long grey staff of shaven wood" — a line of quiet skill that comes only after years of deliberate effort, and then this description of the old man begins to release feelings of awe:

> Motionless as a cloud the old Man stood,
> That heareth not the loud winds when they call;
> And moveth all together, if it move at all.

Every reader will feel the effect, yet it is not easy to trace this sudden intensification to its verbal sources. The verse is tightened by the quick play of "o" sounds and the internal rhyme ("cloud-loud"). There is the slight allusive value of the Biblical form, "heareth." The periodic structure of the main clause puts a typically Wordsworthian stress on the primary fact, "stood." Finally, there is the metaphor that compares the old man to a cloud, releasing motor responses of looking up and imaginatively uniting previous impressions of the old man — his integrity, detachment, and unshakable fixity. The shift of mood is dramatic, but it conveys itself through minute alterations of the verbal texture. In a passage such as this, Wordsworth's style makes use of all his poetic resources to achieve an exact responsiveness, to catch and render slight shades of constantly fluctuating feeling. As a result, the poetry seems unusually alive. It keeps the weight and steadiness we usually associate with Wordsworth, yet it also ripples with unpredictable motions of spontaneous consciousness.

– 6 –

Whatever analogies we may find with other writers, the poetry of Wordsworth, like that of every major figure, preserves its own identity. Only a minor craftsman can show verses of accomplished anonymity. Wordsworth's special note emerges in the union of diverse qualities: free excursiveness of thought that is also ordered and inevitable; intimacy that combines with a public manner; description that dawns into symbolism; spontaneity that breaks from a massive background of reflection and assimilation; generalization that becomes personal emotion. Meanwhile the verse keeps a strong forward surge, so that Wordsworth involves the reader in an act of mind that always pushes on and yet is massively dense at each moment. Hence his distinctive manner cannot be fully exhibited in detached phrases or lines, yet some great passages are always remembered. There are the lines that haunted Keats, as they do every reader, in which Wordsworth speaks of "the burthen of the mystery."

> the heavy and the weary weight
> Of all this unintelligible world.

Granted that these lines draw power from their context, they are also — and this is typical of Wordsworth — partially lost in it. If one asks why they are unforgettable, it is partly that they tell a truth we all know. Yet far from invoking a merely abstract recognition, Wordsworth makes one share his immense personal involvement. A writer must have a giant's grip to wring so much from a poetry of statement.

Then one can turn again to a stanza in "Resolution and Independence," this one famous, or notorious:

> My former thoughts returned: the fear that kills;
> And hope that is unwilling to be fed;
> Cold, pain, and labour, and all fleshy ills;
> And mighty Poets in their misery dead.
> — Perplexed, and longing to be comforted,
> My question eagerly did I renew,
> "How is it that you live, and what is it you do?"

No one else writes this way, incorporating a sweeping, abstract, relentlessly marching summary of human woe with a confession of personal dread. And no one else, it may be, would so descend into anticlimax in questioning the old man. For Wordsworth, it is always pointed out, can be astonishingly uneven. But then he was involved and confident in the experience he was creating; writers less pressed upon by meaning and feeling can more easily stand watchful over their work. And possibly the lapse also reveals something of the integrity that would assert itself at the expense of aesthetic felicities. As a final example, we can take a passage from the great ode, where Wordsworth evokes moments in childhood that revealed the soul's infinitude:

> those obstinate questionings
> Of sense and outward things,
> Falling from us, vanishings;
> Blank misgivings of a Creature

> Moving about in worlds not realized,
> High instincts before which our mortal Nature
> Did tremble like a guilty Thing surprised:
>> But for those first affections,
>> Those shadowy recollections,
>> Which, be they what they may,
> Are yet the fountain-light of all our day.

It is a paean, with its triumphant beat thrusting forward, but it is also an accumulation of synonyms as Wordsworth strives to grasp in language what he remembers. And, to repeat, few poets would submerge a magnificent figure —

> High instincts before which our mortal Nature
> Did tremble like a guilty Thing surprised —

in a swelling tide. For once again Wordsworth is not holding forth phrases to be admired. He is using them in the struggle to express something urgently meaningful. Perhaps that is why they came to him.

IX

THE LATE POEMS

IN THE endlessly accumulating commentaries on Wordsworth no judgments go unchallenged, but there is wide
agreement that the work of his middle and old age marks
a decline. Reading the later verse, most persons seem at
best to feel what Keats felt one autumn afternoon in Win-
chester: "I never lik'd stubble fields so much as now." In
fact, the impression (or it may sometimes be a premise)
has been so generally shared that few critics have wished to
discuss the late poetry in any detail, but have hurried on to
consider the poet's life asking, in effect, what caused his
powers to dwindle. This resort to biography has naturally
led to various answers: estrangement from Coleridge, the
"very rain & air & sunshine" of Wordsworth's intellect, according to Southey; a depleted supply of the vivid recollections that inspired his greatest poetry; remorse from his
affair with Annette Vallon; domestication and then distracting family responsibilities; encroaching religious, moral,
and political conservatism. These speculations cannot be
very conclusive; at best they merely put the late poetry
beside some other observation about Wordsworth's middle
age, not showing any necessary connection. Perhaps this is
the most one can do. At any rate, the present chapter attempts to approach the question in another way, concentrat-
ing on the poetry itself, and seeking first an unprejudiced
appraisal. We can, however, offer one conclusion at the start.

If Wordsworth had written only the later poems (here arbitrarily defined as poems composed after 1815), he would still be read, but as a minor poet and for a few poems: examples are "Ethereal Minstrel," "After-thought," or the "Extempore Effusion upon the Death of James Hogg." Some of these poems are sudden midwinter thaws or late resurrections of an earlier style, but there are also achievements of a relatively new kind. If one were content to leave it at that, one would have only to define the later mode and the vision informing it, evaluating these poems, as one does all others, from within and without, for their integrity as self-enclosing artifacts, and for the justness of whatever sense of reality they evoke. But since Wordsworth's manner did change, I have also tried to compare the later verse with that written before, hoping to suggest once again what Wordsworth so triumphantly does in the poems we have been talking about hitherto, and hoping also to show in the later poems an altered attitude toward his art, and a new use of it.

— 2 —

Perhaps the most obvious note of Wordsworth's later poetry is the return to convention. It does not, however, appear primarily in the revival of Augustan diction. That is only a symptom, though likely to be exclusively stressed if one allows Wordsworth's own critical emphasis on diction to dominate. The deeper significance lies in the fact that a poet, once so deeply personal and relatively original, should adopt sentiments, attitudes, and forms of expression he finds stored and available in the literary milieu. A general example is the way Wordsworth defines his rôle and inspiration as a poet. When one recalls that several of the *Lyrical Ballads* are ostensibly told by literal-minded, "loquacious" narrators, speakers not "poetic" but created in defiance of convention, and that the voice heard in most of the early poems can be summed up as that of a "man speaking to men," it is rather a shock in the later verse to come upon frequent references to the poet as a bard, a votary of the muse playing a harp or lyre, and the like. One might also instance the new, occasional derivation of subject matter from the classics, with the approach, now and then, to something of their style and tone, especially that of Virgil.[1] At one time, as he says in the Fenwick note to the "Ode to Lycoris," Wordsworth avoided "mythology and classical allusion," fearing that they might seem "unnatural and affected," and so "tend to unrealize the sentiment." In other words, they might lead the reader to doubt his sincerity. He now feels, however, that "pagan fable . . . may ally itself with real sentiment," as indeed it may, but only for a poet steeped in the classics.[2] And, of course, Wordsworth's mode having changed, the late poems do not always require that we trust or even think about the sincerity of the speaker. In fact, "Dion" and "Laodamia" show Wordsworth exploiting the classics as Milton does in "Lycidas." That is, by classical allusion he avoids a merely personal expression. The man speaking to men disappears in the familiar symbolism. No doubt, as Christopher Wordsworth says in the *Memoirs*,[3] the matter and style of the classics were still more deeply fixed in his mind by the labors of preparing his oldest son for college. He also translated portions of the *Aeneid* between 1819 and 1823. But these efforts may be viewed as typifying some of the causes for an increasingly conventional art: the loss of an urgent, personal use for poetry with the accompanying (though never complete or exclusive) sense of verse as artifice, and the commitment to family and public responsibilities in which he gradually became a spokesman or prop for orthodoxies, a poet, as Yeats put it, "cut and sawn into planks of obvious utility."

A purely conventional poem can, of course, be a very good one, but at its best it is likely to seem almost anonymous. It is the voice of a tradition, and will be enjoyed for the grace with which it assumes the appropriate habits. For example, the "Ode Composed on May Morning" (1826) begins:

> While from the purpling east departs
>   The star that led the dawn,
> Blithe Flora from her couch upstarts,
>   For May is on the lawn.

The reader at once understands that he is encountering one of the platitudes of lyric verse, a welcome to spring. The diction is general and conventional, showing the direct influence of the classics more than anything else. Such an opening makes novelty almost an intrusion; it certainly precludes any struggle with experience in the discovery of meaning. We are not to be led into intimate sympathy with a man different from ourselves, and, through that outgoing sympathy, into a previously alien way of viewing things. In one sense, the verse is too sophisticated for this; it comes close to suggesting poetry is a game. The challenge and the fun lie in recognizing and abiding by convention, and yet also being able to refresh a stock poem. From this point of view, the ode succeeds:

> Thy feathered Lieges bill and wings
>   In love's disport employ;
> Warmed by thy influence, creeping things
>   Awake to silent joy:
> Queen art thou still for each gay plant
>   Where the slim wild deer roves;

And served in depths where fishes haunt
Their own mysterious groves.

The personification of May as a Queen, with the periphrasis
that makes the birds her Lieges, evokes the feudal pageantry
of the Middle Ages, at least as re-created in the romantic
imagination. Under the influence of this metaphor, the love-
making of the birds become a courtly game ("disport"
meaning, of course, play or diversion), distanced for the
reader and contemplated aesthetically. And then there is
the delicate particularity of the reference to the "slim wild
deer." It implies the poet's affectionate appreciation, while
the verb "haunt" suggests the elusive, shadowy, flitting appearance of the fish in that other world of water which has
its own "groves" and which must always seem mysterious
to human observers. If, as W. P. Ker remarks, description
is the poet's act of love, the love here is of a quality different
from that in Wordsworth's earlier work. There was then a
felt communion, a dynamic interrelationship. Here description is much more objective; the love is aesthetic and detached. The one especially Wordsworthian moment occurs
in the reference to "creeping things" that "awake to silent
joy," a reminder wonderful in itself but possibly out of
place here.

In the Preface to the *Lyrical Ballads* Wordsworth remarks
that by writing in verse one enters into an engagement, an
implicit agreement that the poetry will fulfill definite anticipations. Without some such understanding between a
poet and his audience, he can hardly communicate; at least,
he will have to educate a public in his own particular conventions, and until this has been accomplished, his verse
may seem charged with a shock of novelty likely to provoke
pained outcries. At the same time, the agreement Words-

worth has in mind can, as we have seen, be extended to refer
not merely to ways of speaking, but to feelings, attitudes,
ideas, and the like. Hence if Wordsworth's early verse indicates, to quote the lush, monitory phrasing of his nephew,
"a temper which would hurl defiance against public opinion
with wayward wilfulness, petulant pride, and random reck-
lessness," it is also true, as the future bishop adds, that
Wordsworth "would not have written such lines" in his
"maturer years." [4] He no longer seeks to reform the state
of mind supposed in the reading public. Instead, the later
verse exists in a bond of agreement and seeks rather to remind us of what we already accept and know. There is none
of what Yeats called an "old man's frenzy" in the aging
Wordsworth, no "ravening, raging, uprooting that he may
come" to some reality. To write as he writes is to assert that
in tradition and convention repose the truth and wisdom
needful for man, and to this wisdom and truth he naturally
subordinates himself.

– 3 –

Perhaps this is one reason why the later verse tends to be
relatively impersonal. In the first place, Wordsworth frequently exploits a new subject matter. Where he used to
speak of events in his own life, he now talks more about
political affairs, works of painting or architecture, widely
known sites, events drawn from history or literature, and
whatever else has a more obviously public existence. Such
subjects are appropriate to the purposes of his later art, as
I will try to show, but their prevalence also helps distinguish
it. More than it refers to a subject matter, however, the notion of impersonality suggests a way of speaking about any
subject, an attitude of disengaged, objective contemplation.
This high serenity always appealed to Wordsworth; it grew

on him as he aged, and is most noticeable, because most
surprising, in those poems where he does talk of himself,
his family, and friends. For one thing, when he now draws
on the events of his own life, he usually translates them into
general, widely familiar human situations, the generality
maybe allowing or making acceptable a lack of involvement
and concern. Old age, he says in the *Excursion*, may be compared to an "eminence" or mountain top;

> on that superior height
> Who sits, is disencumbered from the press
> Of near obstructions, and is privileged
> To breathe in solitude, above the host
> Of ever-humming insects.   (IX, 69–73)

He likes the thought; from this altitude one sees more
clearly; but to some readers such serenity, "held," as Wordsworth puts it in *The White Doe of Rylstone*, "above/The
infirmities of mortal love" (ll. 1625–26), will always seem
morally questionable, perhaps a little inhuman. Wordsworth
might say it is angelic; for angels, the Priest reminds us in
the *Excursion*,

> perceive,
> With undistempered and unclouded spirit,
> The object as it is.   (V, 486–488)

The angelic point of view, as John Jones demonstrates,[5] is
embodied and expressed in a very beautiful poetry that sees
the world as jeweled, miraculous artifice, and that with its
"armed vision," to borrow Coleridge's phrase, displaces the
ordinary proportion and scale that centers on human life to
treat all objects, whether human or not, with equal attention; all alike express the Divine Artificer. It may be, however, that to relish this poetry one must stand with Words-

worth somewhere near the top of Jacob's Ladder. As with
the poetry of Shelley, angelic notes may grate on unregen-
erate ears. In fact, one may feel that a man, while he is a
man, does well to cling to his warm, vital, maybe blind,
earthly interests, not seeking to rise toward another sphere
until he is dead. Had old Wordsworth been in the Garden
of Eden, he would not have touched the apple; Eve would
have suffered all by herself. The suggestion is not merely
facetious. It refers to a state of mind in Wordsworth that,
however admirable some persons may find it, blocks not
perhaps our appreciation but our involvement in many of
the later poems. "We desert our master," Johnson said of
Milton's *Paradise Lost*, "and seek for companions."

Much of what I have been saying can be illustrated in
Wordsworth's "Farewell Lines" (1828), written to Charles
and Mary Lamb shortly after Lamb, having retired from
the India House, moved from London to Enfield. The poem
does not name Lamb or Wordsworth, nor does it describe
anything in a particular way. It becomes, instead, more a
meditation on the solitary peace of country dwellers:

> Most soothing was it for a welcome Friend,
> Fresh from the crowded city, to behold
> That lonely union.

The welcome friend was, of course, Wordsworth, and at
one time he would have said so, making the poem a very
intimate, personal expression. But he now seeks to generalize, and the poem suggests what must have been one motive.
In a poem of 1824, "A Flower Garden," Wordsworth introduces a peculiar and characteristic being: "Thus spake the
moral Muse — her wing/Abruptly spreading to depart."
But the moral muse did not depart; she haunted most
of his later years, and inspired an anxiety to judge. That is

why he so often writes about more public objects or events. The wish is now to comment and pass sentence. But granted the moralistic intentions, the impersonal tone is necessary; it is, perhaps, the only thing that saves, if they can be saved, many of the poems the moral muse obviously prompts. If one knows that the "Farewell Lines" were written to Charles Lamb, one is likely to protest that the tone is unattractive. One assumes this retirement might have been an occasion for affectionate well-wishing. Instead, it first gives rise to a grave, unintentionally condescending appraisal:

> if severe afflictions borne
> With patience merit the reward of peace,
> Peace ye deserve.

Before he can wish that his friends may have peace, he must, it seems, assure himself that it would be deserved. It is hard to sympathize with such heavy scrupulosity at the expense of more generous emotions. And his later remark that the retirement to the country was "wise though late" again intrudes a rather grudging evaluation. Of course, Wordsworth ends with a "hope that we, dear Friends! shall meet again," but in the circumstances it is a rather modest flourish. What is more important is that the poem does not raise these difficulties so urgently unless one remembers that it refers to Charles and Mary Lamb. Hence it may, as I said, suggest why Wordsworth was tempted to generalize and to write impersonally. His verse is now controlled by a need to offer religious and moral guidance.

The presence of an impersonal voice has been stressed because it is new in Wordsworth's poetry, but it never became dominant. At least since the first half of the nineteenth century, intimacy is the most common tone of poetry, and the art of Wordsworth's later years is no exception. What one finds, often, is a quietly intimate manner that changes and becomes impersonal when Wordsworth states a moral message. The shift in tone may be very gradual. A typical example is the first of the "Evening Voluntaries." It begins in what seems to be the usual intimacy, the poet speaking to some companion:

> Calm is the fragrant air, and loth to lose
> Day's grateful warmth, tho' moist with falling dews.
> Look for the stars, you'll say that there are none;
> Look up a second time, and, one by one,
> You mark them twinkling out with silvery light.

As the poem continues, however, references to the companion are dropped. The speaker calls attention to one impression after another — the birds now silent, the flowers scarcely visible, the sound of the church-clock — and then begins to add associations and fancies to the objects he names. And then, as the poem works toward a conclusion, the tone seems to change again, a shift marked, though very faintly, by a reliance on passive constructions:

> A stream is heard — I see it not, but know
> By its soft music whence the waters flow:
> Wheels and the tread of hoofs are heard no more.

The speaker does not now seem to be addressing a companion, or even himself. He simply notes, in an impersonal and objective way, that "a stream is heard." It would not, of course, be proper to infer much from such slight indications, but the shift is representative, and the tone, approaching that of a descriptive monograph, lends force to the statement. It gives to the religious or moral reminders something of the authority always granted to what seems a

totally impersonal utterance. To some extent, this occurs
here:

> One boat there was, but it will touch the shore
> With the next dipping of its slackened oar;
> Faint sound, that, for the gayest of the gay,
> Might give to serious thought a moment's sway,
> As a last token of man's toilsome day.

Perhaps the strategic values of impersonality are most clearly
symbolized in the "Vernal Ode" (1817). We are again
drawing upon the notion of angelhood; for in the ode
Wordsworth introduces an angel and quotes his speech. It
would be hard to find a more impersonal, authoritative mask
for your own doctrine and exhortation. And, of course, to
do this implies an enormous confidence in your beliefs.

– 4 –

In the *Recluse*, according to Coleridge, Wordsworth was
to "assume the station of a man in mental repose, one whose
principles were made up, and so prepared to deliver upon
authority a system of philosophy." [6] Perhaps this projected
work was more ardently wished by Coleridge than by
Wordsworth, and it may be that Coleridge, fretting his
friend to write this long philosophic poem, injured Wordsworth's gift as much as he earlier fostered it. I am not thinking only of the time Wordsworth spent resolving and preparing for the never-written *Recluse*, or of the gloom he
sometimes felt as a result of repeated failures to get under
way, but also of the *Excursion* (part of the *Recluse*) and the
later poetry generally. An introspective, emotional brooder
may think profoundly when his mind centers on some particular event; he can scarcely be made to "deliver upon
authority a system of philosophy." Yet Wordsworth comes

near this goal in the late poems. Or, rather, there may be little philosophy, but there is much "mental repose"; his principles are "made up."

During the years of his greatest poetry, Wordsworth possessed no integrated system of belief. The fact is often forgotten; it is easy to see why. In the first place, if Wordsworth had no single creed, he expounded a number of doctrines separately. One may think of him as a philosophic poet simply because one does not read poetry as though it were philosophy. No reader needs ask whether his doctrines are consistent with each other; it makes no difference to the poetry. And then, too, we know that Wordsworth went through a period of desperate intellectual uncertainty between approximately 1794 and 1796, from which, the *Prelude* says, he gradually recovered. Reading his poetry in the light of this biographical information, we naturally pay less attention to the uncertainty and many-sided debate that show themselves in the poetry of 1798–1807. In a grand moment already cited from the *Prelude* Wordsworth asserts that

> Our destiny, our being's heart and home,
> Is with infinitude, and only there;

but later in the same poem he says that in the world of common experience "We find our happiness, or not at all." Here Wordsworth swings between romantic transcendentalism and naturalism. The *Prelude* certainly urges that the imagination gives us our only reliable knowledge, and hence, one supposes, our best moral guidance. The poem was finished in 1805. But Wordsworth felt misgivings even while he was writing it. In 1804 he pledged himself to a stoic life of duty. In 1798, to take another example, he found in "nature and the language of the sense"

> The guide, the guardian of my heart, and soul
> Of all my moral being;

for he was certain that nature "never did betray/The heart that loved her." But four years later, while the great celebration of nature was still going forward in the *Prelude*, he took time off to reflect that

> My whole life I have lived in pleasant thought,
> As if life's business were a summer mood;
> As if all needful things would come unsought;

and he admired the old leech-gatherer with his stony independence and fortitude. In a more trivial instance, Wordsworth scolded in 1807 because a group of gypsies had rested one whole day. A "torpid life," he calls it. But when old Matthew asked him,

> Why, William, on that old grey stone,
> Thus for the length of half a day,
> Why, William, sit you thus alone,
> And dream your time away?

William replied that

> we can feed this mind of ours
> In a wise passiveness.[7]

And we saw that "I Wandered Lonely as a Cloud" and "The Solitary Reaper" imply opposite views of man in the cosmos, yet at most only twenty-three months separate the two poems.

One does not usually go to poetry for an intellectual system. In fact, a readiness to explore diverse points of view may be as far as our honesty can go; for all philosophies must fail before the vast mystery. But throughout these years of unsettlement, Wordsworth was striving for a unified system of belief. In a sense, his poetry from 1795 to approximately 1815 embodies a prolonged self-criticism working toward what Arnold held to be the function of criticism in general — the acquiring of true ideas and the ordering of them, and of the self with them, which, as Arnold remarks, calms and satisfies us as nothing else can. According to Arnold, this critical effort is a necessary prior condition of major creative achievement. We have now to see what happens, or, at least, what happened to Wordsworth, at the close of such an effort. If Wordsworth ended as a minor poet, his life may argue the advantage for poetry of a mind playing freely. Though Yeats had a more complex idea in mind, the well-known lines may make the point:

> Throughout the lying days of my youth
> I swayed my leaves and flowers in the sun;
> Now I must wither into the truth.[8]

Had Wordsworth clearly recollected former sentiments, he might have repudiated the "lying days" of his youth far more earnestly than Yeats does here. For, of course, the irony that puts a gap between truth and poetry applies much more to Wordsworth than to Yeats, who never made up his mind, and never withered.

– 5 –

Making the point less obliquely, one might say that Wordsworth's late verse illustrates the potential liabilities of a militant ideal of sincerity. It is not simply that in the deliberate pursuit of sincerity the eye swivels and stays fixed upon the self, perhaps so much so that we become almost unaware of anybody else. Neither is it simply that the urge to honesty, creating at every moment a sense of responsibility, can compel us to give up sportive poses and speculations, tryings-on and free rangings. These risks are obvious. But if it dominates sufficiently, the thirst for sincerity may actually drive one to adopt a creed, even if it also makes a commitment more difficult. Wordsworth might feel that belief ought not so much to be adopted as to rise organically out of past feelings and experience, but this, as I hope to show, was not what finally happened to him. One must account in other ways for the shackles of self-mutilating dogma Wordsworth had put on by 1815; and the main explanation is his desperate need for certitude. When Keats praised the quality he called Negative Capability — "that is when man is capable of being in uncertainties, Mysteries, doubts, without any irritable reaching after fact & reason" [9] — the praise would have seemed shocking to Wordsworth. He would not, of course, have disputed Keats's remark as it is phrased. He knew that truth could not be obtained by "reaching after fact and reason." But he would have deplored any acquiescence in a state of doubt. What is the object of life if it is not to seek the truth and to align oneself with it? How can we summon the energy for moral effort if we lack an assured belief? Responding to the influence of Wordsworth, Keats himself was later to feel that there could be no integrity or consistency of character (he calls it "identity") without the continuing effort of reflection that leads to a settled view of things. One might even suggest that a man obsessed with sincerity may have an unconscious interest in excluding doubts, if only because, once admitted or recognized, they bring on acute anxiety and exhausting toil as he tries to resolve them. When Dr. Adams told Samuel Johnson, who was then seventy-five, "You have evidence enough" of the spiritual world, Johnson characteristically replied, "I like to have more." The aging Wordsworth would not have admitted this. Toward the end of his life he does not exemplify the struggle to believe that one may find even in a believer. Or rather he exemplifies it in a negative way, by a denial and retreat from whatever might threaten his faith.

One of the noblest of Wordsworth's qualities is his constant effort to keep in mind whatever he thought essential, banishing trivial interests and activities. The example can have a powerful influence on his readers. It makes his poetry unusually bracing and emancipating. Even if we did not notice Wordsworth himself, present as an example in his poetry, it is hard not to be shaken by the loud blasts of contempt for all that he deems petty and affected, and for ourselves when we waste our powers chasing unworthy objects. Yet this very sincerity, if pursued too long and too intensely, threatens another sort of waste, as more and more may come to seem unessential. Milton offers a quick instance. The baroque achievement of *Paradise Lost* rests on the Christian-humanist synthesis that allowed Milton, though a Christian, to regard classical writing as a source of true inspiration supplementary to the Bible. But persons such as Milton or Wordsworth cannot rest in a complex synthesis; they will continue to probe and question until they reach what cannot possibly be questioned. In other words, Milton confronted and resolved difficulties which a more easy-going person would not have raised. Hence there is the famous moment in *Paradise Regained* when classical culture is set in opposition to the Bible, and, of course, once set in opposition it had to be rejected. Wordsworth himself recognized that he was narrowing. There is a brooding, rather melancholy passage in the "Essay, Supplementary to the Preface" of 1815: "as the mind grows serious from the weight of life, the range of its passions is contracted" and "its sympathies" become exclusive.[10]

More than anything else, then, the "mental repose" accounts for the changed character of his verse. The greater poetry of his early manhood creates its drive and power in struggling with personal experience; it tries to grasp experience in the concrete and to build from it what Josephine Miles calls "structures of deliberation," [11] seeking a conscious understanding. Now, however, with Wordsworth's more rigid structure of belief, one finds poems dramatizing a rejection of inspirations from experience, refusing to be led by the imagination, and compelling encountered objects or circumstances to illustrate truths he already possessed. If the later poetry still embodies a struggle, the struggle is not what Keats termed a "search after Truth," but an effort to rally and marshal the inner man. Putting it another way, we can again turn to the "Essay, Supplementary to the Preface" (1815). Here Wordsworth describes the limitations of pious and devout persons in reading poetry, and the point is that he now confronts in a similar state of mind whatever impressions and promptings occur to him. "Religious faith," he says, "is to him who holds it so momentous a thing, and error appears to be attended with such tremendous consequences, that, if opinions touching upon religion occur which the Reader condemns, he not only cannot sympathize with them . . . but there is, for the most part, an end put to all satisfaction and enjoyment." [12]

It is, nevertheless, somewhat accidental to our theme that the mental repose rooted itself in Anglican orthodoxy. The point is rather that Wordsworth finally obtained a settlement, and that the settlement naturally resulted in a different kind of poetry. Any firmly held system of belief might have produced a similar poetry. But that the final placement was religious creates an embarrassment. It means that in talking about the poetry one cannot avoid evaluating, at least by implication, the religious moods it expresses. The ideal aim of man may not be to create art, but for human beings the life of the spirit can be tested only as it flows into activity, and the quality of Wordsworth's later poetry must be a comment on the quality of his religious experience. It often seems, in the later work, that religion presides as a governess among impulsive gestures of the heart. It is true that there is not always much strength in the impulse, but, on the other hand, there is a very exacting monitor, and hence the poems often show the religious conscience scrutinizing random feelings. An example is the not very good poem that pretends to have been written "At Vallombrosa," one of the *Memorials of a Tour* in Italy in 1837. Here Wordsworth tells how, having associated Vallombrosa with Milton and formed an imaginative picture of it, he has longed to see it. The wish is now granted, and the happiness he feels would seem sufficiently innocent. But the poem at once undertakes to consider whether such pleasures are justifiable, characteristically generalizing the event and passing judgment on it:

> Even so, and unblamed, we rejoice as we may
> In Forms that must perish, frail objects of sense;
> Unblamed — if the Soul be intent on the day
> When the Being of Beings shall summon her hence.

The "objects of sense" contemplated here would not often be thought a menace to religion or morals, but the point is that any enjoyment which distracts us from God may be blamed and should be checked. If we find pleasure in natural forms, we must at the same time be intent on the truths of religion. Ultimately, we shall see, man responds to nature properly to the extent that he finds in it religious illustrations, reminders, and spurs. In fact, such a reminder is embedded here; for, of the many traits that might distinguish "objects of sense," the speaker chooses to emphasize only that they are "frail" and "must perish," and thus leads himself to think of the day when the "Being of Beings shall summon" him. But even at this point, scruples excited by rejoicing in shady woods, meadows, and brooks have not been allayed, and the poet goes on to stress that

> he and he only with wisdom is blest
> Who, gathering true pleasures wherever they grow,
> Looks up in all places, for joy or for rest,
> To the Fountain whence Time and Eternity flow.

"My heart leaps up when I behold/ A rainbow in the sky," Wordsworth wrote in 1802, and he went on to pray "So be it when I shall grow old,/ Or let me die." The poem ended with a reference to "natural piety." Now, at the age of sixty-seven, a great deal weighs down the heart, and it is mainly a different sort of piety.

When impulses so innocent are questioned, Wordsworth would naturally repress those other impulses or impressions he used to feel so strongly that they seemed undeniable revelations. Or if they are entertained, it is, as I said, mainly for the sake of denying them, the poem becoming an exemplification of the religious conscience rejecting error, seeking to curb wrong yearnings and create "a second Will more wise," to quote from a rejected stanza of the "Ode to Duty." There is, for example, the impression that natural objects such as flowers can themselves feel pleasure. In "Lines Written in Early Spring" (1798) Wordsworth speaks of a moment when his "human soul" was linked to nature, and he was made aware of its essential life, or being, that "grand elementary principle of pleasure," by which everything, including man, "knows, and feels, and lives, and moves." [13] Of course, he still remains conscious of a separate human identity, still exists outside the natural objects. He "cannot measure" the thoughts of the birds, but "the least motion which they made,/ It seemed a thrill of pleasure." His sense of this is so urgent that it cannot be repudiated:

> The budding twigs spread out their fan,
> To catch the breezy air;
> And I must think, do all I can,
> That there was pleasure there.

It is altogether characteristic of Wordsworth, or at least of his rhetorical strategy of persuasion, to struggle against the dominance of impressions leading to strange insights, sometimes called "mystical." Such discoveries are never shown to be easily won. But in the early poetry his imaginative impressions are not subjected to the control of prior belief or knowledge. So here the hesitating gestures ("do all I can") are framed within an initial premise that the soul was linked to nature, and the poem leaves no question that the poet accepts as a belief sent from "heaven," as a "faith," that "every flower/ Enjoys the air it breathes."

Forty-six years later Wordsworth returned to the same theme in a poem that begins

> So fair, so sweet, withal so sensitive,
> Would that the little Flowers were born to live,
> Conscious of half the pleasure which they give.

Here he presents himself briefly contemplating a thought he knows to be impossible ("Would that"). He continues to play with the notion, or "bold desire," as he calls it. What, he says, if the sun might see "all that issues from his glorious fount"; and if the moon were equally "privileged,"

> what a countenance of delight
> Would through the clouds break forth on human sight!

(We may recall "Intimations of Immortality" where "The Moon doth with delight/ Look round her," a thought here renounced.) The point of the poem comes in the last two stanzas. Such wishes have been uttered that the poet may have occasion to judge and reject them, and hence to state how man ought to respond to nature:

> Fond fancies! whereso'er shall turn thine eye
> On earth, air, ocean, or the starry sky,
> Converse with Nature in pure sympathy.

"Pure sympathy" suggests, of course, the "undistempered and unclouded spirit" possessed by angels, who, as we noted, see "The object as it is." In Wordsworth's poetry, the adjective "pure" usually means not "touched by welterings of passion," and perhaps a "pure sympathy" should be contrasted with the former, impure sympathy that, he might now sense, projected human feeling into the natural world. So the poem concludes:

> All vain desires, all lawless wishes quelled,
> Be Thou to love and praise alike impelled,
> Whatever boon is granted or withheld.

The poem is, of course, slighter than we have made it out to be, and it is also more complex. It expresses a genuine wistfulness that such desires or fancies cannot be allowed, and the mood of regret brings out a rather moving conflict between what the poet wants to believe and what he knows he must believe. The "lawless wishes" are "quelled" on the level of assertion and resolve; but they still tug at the poet's emotions.

– 6 –

To contrast poems written after 1815 with those preceding them may be to risk suggesting that the imprisonment in orthodoxy was rather sudden. This was not the case; it took place over many years, and it is doubtful whether at any point Wordsworth clearly perceived how far he had receded from notions espoused in his youth. As far as I know, he never made any thoroughgoing acknowledgment, and, what is more significant, he did not much tinker with the poems published earlier. For since he held with utter seriousness that "every great Poet is a Teacher," and since he had pledged himself to orthodoxy, he would very likely have modified or suppressed any lines that could threaten piety or challenge received truth, as, in fact, he did in the unpublished *Prelude*. Instead, he seems to have dealt with such youthful, potentially distressing utterances by gradually reinterpreting them, or by stressing only one of many possible interpretations. We are, like Wordsworth, false to his early vision unless we understand that when he says "every flower/ Enjoys the air it breathes," he reports what he holds to be a reality. It is, as the poem concedes, strange, paradoxical, and hard to accept, but the poem seeks to make us accept it. Now, however, Wordsworth urges an alternative way of reading such verses. One illustration comes in a letter of 1829 to W. R. Hamilton in which Wordsworth criticizes some poems written by Hamilton's sister. She, like Wordsworth, had evidently been tempted to endow nature with human attributes. "We have had the *brow* and the *eye* of the moon before, both allowable," Wordsworth exclaims, "but what have we reserved for human beings, if their features and organs etc., are to be *lavished* on objects without feeling and intelligence?" He at once concedes that this observation may come "with an ill grace from one who is aware that he has tempted many of his admirers into *abuses* of this kind," but, he goes on, "I assure you, I have never given way to my own feelings in personifying natural objects, or

investing them with sensation, without bringing all that I
have said to a rigorous after-test of good sense." The test,
one knows from many sources, lies in determining whether
the personifications are dramatically appropriate to a man
in the mood supposed in the poem. The letter of 1814 to
Catherine Clarkson has already been cited. It was written
in response to Mrs. Clarkson's instance of a friend of hers
who thought Wordsworth a worshiper of nature. "A passionate expression, uttered incautiously in the poem upon the
Wye," he explains, "has led her into this mistake; she, reading in cold-heartedness, and substituting the letter for the
spirit." He adds that "there is nothing of this kind in *The
Excursion*," except possibly the "simile of the Boy and the
Shell and what follows" has "something ordinarily (but absurdly) called *Spinosistic*. But the intelligent reader will
easily see the *dramatic* propriety of the passage." [14] In other
words, such ebullient utterances cannot offend because they
do not pertain to objective realities. They merely portray a
state of mind. The rationalization is not ineffective, and,
moreover, it is consistent with other premises urged by
Wordsworth while he was habitually investing natural objects with sensations, for example, that poetry studies and
portrays man's emotional nature — it is "the history or science of feelings" — and that the "earliest poets" used personifications because they were spontaneously created by passion, and hence they can still be employed if they arise naturally rather than by "mechanical adoption." [15]

-7-

Of course, it was Wordsworth's complex theory of the
imagination that allowed him to accept, or to justify accepting, impressions and promptings such as those in "Lines
Written in Early Spring." But in his later belief, the imagina-

tion no longer has any important function. It cannot be an organ of truth, for the truth is known, and therefore what Wordsworth used to call "imagination" he now regards as a potential source of error. In one example ("Processions," 1820), he describes a religious procession circling the outside of a church. It was seen in the "vale of Chamouny" and as the white-robed marchers moved in silence, they seemed to Wordsworth, viewing them from a distance, to resemble the glaciers he simultaneously observed coming down from Mt. Blanc:

> Still in the vivid freshness of a dream,
> The pageant haunts me as it met our eyes!
> Still, with those white-robed Shapes — a living Stream,
> The glacier Pillars join in solemn guise
> For the same service.

And as, in this optical illusion, the glaciers seem to join in the religious ceremony, the human figures also seem to have issued from "The impenetrable heart of that exalted Mount." Perhaps at one time this visual impression, this instance of the modifying power of the imagination, might have been taken as a revelation, and the poem might have proceeded to meditate upon it. Now, however, the response is very different. He is afraid of the imagination and uses the occasion to deplore it:

> Trembling, I look upon the secret springs
> Of that licentious craving in the mind
> To act the God among external things,
> To bind, on apt suggestion, or unbind;
> And marvel not that antique Faith inclined
> To crowd the world with metamorphosis.

But what he now terms a "licentious craving" he formerly called "imagination," a word "denoting operations of the

mind upon" external objects, endowing them "with proper-
ties that do not inhere in them." "To act the God among external things" is only to exert the imagination that "shapes
and *creates*" (the italics are Wordsworth's) "proceeding from,
and governed by, a sublime consciousness of the soul in her
own mighty and almost divine powers." [16] And the poem also
suggests a source or reason in Christian belief for this "trem-
bling" fear of imaginative processes. The imagination is
not prompted by faith; it remains a merely natural faculty;
it created, and, if unchecked, might still create erroneous
faiths, like those of Greece and Rome. Its "insolent temptations" lead to *hubris* and must be shunned. The temptation,
at least in part, would seem to lie in a suggestion that the
mountain sends forth "pure and silent Votaries," cooperat-
ing with man in his worship. But the implications of the
imagery may go much further; for to see human beings as
"a living Stream," and to identify the stream with a glacier,
may reveal something about the character and source of worship, perhaps that it does issue from the "wintry fount" of
an "impenetrable heart," perhaps that man as a worshiper
loses individual identity and becomes only a vague "Shape,"
part of a "living Stream," pure, cold, still, awful, and remote
from any participation in human life. This interpretation
may not seem very far-reaching or well-founded, but the poetry does suggest that Wordsworth was finding some symbolic meaning in the scene. Certainly he recollects it with an
emotion ("Still . . . haunts") that seems excessive to its
occasion. Hence if one cannot go very far in explaining the
emotion, that may be because the scene creates insights the
poet will not bring to consciousness, that, in fact, he may be
suppressing. If this is merely speculative, at least it is clear
that the poem shows Wordsworth withdrawing from imaginative vision.

– 8 –

Partly because he repudiated and suppressed what he used
to call imagination, Wordsworth now sometimes writes a
poetry of wit. He still builds poems about his response to
natural objects, but they are used in a different way. Where
once they could be described as symbols of a peculiar kind,
"consubstantial," to cite Coleridge again, "with the truths of
which they are the conductors," they now *illustrate* truths
derived from other sources. That the poems are no longer
produced by the "imagination" — in Wordsworth's general
sense of the word — appears most obviously in his attitude
to metaphor. For when the imagination frames a metaphor,
the objects compared tend to "unite and coalesce," Wordsworth says, and a "sense of the truth of the likeness" grows
upon the mind of the reader.[17] This is exactly what Wordsworth no longer desires, if only because nothing can be a
true "likeness" to the objects of religious faith. Hence he
will often disown a metaphor as soon as it is used. The "Vernal Ode" (1817), for example, employs stars as a figure
of heaven, bright, ordered, and "unsusceptible of change."
But the poetry at once corrects the metaphor by a plain statement of fact: stars are "subject to decay." It is only to the
"mortal eye" that they seem to possess an "absolute serenity
. . . free from semblance of decline." Such scrupulous literalness in exploiting a figure so conventional suggests as well
as anything else the damaging responsibilities Wordsworth
has shouldered. Metaphor is no longer a way of expressing
imaginative impressions and feelings which may then be interpreted. The interpretation is present to his mind from the
start; it is given in his creed. As a result, metaphor becomes
an ornament, or, at best, an illustration, perhaps most honest
and trustworthy when it is also understood to be playful.
To use Wordsworth's own vocabulary, his poetry now ex-

ploits the faculty of fancy, to which nature, as he says in the *Prelude*, presents

> Apt illustrations of the moral world,
> Caught at a glance, or traced with curious pains.
>
> (XIV, 319–320)

The workings of "fancy" are more precisely described in the Preface of 1815. Following what Wordsworth says, one can note that in the late verse associations connected with natural objects tend to be capricious and accidental — a point to be exemplified later on — and the effects of the comparison are usually "surprising, playful, ludicrous, amusing, tender, or pathetic." A line from "Love Lies Bleeding" (1842?), " 'Tis Fancy guides me willing to be led,/ Though by a slender thread," describes many of the late poems. In them, he detects what he calls "lurking affinities" with "curious subtilty" and "successful elaboration," while he maturely dominates his expressive tools.[18]

The wit is more that of Dryden than of Donne; it knows, as Dryden put it, what it "designs to represent" and moves "like a nimble Spaniel" to spring "the Quarry it hunted." It shows itself partly in that "heterogeneous ideas are yoked by violence together," to quote Johnson on metaphysical wit; but of this Wordsworth was always capable. What is new in the late poetry is a more deliberate "alliance of levity with seriousness," to borrow Eliot's phrase describing Marvell. The word "levity" may put it too strongly, but at least the verse usually acknowledges that the metaphors are farfetched and makes only a qualified commitment to them. In the "Farewell Lines," Charles and Mary Lamb are compared to "a pair of herons . . . Drying their feathers in the sun" after a storm, and then, in a still more extreme juxtaposition, to

> Two glow-worms in such nearness that they shared,
> As seemed, their soft self-satisfying light,
> Each with the other.

Usually these metaphors are most successful when they illustrate religious conceptions. The first stanza of a poem
called "Devotional Incitements," a title summing up the
more serious use of this wit, tells how the odors of herbs and
flowers travel along the breeze, always ascending from the
ground and making "mute aerial harmonies" as they rise.
"Where will they stop," he asks; they climb "As if no space
below the sky/ Their subtle flight could satisfy." And, of
course, the odors in their windings and aspirings are a figure
or model for the thoughts of man, which ought also to mount
heavenward. But Wordsworth makes the point in a modestly
ironic understatement — "Heaven will not tax our thoughts
with pride/ If like ambition be *their* guide" — and both the
elaborate conceit and the light yet earnest use of it are characteristic.

Many of these points can be put in a wider context in discussing "The Cuckoo at Laverna" (1837), a poem, like so
many of Wordsworth's, taking for one of its themes the
poetic imagination itself. In the opening sections, Wordsworth presents himself approaching a Franciscan monastery.
He has been touring Italy, and during that "long/ And
pleasant course" has heard various familiar birds, but not
the cuckoo, and it seems, for reasons not immediately clear,
particularly appropriate that he should first catch "that vagrant Voice" as he sees the monastery. Among the "sterile
heights of Appenine," the monastery is a "Christian Fort-
ress, garrisoned/ By a few Monks . . . Dead to the world
and scorning earth-born joys." The monks, conforming to
"severe restraints/ Of mind," a "dread heart-freezing dis-

cipline" (one may recall the glacial figures of "Processions") may show the religious conscience in full control, man's obligations to God framed and lived to the utmost of human power in "rules/ Stringent as flesh can tolerate." If so, a total faith has no room for "earth-born joys" (we remember Wordsworth's scruples in "At Vallombrosa"), and in that "heart-freezing discipline" among "sterile heights," there is no source or use for poetry. But this is a Franciscan monastery, and the poet reminds himself that St. Francis was "wont to hold companionship" with "sun, moon, stars, the nether elements,/ And every shape of creature they sustain." His heart having been "cleansed," the genius of St. Francis worked "through heaven" on behalf of earthly things, making it possible and right that they should be loved. And to St. Francis the "changeful earth" illustrated things of heaven. Hence, to sum up, his love of God made "Divine affections" overflow on "beast and bird," and his love for creatures of the earth led back to heaven.

It seems reasonable to suggest, then, that if in this late poem something of Wordsworth's brooding power revives, its source is again an urgent, personal concern. Granted both the terms in which he conceived man's religious duty and his own intense sincerity, he, like many poets, must have felt that his faith threatened his calling. To a puritan conscience, if poetry cannot serve man's highest needs it cannot justify the energies spent in it, and there is the further anxiety that poetry may be not merely irrelevant but also distracting. That is why Wordsworth's later writings, adopting Herbert's premise that "all good structure" is not "in a winding stair," are often a direct statement of religious thoughts with no mediating imagery. But here he finds in a model a different answer. The "milder Genius" of St. Francis reveals what gifts and service the imagination (or fancy, as it ought now

to be called) can bring to religion. Wordsworth puts it in
three condensed lines from which I have already quoted:
the imagination works by "unsought means," in other words,
suddenly and spontaneously, "for gracious purposes" —
the word "gracious" here denoting Divine grace — "For
earth through heaven, for heaven, by changeful earth,/ Illustrated, and mutually endeared." It is ironic that the "Essay, Supplementary to the Preface" (1815) had argued that
"Pious and devout" persons are likely to be incompetent
critics of poetry, for the Essay can be used to interpret both
Wordsworth's account of St. Francis and his own practice.
"The religious man," he remarks, "values what he sees chiefly
as an 'imperfect shadowing forth' of what he is incapable of
seeing." Since "the concerns of religion refer to indefinite
objects," the "commerce between Man and his Maker cannot be carried on but by a process where much is represented
in little," religion "submitting herself to circumscription,
and reconciled to substitutions." [19] In other words, faith and
worship must make use of images, though since they do not
partake in the reality, they would seem to be merely icon-
ographic. Such images or illustrations can be found in natural objects. Later in the poem Wordsworth speaks of the
"baptized imagination," prompt "To catch from Nature's
humblest monitors/ Whate'er they bring of impulses sublime." The phrasing is not very precise, but the meaning becomes clear as the poem exemplifies the workings of the
"baptized imagination." "Impulses sublime" are religious
emotions prompted by natural objects, the imagination having perceived these objects as illustrations of religious truth.

Wordsworth attributes this activity of imagination to two
monks noticed as he approached the monastery, one "Seated
alone" in "musing mood," and the other "Looking far forth
from his aerial cell," both of them bringing to mind descriptions of poets or visionaries typical throughout Words-

worth's career. The voice of the cuckoo, he suggests, may have moved them to think, as he did, of "the great Prophet, styled *the Voice of One/ Crying amid the wilderness*." This striking leap that connects the cuckoo to John the Baptist is obviously an act of the "baptized imagination." It is also an instance of the use of metaphor I have been trying to describe. The comparison is sudden, unprepared, and dependent on a "slender thread." It is, moreover, not developed, except that the poem goes on to name associative links between the cuckoo and Saint John: the cuckoo wanders "in solitude . . . Foretelling and proclaiming" the coming of spring as Saint John foretold the coming of Christ. The "baptized imagination" ought, perhaps, to suggest an imagination informed by grace, but defined as it displays itself in poetry, it means something rather different. It means fancy guided, controlled, corrected, and sometimes blocked by a prior acceptance of Christian doctrine.

-9-

Obviously the late poetry has less need of the colloquial matter-of-factness that used to work so finely. The exactitude, as I said, emerged in a personal use of art; searching after truths hidden in particular events, "spots of time" such as those cited in the twelfth book of the *Prelude*, Wordsworth had to begin with a scrupulous honesty to experience. Otherwise, he could scarcely trust the beliefs he derived. Lacking such pressure to "look steadily" at his subject, Wordsworth, for all his skill, tends at times to become rather plodding and mechanical. The impression can perhaps be summed up in the account a servant gives of the older poet at work: "He would set his head a bit forrad, and put his hands behint his back. And then he would start a bumming, and it was bum, bum, bum . . . and goa on bumming for long enough." [20] Similarly, Wordsworth could no longer summon in meditation his former language of weighty passion. However sincerely he felt his religion, there was not the same sense of meaning or new understanding suddenly breaking upon the mind as he interrogated his experience. His emotions were no longer roused to the same degree in the process of writing. And if his late poems are looser structures, that too may be a function of settled belief. Just as the younger Wordsworth reached so often into his own past, attempting to link it with the present and find a continuing identity, each poem worked out its own unified being in a step-by-step progression. At any point, the motive and source for succeeding lines lay in those that went before. I am, of course, overstating the point; there were plenty of intrusions. But the tighter integration of the early poems must be related to the uncertainties in Wordsworth's own mind. It is not an order of ideas, but the need for it, that makes for close, integrated thinking. Like other finished monuments, structures of thought can only repose, and a mind that dwells secure in them may become unbuttoned and loosely garrulous. One instance is described in the Fenwick note to "Lines Suggested by a Portrait from the Pencil of F. Stone" (1834). In the poem, Wordsworth tells of a monk's remark that in a painting by Titian one could almost think the figures "are in truth the Substance, we the Shadows." The note explains that the anecdote "was told in this house by Mr. Wilkie, and was, I believe, first communicated to the Public in this Poem, the former portion of which I was composing at the time." [21] The plain implication is that he heard an anecdote and stuck it in. This may not necessarily argue that it does not belong, but it at least suggests that no urgent concern animates the poem. Wordsworth did not create the earlier poetry by stitching in random scraps.

As a matter of fact, the "unity indispensable to every work of art," to quote Wordsworth, is now often achieved in a rather different way. What holds the poems together, as in much verse of the nineteenth century, may be the dominance of a mood. The fine "Extempore Effusion on the Death of James Hogg" is mainly a static listing of dead friends — Hogg, Scott, Coleridge, Lamb, Crabbe, and Felicia Hemans — in a mood of nostalgia and regret. And the evening voluntary already cited, "Calm is the fragrant air," establishes a gentle tranquillity and then goes on to sustain the feeling by naming appropriate objects. The intention can be shown in a revision. In an early draft Wordsworth wrote:

> The Labourer wont to rise at break of day
> Has closed his door, and from the public way
> The sound of hoof or wheel is heard no more.

But this was changed:

> The shepherd, bent on rising with the sun,
> Had closed his door before the day was done,
> And now with thankful heart to bed doth creep,
> And joins his little children in their sleep.

The transformation of the laborer to a shepherd and the added references to a "thankful heart" and "little children" indicate well enough why the lines were altered.

— 10 —

It may be that, trapped in the wish to compare this verse with the greater poetry that went before, I have suggested an evaluation I do not intend. It is not simply that one is reluctant to begrudge, persecuting poems for not accomplishing what they do not, in fact, attempt. On the whole, the late poetry is very good. It suffers only when measured against standards met rarely in English poetry. If Wordsworth, writing from the high plateaus of old age, sometimes seems inhumanly remote, that very remoteness can be curiously liberating in its impartial vision. And what sometimes seems to be smug self-approval can manifest itself as an old man's earned authority. Even the readiness that could produce lumps of inert material may become bravura deftness and ease. There is no longer the same pressure and power, but skills of all kinds have been accumulating in this lifetime of devoted workmanship, and the reader may often have much pleasure in watching the mature poise of a great artist. Yet it is not easy to demonstrate the excellence of these late poems; to the extent that it is present, it will quietly sustain a poem as a whole, seldom issuing in memorable lines or phrases that can be plucked from their context. Summing up, one can say that at its best the late poetry is quiet, grave, limpid, and very delicately hued. As an example, we can turn to some well-known lines in the *White Doe of Rylstone*; for though written in 1807, the lines anticipate the particular kind of excellence one finds in the poetry of Wordsworth's old age.

> And through yon gateway, where is found,
> Beneath the arch with ivy bound,
> Free entrance to the churchyard ground —
> Comes gliding in with lovely gleam,
> Comes gliding in serene and slow,
> Soft and silent as a dream,
> A solitary Doe!　　　　　　　(ll. 52–58)

"My ear," Wordsworth once told Crabb Robinson, "is susceptible to the clashing of sounds almost to a disease," and such passages would bear him out. For another instance (from "Memory," 1823) there is:

> With heart as calm as lakes that sleep,
> In frosty moonlight glistening;
> Or mountain rivers, where they creep
> Along a channel smooth and deep,
> To their own far-off murmurs listening.

If, in conclusion and summary, one asks again what happened to the poetry as Wordsworth aged, it is at least clear that simple answers do not work. Taking into account what has been emphasized — stable belief that limits free excursions and creates a poetry of wit, combined with an altered relation with his audience that leads him to be impersonal and hortatory — one may begin to describe the later poetry and to see why Wordsworth could not have continued in the mode of his youth. Still, however, one does not know why Wordsworth could not write a great Christian poetry, as persons like Keats's friend, Benjamin Bailey, expected him to do — a poetry different in kind but comparable in worth to all but the finest passages of his earlier achievement. The mode could certainly support such a poetry, as, in fact, it does in Johnson's "Vanity of Human Wishes."

The main reason, I think, lay in an acute split between his religious beliefs and his instinctive emotions, which never came into line with his belief. In other words, the step into Christian orthodoxy was not an organic completing of instincts and past experiences. As a result, the unconscious and assimilative processes that formerly did much of the work in poetic creation could no longer be trusted; for they would suggest poems that his conscience would not allow him to write. The ideal of sincerity remained as strong as ever, but it now exacted a vigilant self-watchfulness as he compelled his poetry to express his faith. Naturally Wordsworth was at least half-aware of this. Yet, characteristically, he approached the trouble from the other side, wondering why he could not write an even more emphatically Christian verse. Once when he was about seventy-four years old he remarked to Aubrey de Vere on the fact that the religion of his poetry was "not as distinctly 'revealed religion' " as might be expected. He explained it

by stating that when in his youth his imagination was shaping
for itself the channel in which it was to flow, his religious convictions were less definite and less strong than they had become
on more mature thought; and that, when his poetic mind and
manner had once been formed, he feared lest he might, in attempting to modify them, become constrained.[22]

The point is that he did alter his "poetic mind and manner,"
and he was constrained.

Perhaps also one should stress the fatigue one feels almost
everywhere, an intellectual weariness that matches the aged
and worn appearance of Wordsworth when he was not yet
very old. He who "would keep/ Power," Wordsworth wrote
at the age of seventy-one, "must resolve to cleave to it through
life,/ Else it deserts him, surely as he lives." But he was not
inwardly willing to make the struggle; and he goes on in
"Musings near Aquapendente" to accept the leaning tower
of Pisa as an image of old age. To the "mind's consenting
eye" it is a "type of age in man,"

> Bearing the world-acknowledged evidence
> Of past exploits, nor fondly after more
> Struggling against the stream of destiny,
> But with its peaceful majesty content.

And perhaps the fatigue also lies behind his particular
form of religious acceptance. It is easy to make such a remark. But if the late poetry can be used to comment on
Wordsworth's faith, it suggests that the belief was taken up
for motives which, however understandable, may be unfortunate. Wordsworth's own massive integrity forced him
to search amid the shocks of experience for final, all-em-
bracing answers, and the frustration of this search once, at
least, brought him to be "sick, wearied out with contrarie-
ties," and despairing. But the very integrity that drives so

urgently toward a settlement can create a temptation to settle prematurely. It may be, then, that Wordsworth's faith did not result from repeated inquest of experience and ceaseless thought so much as from a yearning for assurance, stability, and repose. It may have been not so much a gradual conversion as a sad transaction in which the free, inquiring spirit was exchanged for peace. As a result, the belief was, we have seen, controlling and imprisoning. Once he had accepted it, Wordsworth spent the rest of his life in attitudes of contraction and defense, curbing and rallying himself to the faith he espoused. In a sense, one moral emerging from Wordsworth's life may be that the effort for integrity, wearing out the energies it calls into play, can lead to exhaustion and surrender. But whoever imposed such a judgment would, like Wordsworth, be taking an excessively angelic point of view. It is scarcely justifiable for human beings to cast an unsympathetic eye on a struggle so noble. Yet the poetry itself reflects the limitations of a continuously willed belief, and the fatigue. But as Fuller remarks of Ben Jonson's plays, "If his later be not so spriteful and vigorous as his first pieces, all that are old will, and all that desire to be old should, excuse him therein."

– II –

Wordsworth is only one instance — though the greatest in English — of the ideal of sincerity powerfully at work in the poetry of the romantic age. Unquestionably, this ideal and example could lead toward kinds of literature Wordsworth would have deplored. From one point of view, he writes a poetry of impressions, in which the visible begins to be replaced by the visionary, and the objective world starts to get lost in personal mood. From this to an art of reverie and escape is only a step. Moreover, Wordsworth helped to open the door to the willful pursuit of the emotionally bizarre in the writers of the late nineteenth century; for this was simply the *reductio ad absurdum* of Wordsworth's premise that poetry is the "science of feelings." But in Wordsworth himself these and other tendencies were submerged in the struggle for honesty, and this example has challenged as well as burdened writers ever since. Later poets have repeatedly urged one another to adopt what may be called indirect approaches, through symbol, myth, "objective correlative," or (in Arnold's version) the heightened rendering of significant actions. But the larger figures have seldom been able to embrace these ideas in a wholehearted way. Constantly oblique approaches trouble the poet's conscience; there is a yearning for a direct assault. Wordsworth's haunting ideal of honesty has become a thing which the modern poet can neither live with nor live without.

Moreover, the romantic dream of sincerity has influenced not only poetry but all the arts since the romantic age. It has encouraged a sense of guilt in the use of forms, and a consequent relaxation of forms. It has raised an accelerating alarm over the adequacy of the medium, so that there has been a conscious effort to enrich with new resources — novel sounds in music, sculpture in wire or stainless steel — and to distort the common resources into new expressive possibilities. Again, the zeal for sincerity has fostered a turning away not only from past models but even from newly created conventions. When in 1802 John Constable, then only twenty-six and just starting his career, felt that the trouble with his recent studies was that he had "tried to make his performances look like the work of other men," and that "the great vice of the present day is *bravura*, an attempt to do something beyond the truth," he forecast the future course of painting. Most major revolutions in the art were to be waged in the name of truth, and the "truth" pursued was to be the painter's individual consciousness or perception. It is significant that Hazlitt could make much the same grumble over Turner's paintings — they are "a waste of morbid strength" and "give pleasure only by the excess of power triumphing over the barrenness of the subject" — that he and others lodged against Wordsworth's poetry. Also, since the romantic age it has seemed shameful to defer to the wishes or expectations of an audience, or even to be too much influenced by them. The consequences of this honorable selfishness appear everywhere, including, for one example, what many thought the extreme indecency of Rousseau's *Confessions*, and, for another instance, modern functional architecture, which has sometimes shown more concern for a certain kind of integrity than for people. And finally, the very wish to be sincere inevitably burdens artists with a new self-consciousness and thus serves as a subtle source of insincerity. All of the arts have been troubled by a persisting thought that we can be most honest when we are least thinking about it, that is, when we are spontaneous.

Yet at least in the literary arts, the struggle for sincerity has usually been linked to a quest for stable belief, for moral and metaphysical answers. Every age and generation naturally sees itself as modern, and, at least for the last two centuries, to be modern has meant to be assailed by complexities unknown before, to feel that the verities or certainties of the last generation are crumbling underfoot. Often this sense that our fathers grew up in a simpler world may result only from something structural or necessary in the relation of children to parents. We do not know our parents in their youthful times of unsettlement; they are the first and most important enforcers of the standards we later come to question. Nevertheless, it seems undeniable that Wordsworth's generation was jolted into a moral, intellectual, and religious perplexity unknown by their fathers. There was a heightened sense of the vastness and fluid diversity of the cosmos, and, correspondingly, a new realization of the ambiguity and infinite ramification of the events we ourselves experience, and of the uncertainty of one's hold upon anything. The human mind found itself in the center of a mystery stretching in every direction; men were "straining for particles of light," as Keats put it, "in the midst of a great darkness." In this situation, a search for belief must naturally go back and start once more in the immediate facts of personal experience. And, of course, we will desperately strive to be faithful in recollecting our experience; for how else can we draw a true philosophy from it? It is the quest for general meaning that brings literature back to personal experience and then beyond the particular experience, tracing a characteristic movement from recollection to introspection, from narration to interpretation. In its fullest development, then, the literature of sincerity presents a peculiar union of concrete, personal experience with meditation and generalization, as we find it in Thoreau, Rousseau, Proust, Lawrence, the later Eliot, Wordsworth. Its characteristic formal process might be described as the drama of a certain mode of intellectual discovery — the general rising from the personal while still anchored in it, the abstract still living and convincing because it is embodied in a vivid moment of actual experience.

But for these writers, to retrieve and contemplate one's own past naturally does not imply an indiscriminate recall. They do not suppose that belief can be based on the slow and anxious minuteness of inference, even on inference from one's own direct experience. They feel instead that belief is given in special moments of illumination, happenings that come to us with a peculiar weight and clarity. Chance glimpses — in Wordsworth the stretch of a field of daffodils, the sight of a drowned man raised from a lake; in Proust three spires seen on a carriage ride, or the hawthorns, or the little phrase in Vinteuil's Sonata; in Eliot the garden inhabited by "echoes" in the "first world" of childhood — are felt to have reaches of meaning beyond any significance we can name at the time they occur. And the quest of the meaning of life is a meditation on these moments, a meditation that, as it seeks to interpret, will also keep in mind the context of experience surrounding such moments. Of course, one must also understand — as perhaps Wordsworth did not wholly — that the moment of vision, or "spot of time," is composed retrospectively. Sober contemplation will tell most of us that experience as we undergo it does not incandesce into special illumination or completed joy, that it takes on visionary brightness only afterward, as memory is able to transfigure what it keeps. And of course the same processes work more intensely when recollections are written into poetry. When Wordsworth described childhood appearances of shepherds, or the unforgettable episodes in the first book of the *Prelude*, he was not recapturing actual events so much as he was creating symbolisms powerfully urging what he sought to believe. This, indeed, is one of the functions of art generally, not only for the artist, but for mankind.

The poetry of sincerity must run risks, and, even in its greatest success, will not achieve much that we admire in the poetry of earlier times. Simply because it deals with the feelings and experience of the writer, it hazards becoming obscure; it pursues the accidents on one man's way, rather than what Coleridge, in his praise of Shakespeare, called the "high road of life." Moreover, because it stands relatively close to its subject matter the poetry of sincerity tends, as compared with the older poetry, to be less sweeping in its purview. It gains, perhaps, in immediate vividness as it handles experience directly, but it often lacks the ranging allusiveness that may come when a writer does not feel compelled to speak of himself, or, at least, for himself. Poets in the Renaissance were free to use all that tradition and culture made available to them; their theme was man. But when the theme is a man, the situation is very different. Keats's comparison of Wordsworth with Milton discloses, at the setting forth of modern poetry, one of the large dilemmas in which it still finds itself; for in making this comparison Keats speaks out of his own questioning. He did not know which direction he should try to take. "The antients," including the Elizabethans and Milton, "were Emperors of vast Provinces," but "Each of the moderns like an Elector of Hanover governs his petty state, & knows how many straws are swept daily from the Causeways in all his dominions." A similar thought was expressed by Yeats:

> Shakespearean fish swam the sea, far away from land;
> Romantic fish swam in nets coming to the hand;
> What are all those fish that lie gasping on the strand? [23]

And so, Keats goes on, "I will have no more of Wordsworth." But this is bravado. Wordsworth continues to trouble his conscience. Milton "did not think into the human heart, as Wordsworth has done." Though Milton has certainly an "extended vision," like an eagle on the wing, and Wordsworth may be only an "eagle in his nest," brooding perhaps, "I must think Wordsworth is deeper than Milton." [24]

Yet the poetry of sincerity appeals not only by its profound and close confronting of experience. We can remind ourselves again that it draws the reader into a special relation with the poet. Its appeal lies partly in the human intimacy, partly in the trust generated by sincerity, partly in our admiration for a determined exploration. Moreover, if our enagagement with a work of art has any subsequent effect upon us, the poetry of sincerity is peculiarly liberating. It tends to free us from stock opinions and judgments blindly accepted, and calls us to go back in honesty to our own experience. The sincerity of another man increases our own.

NOTES   INDEX

ABBREVIATIONS USED IN NOTES

D. W. J.   *Journals of Dorothy Wordsworth,* ed. Ernest de Selincourt, 2 vols. (London, 1941).

E. L.   *The Early Letters of William and Dorothy Wordsworth* (1787–1805), ed. Ernest de Selincourt (Oxford, 1935).

Grosart   *The Prose Works of William Wordsworth,* ed. Alexander B. Grosart, 3 vols. (London, 1876).

L. Y.   *The Letters of William and Dorothy Wordsworth: The Later Years,* ed. Ernest de Selincourt, 3 vols. (Oxford, 1939).

M. Y.   *The Letters of William and Dorothy Wordsworth: The Middle Years,* ed. Ernest de Selincourt, 2 vols. (Oxford, 1937).

Prel.   *The Prelude, or Growth of a Poet's Mind,* ed. Ernest de Selincourt, 2nd ed., rev. Helen Darbishire (Oxford, 1959).

P. W.   *The Poetical Works of William Wordsworth,* ed. Ernest de Selincourt and Helen Darbishire, 5 vols. (Oxford, 1949–1958).

NOTES

CHAPTER I

THE CHALLENGE OF SINCERITY

1. *La Nausée* (1938), p. 162.
2. Interview in *The Paris Review*, XXV (Winter–Spring, 1961), 71.
3. *Collected Letters*, ed. E. L. Griggs (1956–1959), III, 112.
4. *Essays and Introductions* (1961), p. 522.
5. *The Paris Review*, XXV, 67, 69.
6. *Letters*, ed. H. E. Rollins (1958), I, 279.
7. *E. L.*, p. 95.
8. B. R. Haydon, *Diary*, ed W. B. Pope (1960), II, 148.
9. De Quincey, *Literary and Lake Reminiscences*, in *Collected Writings*, ed. D. Mason (1896), II, 246.
10. De Quincey, *Collected Writings*, II, 246; Hazlitt, "My First Acquaintance with Poets," *Works*, ed. P. P. Howe (1933), XVII, 118; Hunt, *Autobiography*, ed. R. Ingpen (1903), II, 21.
11. Sara Hutchinson, *Letters*, ed. K. Coburn (1954), p. 111.
12. *Works*, XVII, 118.
13. *Reminiscences*, ed. J. A. Froude (1881), p. 531.
14. *Diary*, II, 148.
15. *Autobiography* (1885), I, 149.
16. *M. Y.*, I, 296.
17. *Collected Letters*, III, 304–305.
18. Sara Hutchinson, *Letters*, pp. 107, 151.
19. *D. W. J.*, II, 333.
20. *M. Y.*, I, 321.
21. *Collected Letters*, III, 9.
22. *Collected Letters*, I, 410; II, 977.
23. *P. W.*, I, 362.
24. *Collected Letters*, IV, 938.
25. *Autobiography*, I, 149.
26. *E. L.*, pp. 460, 463.
27. *Collected Writings*, II, 287; *D. W. J.*, I, 103.
28. *E. L.*, p. 162.
29. *D. W. J.*, I, 129.
30. *E. L.*, p. 58.
31. *Collected Letters*, II, 1033.
32. *Essays Chiefly on Poetry* (1887), I, 153.

CHAPTER II

SINCERITY AND COUNTER IDEALS

1. "Sacred Poetry," in *English Critical Essays (19th Cent.)*, ed. E. D. Jones (1947), p. 171.
2. *Hours in a Library*, III, 139.
3. *Edinburgh Review*, XXXVII (1822), 450.
4. Elsie Smith, *Estimate of Wordsworth by his Contemporaries* (1932), p. 36.
5. Grosart, I, xxxviii.
6. Grosart, II, 12–13, 15.
7. *E. L.*, p. 517.
8. *P. W.*, III, 503.
9. *P. W.*, IV, 415.
10. Grosart, II, 36.
11. *Ibid.*, p. 35.
12. *Ibid.*, p. 54.
13. *Ibid.*, p. 38.
14. *Ibid.*, pp. 44, 45.
15. *Ibid.*, pp. 47–62, *passim*.
16. *Ibid.*, p. 48.
17. *P. W.*, III, 489.
18. Grosart, II, 69, 53.
19. *Collected Letters*, III, 95.
20. *Letters*, ed. E. V. Lucas (1935), I, 95.
21. *Autobiography*, ed. E. Blunden (1927), p. 279.
22. *Notebooks*, ed. K. Coburn (1957), entry 609.
23. *P. W.*, II, 386, 388n.
24. *P. W.*, II, 512.
25. *M. Y.*, I, 128–129.
26. *P. W.*, II, 487. I have quoted only a small part of this lengthy analysis.
27. *Works*, ed. Mrs. Russell Barrington (1915), IV, 288.
28. *Dissertations and Discussions* (1874), I, 111.
29. *Works* (1857), VII, 311.
30. For ample discussion of the implications for romantic poetry see Earl R. Wasserman, *The Subtler Language* (1959).
31. *P. W.*, II, 513.
32. Grosart, II. 64; *Prel.*, I. 249.
33. Grosart, III, 462.
34. *Prel.*, p. lvi.
35. *E. L.*, p. 295.
36. *P. W.*, II, 394n.
37. Grosart, III, 426.
38. *P. W.*, II, 386–387.
39. Grosart, III, 426; *P. W.*, II, 392.
40. For more extended discussion see W. J. B. Owen, *Wordsworth's Preface to Lyrical Ballads, Anglistica*, IX (1957), 59–79.
41. Grosart, II, 51.
42. *Collected Letters*, II, 812.
43. *P. W.*, II, 52, 2.
44. "Sleep and Poetry," ll. 193–195.

CHAPTER III

THE PROCESS OF COMPOSITION

1. *Dissertations and Discussions*, I, 113.
2. *L. Y.*, I, 537.
3. *Collected Letters*, II, 814.

4. *Works*, XI, 32, 37.

5. *Shakespearean Criticism*, ed. T. M. Raysor (1930), II, 124.

6. *P. W.*, II, 393.

7. *P. W.*, II, 387–388, 393.

8. *Collected Letters*, I, 612; II, 668.

9. *P. W.*, II, 388.

10. *L. Y.*, III, 1231.

11. *Essays Chiefly on Poetry*, II, 280.

12. *D. W. J.*, I, 104.

13. H. D. Rawnsley, *Lake Country Sketches* (1903), pp. 47–48.

14. *D. W. J.*, I, 106.

15. *P. W.*, III, 542.

16. *E. L.*, p. 204.

17. *P. W.*, III, 432.

18. *P. W.*, I, 361–362.

19. *Essays Chiefly on Poetry*, II, 276–277. Cf. F. W. Bateson, *Wordsworth* (1956), pp. 164–165.

20. P. W., II, 400–401.

21. *Letters*, I, 238; *The Keats Circle*, ed. H. E. Rollins (1948), I, 129.

22. *M. Y.*, II, 760; *L. Y.*, I, 136, 348.

23. *Letters*, ed. E. H. Coleridge (1895), II, 734.

24. *P. W.*, IV, 427.

25. *P. W.*, II, 387.

26. *P. W.*, II, 388.

27. *L. Y.*, I, 275; *M. Y.*, II, 614.

28. *Prel.*, p. lvi.

29. *P. W.*, II, 432.

30. *P. W.*, II, 511.

31. *P. W.*, IV, 422; II, 478.

32. *P. W.*, II, 422.

33. *M. Y.*, II, 717; *P. W.*, II, 512.

34. *Prel.*, IV, 118–120.

35. *Lake Country Sketches*, pp. 38–39.

36. *P. W.*, II, 494; III, 429–430.

37. *E. L.*, p. 274.

38. *P. W.*, II, 259; V, 316; *Prel.*, IV, 131–132; *P. W.*, V. 316; III, 202–203; *Prel.*, V, 293–294; VII, 668–669; VII, 400–401.

39. *P. W.*, V, 347; *Prel.*, VIII, 466–467; *P. W.*, III, 156.

40. *L. Y.*, II, 586.

41. *Correspondence of Henry Crabb Robinson with the Wordsworth Circle*, ed. E. J. Morley (1927), I, 111, 114.

42. *P. W.*, III, 198–199.

CHAPTER IV

THE ADEQUACY OF LANGUAGE

1. This general argument with respect to symbolic forms is especially urged by Ernst Cassirer through all of his major writings.

2. *Grosart*, II, 57.

3. *Prometheus Unbound*, IV, 415–417.

4. *Aids to Reflection*, ed. H. N. Coleridge (1848), I, xx; *Biographia Literaria*, ed. J. Shawcross (1958), II, 41.

5. *Aids to Reflection*, I. xvii. In effect Coleridge is suggesting at this point that a word is a symbol. This, of course, would be the most commonplace of remarks except

that Coleridge attached a special sense to the term. A symbol fuses such opposites as sensation and thought, matter and spirit, the individual and the universal, and is more real, so to speak, than either its subjective or its objective components taken separately. For further possible implications, one could turn to the well-known, orphic passage in the *Statesman's Manual*, App. B, *Works*, ed. H. N. Coleridge (1839), p. 229; the imagination "gives birth to a system of symbols, harmonious in themselves and consubstantial with the truths of which they are the conductors. These are the *wheels* which Ezekiel beheld, when the hand of the Lord was upon him . . ." See also *Shakespearean Criticism*, II, 104, where Coleridge suggests that Horne Tooke's book should have been entitled "living words"; "for words are the living products of the living mind and could not be a due medium between the thing and the mind unless they partook of both. The word was not to convey merely what a certain thing is,

but the very passion and all the circumstances which were conceived as constituting the perception of the thing by the person who used the word."

6. *Grosart*, II, 64; *P. W.*, II, 385; *L. Y.*, I, 437; *Grosart*, II, 65.

7. *Grosart*, II, 65.

8. *Prel.*, VI, 304–305, 300; VIII, 435–437.

9. *P. W.*, II, 402, 428.

10. *Prel.*, V, 13; II, 308–309; VII, 756–758; I, 586–588; I, 335–338.

11. *Prel.*, XIII, 267–273.

12. *Prel.* (1805), XII, 303–311.

13. *Prel.*, X, 288–290.

14. *Prel.*, VI, 593; III, 241–242, 187; my italics.

15. *P. W.*, II, 435, 428.

16. *Prel.*, I, 55–56.

17. *P. W.*, II, 428.

18. *Prel.* (1805), XIII, 311–312

19. *Collected Letters*, IV, 559–560.

20. *Prel.*, III, 180–194.

21. *Works*, II, 268.

22. See Geoffrey Hartman, *The Unmediated Vision* (1954), pp. 29–33, 42–43.

CHAPTER V

THE PSYCHOLOGY OF BELIEF

1. *Works*, ed. J. Spedding, R. L. Ellis, and D. D. Heath (1864), VIII, 98.

2. *Prel.*, II, 206–207, 229–232.

3. *Prel.*, VIII, 501–502.

4. *Letters*, II, 146.

5. *Aids to Reflection*, I, 19.

6. *Prel.*, VIII, 340–426. I have quoted from both the 1805 and the final text.

7. *Prel.* (1805), VIII, 624–640. When Wordsworth later espoused Christian orthodoxy he revised the passage.

8. *Grosart*, I, 29.

9. *Prel.*, VII, 594; VIII, 646, 545–547.

10. *Prel.*, VIII, 650–654, 644–645.

11. *Prel.*, VIII, 642–643; *Prel.* (1805), VIII, 754–755; *Works*, XI, 56; *Prel.* (1805), VIII, 756–760.

12. See Wordsworth's use of the term at *Prel.*, VIII, 673, a significant revision of the 1805 text where, instead of "a sublime *idea*," he had previously written "this sensation."

13. "On Poesy or Art," printed with *Biographia Literaria*, II. 259; *Miscellaneous Criticism*, ed. T. M. Raysor (1936), p. 44. For aid at this point I am indebted especially to J. H. Muirhead, *Coleridge as Philosopher* (1930), pp. 97–102, and W. J. Bate, "Coleridge on Art," in *Perspectives of Criticism*, ed. Harry Levin (1950), pp. 125–141. To see how baffling Coleridge can be in defining what he means by an idea, and possibly to obtain clarification, one might consult the

long footnote in *Aids to Reflection*, I, 135–138.

14. *Prel.*, VIII, 592–627; (1805), VIII, 765–766.

15. *Prel.*, VIII, 307; (1805), VIII, 78; X, 271–273; XI, 288–291.

16. *Prel.*, VIII, 279–281.

17. *Prel.* (1805), VIII, 82–85, 93–96.

18. *Prel.*, VIII, 128, 316, 117–118; (1805), VIII, 173.

19. *Prel.*, VIII, 289–327.

20. *Prel.*, p. 575, ll. 153–154; *Prel.*, XIII, 377–378; *Prel.*, XII, 284–286.

21. *Prel.*, XI, 203, 243–244, 297–314.

22. *Collected Letters*, II, 961.

23. *Aids to Reflection*, I, 287–288.

24. *Grosart*, II, 29–30.

25. *Aids to Reflection*, I, 149–150.

26. *Prel.*, XI, 86–87; (1805) VIII, 171–172.

27. *Biographia Literaria*, II, 128; *Notebooks*, entry 1616; *Aids to Reflection*, I, 332, 320.

CHAPTER VI

WORDSWORTH AND HIS AUDIENCE

1. *Essays in Criticism, Second Series* (1896), pp. 161–162.

2. Editor's Introduction, *Prel.* p. lxiii.

3. James Russell Lowell, *Works* (1890), IV, 401.

4. *M. Y.*, I, 170.

5. *Prel.*, II, 427–431.

6. *P. W.*, II, 403, 413.

7. *Letters*, III, 203.

8. *E. L.*, p. 295.

9. *M. Y.*, II, 638; *E. L.*, pp. 303–304.

10. H. D. Rawnsley, *Lake Country Sketches*, p. 13.

11. *P. W.*, II, 406, 389.

12. *P. W.*, II, 406.

13. *L. Y.*, I, 127; *Prel.*, XIII, 217–220; *P. W.*, IV, 239.

14. *E. L.*, pp. 298, 295–296.

15. *Correspondence*, I, 53.
16. *M. Y.*, I, 125–126.
17. *P. W.*, V, 336.
18. *P. W.*, II, 410–411, 425–428.
19. *M. Y.*, II, 619.
20. *P. W.*, II, 427–428.
21. *M. Y.*, II, 620; Sara Hutchinson, *Letters*, p. 227; *L. Y.*, I, 448.
22. *M. Y.*, II, 617–620.
23. *M. Y.*, I, 125–131, 170; *E. L.*, pp. 292–298.
24. *Letters*, I, 212–213, 216.
25. *M. Y.*, I, 198; *E. L.*, pp. 306–307.
26. *The Life of Mary Russell Mitford*, ed. A. G. K. L'Estrange (1870), I, 271; *Henry Crabb Robinson on Books and Their Writers*, ed. E. J. Morley (1938), I, 214.
27. *M. Y.*, I, 130–131.
28. *Dissertations and Discussions*, I, 97.
29. *E. L.*, p. 489.
30. *Prel.*, I, 628–629, 618–619; III, 301–302, 322; II, 448, 455.

31. *Prel.*, I, 630, 617–618.
32. *Letters*, II, 126.
33. W. B. Yeats, "Sailing to Byzantium"; Robert Frost, "Birches."
34. *P. W.*, II, 118, 83, 86.
35. *Prel.* (1805), X, 372–373.
36. *P. W.*, V, 133; *Prel.*, XII, 279–282.
37. *P. W.*, III, 16; Gerard Manley Hopkins, "I wake and feel the fell of dark, not day"; W. B. Yeats, "The Tower."
38. Alaric Alfred Watts, *Life of Alaric Watts* (1884), I, 240.
39. Coleridge, *Collected Letters*, I, 584; II, 1013.
40. *Diary*, II, 464.
41. *Memoir and Letters of Sara Coleridge* (1874), p. 305.
42. *Collected Letters*, III, 214; *Notebooks*, entry 62.
43. *Prel.*, VI, 242–247.
44. Charles Cowden Clarke, "Recollections of Keats," *Atlantic Monthly*, VII (January 1861), p. 97.

CHAPTER VII

RESOURCES OF STYLE AND EXPRESSION: I

1. *P.W.*, *II*, 242, 262.
2. *Memoir*, p. 269.
3. Raymond D. Havens, *The Mind of a Poet* (1941), p. 305, lists examples of "quiet humor" in Wordsworth's poetry and letters. Helen Darbishire, *The Poet Wordsworth* (1950), pp. 10, 152, mentions his "peasant" humor. W. P. Ker, *On Modern Literature* (1955), p. 96, cites his "ironical" humor. The subject is surveyed in detail by John E. Jordan, "Wordsworth's Humor," in *PMLA*, LXXIII (1958), 81–93.

4. *Works*, IV, 407–408.
5. *P. W.*, V, 121n. This is an earlier version of *Excursion*, IV, 402–404.
6. *Correspondence*, I, 43.
7. *Prel.* (1805), II, 430.
8. *Biographia Literaria*, II, 109–110. Where Coleridge quotes Wordsworth, I have added the first two lines, which Coleridge did not cite.
9. *P. W.* II, 237.
10. *D. W. J.*, I, 367.

CHAPTER VIII

RESOURCES OF STYLE AND EXPRESSION: II

1. *Eras and Modes in English Poetry* (1957), p. 135.
2. *Prel.*, III, 173–175.
3. *Articulate Energy* (1955), pp. 69–73.
4. *Revaluation* (1947), p. 156.

CHAPTER IX

THE LATE POEMS

1. See Douglas Bush, *Mythology and the Romantic Tradition* (1937), pp. 63–64.
2. *P. W.*, IV, 422–423.
3. *Memoirs of William Wordsworth* (1851), II, 67.
4. *Memoirs*, I, 128–129.
5. *The Egotistical Sublime* (1954), pp. 170–184.
6. *Table Talk*, ed. H. N. Coleridge (1836), p. 175.
7. *Prel.*, VI, 604–605; XI, 144; *P. W.*, IV, 83; II, 262, 236, 227; IV, 56.
8. W. B. Yeats, "The Coming of Wisdom with Time," in *Collected Poems* (New York: Macmillan, 1951), p. 92.
9. *Letters*, I, 193.
10. *P. W.*, II, 411.
11. *Eras and Modes*, p. 129.
12. *P. W.*, II, 412.
13. *P. W.*, II, 395.
14. *L. Y.*, I, 436–437; *M. Y.*, II, 618.
15. *P. W.*, II, 513, 405.
16. *P. W.*, II, 436–439.
17. *P. W.*, II, 438, 441.
18. *P. W.*, II, 441, 167.
19. *P. W.*, II, 412.
20. H. D. Rawnsley, *Lake Country Sketches*, p. 16.
21. *P. W.*, IV, 429.
22. *Essays Chiefly on Poetry*, II, 282.
23. W. B. Yeats, "Three Movements," in *Collected Poems* (New York: Macmillan, 1951), p. 236.
24. *Letters*, I, 224, 280–282.

INDEX

Arnold, Matthew: on self-expression in art, 11; self-proclaimed Wordsworthian, 144; use of meter, 19; on Wordsworth's style, 219–20; other references, 14, 24, 108, 109, 164, 188, 240, 264
Auden, W. H., 18, 88

Bach, J. S., 178
Bacon, Sir Francis, 106, 110
Bagehot, Walter, 48
Bailey, Benjamin, 261
Bate, W. J., 277
Bateson, F. W., 275
Beaumont, Lady, 35, 46, 153, 157
Beaumont, Sir George, 157
Beethoven, Ludwig von, 178
Belief, 131–32; grounds of, 120–21, 135–140; and emotion, 115, 132; and inference, 113, 131
Blake, William, 143, 169, 183, 193
Blunden, Edmund, 74
Browning, Robert, 12
Burke, Edmund, 26
Burns, Robert, 35, 181
Bush, Douglas, 279
Byron, George Gordon, Lord, 25, 59–60, 144, 149, 162, 220

Calvin, John, 59
Carlyle, Thomas, 26
Cassirer, Ernst, 275
Chaucer, Geoffrey, 71
Cincinnatus, 30
Clarke, Charles Cowden, 278
Clarkson, Mrs. Catherine, 155, 157, 249

Coleridge, Hartley, 189
Coleridge, Samuel Taylor: on belief, 136–41; "Christabel," 18; on "Intimations of Immortality," 197–98; on language generally, 87; organic view of poetry, 62; on *The Recluse*, 237, and "Resolution and Independence," 222; comments on Wordsworth, 18, 27, 28, 158–59; and Preface to the *Lyrical Ballads*, 55–58; other references, 17, 29–31, 37–39, 44–45, 63–66, 68, 71, 75, 79, 83, 86, 89, 99–100, 113, 116–17, 121–22, 128, 137, 155, 160–61, 168, 171–73, 178, 187, 190, 208, 217, 227, 233, 259
Coleridge, Sara, 172, 180–81
Constable, John, 264
Convention: sincerity and, 10–11, 36–37; in Wordsworth's late poems, 228–32
Cowper, William, 181
Crabbe, George, 259
Crowe, William, 36
Cummings, E. E., 17

Darbishire, Helen, 278
Davie, Donald, 209
De Quincey, Thomas, 30, 102, 121, 146, 273
De Selincourt, Ernest, 144
De Vere, Aubrey, 31, 66, 69, 261
Diction, in modern poetry, 16–17; Wordsworth's theory, 55–58
Donne, John, 253
Dryden, John, 177, 253